AUTO-BIOGRAPHY

This page enables you to compile a list of useful data on your car, so that whether you're ordering spares or just checking the tyre pressures, all the key information - the information that is "personal" to your car - is easily within reach.

Registration number ....

Model ....

Body colour...

Paint code number ....

Date of first registration...

Date of manufacture (if different).................................

Chassis or 'VIN' number...

Engine number ....

Gearbox number ....

Axle casing number ....

Tyre size: front ....

Tyre size: rear ....

Tyre pressures (normally laden):

Tyre pressures (fully laden):

Front: .... Rear:..................................

Front:................................Rear: ....

Ignition key no. ....

Door lock key/keys no. ....

Fuel locking cap key no. (if fitted).................................

Alarm remote code (if fitted)..

Alarm remote battery type ....

Radio Code No. (if fitted) ....

Insurance: Name, address and telephone number of insurer

....

....

Modifications: information that might be useful when you need to purchase parts

....

....

....

Suppliers: Address and telephone number of your garage and parts supplier

....

....

....

A PORTER PUBLISHING Book

First Published 1994

© Porter Publishing Ltd 1994

Published and Produced by
Porter Publishing Ltd
The Storehouse
Little Hereford Street
Bromyard
Hereford
England HR7 4DE

British Library Cataloguing in Publication Data
Porter, Lindsay
MGB Step-by-Step Service Guide (Service Guide Series)
1. MGB cars
I. Title   II. Series
ISBN 1-899238-00-X

Series Editor: Lindsay Porter
Technical Editor: John Mead
Design: Lindsay Porter and John Rose, TypeStyle
Printed in England by The Trinity Press, Worcester

Other Titles in this Series
Land Rover Series I, II, III Service Guide
Mini (all models 1959-on) Service Guide
VW Beetle (all models to 1980) Service Guide
With more titles in production

Every care has been taken to ensure that the material contained in this Service Guide is correct. However, no liabillity can be accepted by the authors or publishers for damage, loss, accidents, or injury resulting from any omissions or errors in the information given.

Step-by-Step Service Guide to the MGB
by Lindsay Porter

Foreword

The vast majority of MG owners would love to be able to service their cars completely, do their own repairs, and one day totally strip and rebuild their cars to concours condition. But how many actually could even complete a standard service properly without breaking something, losing a part, or cross threading a nut or two?

I know where I would fit in! You are reading about the chap who serviced an MGB roadster on the drive outside his house, cross threaded the oil drain nut and woke up next morning to an oil slick running the length of the road. "This is oil" said my girl friend, "we're rich, we can be married!". Unhappily, the oil was already refined and was the contents of my MGB's sump. I actually tried another service, a few years later, on an MGB GT V8. I could change the plugs, any twit could do that. On removing one, I dropped it and it stuck firmly between the exhaust manifold and the body of the engine bay. I tried everything to shift it bar loosening the engine mounts to jack up the engine. I certainly didn't trust myself to do that. Instead, I fitted the eight new plugs and threw away seven old ones. I was the only owner of an eight cylinder V8 with nine spark plugs.

Still having not learnt to leave well alone, I tried to service an MG TD. Being an older, more basic car, with more than enough room under the bonnet for my fumbling mits, what could possibly go wrong? The service was completed, the car started and I was ecstatic, no more workshop bills for me. At the traffic lights another motorist motioned to me, yes I could smell petrol, what could it be? You've guessed, I hadn't tightened the nut properly on the fuel pump and petrol was spraying out all over the engine.

I used to have two choices, either complete my own services and carry a whole tool kit around backed up by the RAC's Reflex membership, or spend a fortune with mechanics who could do what I could almost do and charge me for the privilege. Now I have a third option, I can buy this book, read it carefully and then go about servicing my MGB in a professional and capable manner. Oh, and if you do see a stream of oil, water or petrol running down the road, it's absolutely nothing to do with me.

Lindsay Porter's MGB, "Guide to Purchase and DIY Restoration" was, and still is, a best seller. The MG Owners' Club has supplied several thousand copies to members worldwide and many more have been sold through bookshops. We now have another essential book for all MGB owners whether they be like me, quietly competent but inept, or as expert as Lindsay himself.

Roche Bentley, **MG Owners Club**

CONTENTS

Auto-biography   1

Foreword by Roche Bentley   4

Introduction and Acknowledgements   6

Using This Book   7

CHAPTER 1:   *Safety First!*   8

CHAPTER 2:   *Buying Spares*   12

CHAPTER 3:   *Service Intervals, Step-by-Step*

Using the Service Schedules   15

500 miles, or Weekly   18

1,500 miles, or Every Month   25

3,000 miles, or Every Three Months   27

6,000 miles, or Every Six Months   41

12,000 miles, or Every Twelve Months   56

Spark Plug Conditions   65

24,000 miles, or Every Twenty Four Months   68

36,000 miles, or Every Thirty Six Months   74

Longer Term Servicing   75

CHAPTER 4:   *Repairing Bodywork Blemishes*   77

CHAPTER 5:   *Rustproofing*   81

CHAPTER 6:   *Fault Finding*   85

CHAPTER 7:   *Getting Through the MOT*   89

CHAPTER 8:   *Facts and Figures*   99

CHAPTER 9:   *Tools and Equipment*   105

APPENDIX 1: *Lubrication Chart*   108

APPENDIX 2: *American and British Terms*   109

APPENDIX 3: *Specialists and Suppliers*   110

APPENDIX 4: *Service History*   111

Keep a record of every service you carry out on your car.

**Lindsay Porter
Porter Publishing Ltd**

Introduction

Over the years, I have run any number of cars, from superb classic cars, modern cars, to those with one foot in the breakers yard. And I know only too well that any car is only enjoyable to own if it's reliable, safe and basically sound - and the only way of ensuring that it stays that way is to service it regularly. That's why we have set about creating a series of books which aim to provide you, the owner, with all the information you might need in order to keep your car in tip-top condition. And if your car is not as reliable as it might be, you will be able to give your car a 'super service', using the information contained in the Servicing section of this book, and bring it back to good, reliable order.

Porter Publishing Service Guides are the first books to give you all the service information you might need, with step-by-step instructions, along with a complete Service History section for you to complete and fill in as you carry out regular maintenance on your car over the months ahead. Using the information contained in this book, you will be able to:

-see for yourself how to carry out every Service Interval, from weekly and monthly checks, right up to longer-term maintenance items.

-carry out regular body maintenance and rustproofing, saving a fortune in body repairs over the years to come.

-enhance the value of your car by completing a full Service History of every maintenance job you carry out on your car.

I hope you enjoy keeping your car in trim whilst saving lots of money by servicing your car yourself, with the help of this book. Happy motoring!

Acknowledgements

This book has been a real team effort, with lots of people contributing time, expertise and no little brain-ache to ensure that it is full of good stuff whilst being easy and straightforward to follow. That the project has worked is due in no small measure to Kim Henson and John Williams who helped with the research for several sections of this book, and my assistant Zoe Palmer who contributed greatly to the Facts and Figures chapter - as well as having spent countless hours on the original concept behind this series of books. Dave Pollard and Jim Patten, other authors in this series, also provided a highly valued input. John Rose of TypeStyle (layout and design) and John Mead (Technical Editor) have also been enormously influential in terms of their expertise and experience. It's a pleasure to work with such people; professionals all and nice folk, to boot!

In fact, one of the great things about this exciting new project is the positive, enjoyable spirit in which the whole thing has taken place. Great enthusiasm and highly valued expertise also came from Graham and Lesley Pearce at Bromsgrove MG Centre, and top mechanic there, Trevor Knight, as well as Alan and Jenny Jones the owners of the beautiful MGB featured in Chapter 3. It's good to report that the enthusiasm and customer care that I experienced at Graham Pearce's business wasn't just put on for show. On the first of my several days there, news came through that Bromsgrove MG Centre had won the coveted Five Spanner Award in the MG Owners' Club annual members' survey of MG specialists - a well deserved accolade!

Others who have provided invaluable assistance include 'Trish Giles, who helped to ensure that the servicing information flowed logically, Peter Stant, who demonstrated the bodywork repair techniques seen in this book and my wife Shan who put her great experience in book-matters to excellent effect. Roy Ford supplied the beautiful MGB featured on the cover and Kevin Brock produced the superb MGB line drawing that appears now and again on these pages.

Specialist expertise also came from Dunlop/SP Tyres, from Kamasa tools, who generously supplied almost all of the great range of tools used here and from David's Isopon who supplied expertise on bodywork repair and body filler that is second to none. Other specialist assistance was kindly supplied by NGK, Dinitrol, Gunsons, Partco and AP Lockheed. And of course, there are our old friends Richard Price and Dawn Adams at Castrol whose advice we are always pleased to receive and whose products we can always unhesitatingly recommend.

Many thanks to everyone listed here as well as to anyone else whom I might inadvertently have missed.

Using this Book

Everything about this book is designed to help you make your car more reliable and long-lasting through regular servicing. But one requirement that you will see emphasised again and again is the need for safe working. There is a lot of safety information within the practical instructions but you are strongly urged to read and take note of **Chapter 1, Safety First!**. To get the most from this book, you will rapidly realise that it revolves around two main chapters. **Chapter 3, Service Intervals, Step-by-Step** shows you how to carry out every service job that your car is likely to need throughout its life. Then, the final Section, **Service History**, in the back of this book lists all of the jobs described in Chapter 3 and arranges them together in tick-lists, a separate list for each Service Interval, so that you can create your own Service History as you go along. When you have completed the three years of Service History included in this book, continuation sheets can be purchased from Porter Publishing. Keeping your car in top condition is one thing; getting it there in the first place may be quite another. At the start of Chapter 3, we advise on carrying out a 'catch-up' service for cars that may not have received the de-luxe treatment suggested here. And then there are four other chapters to help you bring your car up to scratch. **Chapter 4 Repairing Bodywork Blemishes** and **Chapter 5 Rustproofing** show how to make the body beautiful and how to keep it that way - not something that is usually included in servicing information but bodywork servicing can save you even more money than mechanical servicing, since a corroded body often leads to a scrapped car, whereas worn out mechanical components can usually be replaced. **Chapter 6** shows you how to carry out **Fault Finding** when your car won't start and **Chapter 7**, describes **Getting Through the MoT**, an annual worry - unless you follow the approach shown here. With **Chapter 2, Buying Spares** describing how you can save on spares and **Chapter 8, Facts and Figures** giving you all the key facts and figures, we hope that this book will become the first tool you'll pick up when you want to service your car!

This book is produced in association with Castrol (U.K.) Ltd.

"Cars have become more and more sophisated. But changing the oil and brake fluid, and similar jobs are as simple as they ever were. Castrol are pleased to be associated with this book because it gives us the opportunity to make life simpler for those who wish to service their own cars.

Castrol have succeeded in making oil friendlier and kinder to the environment by removing harmful chlorine from our range of engine lubricants which in turn prolong the life of the catalytic convertor (when fitted), by noticeably maintaining the engine at peak efficiency.

In return, we ask you to be kinder to the environment, too ... by taking your used oil to your Local Authority Amenity Oil Bank. It can then be used as a heating fuel. Please do not poison it with thinners, paint, creosote or brake fluid because these render it useless and costly to dispose of."

Castrol (U.K.) Ltd.

CHAPTER 1 – SAFETY FIRST!

It is vitally important that you always take time to ensure that safety is the first consideration in any job you do. A slight lack of concentration, or a rush to finish the job quickly can often result in an accident, as can failure to follow a few simple precautions. Whereas skilled motor mechanics are trained in safe working practices you, the home mechanic, must find them out for yourself and act upon them.

Remember, accidents don't just happen, they are caused, and some of those causes are contained in the following list. Above all, ensure that whenever you work on your car you adopt a safety-minded approach at all times, and remain aware of the dangers that might be encountered.

Be sure to consult the suppliers of any materials and equipment you may use, and to obtain and read carefully any operating and health and safety instructions that may be available on packaging or from manufacturers and suppliers.

IMPORTANT POINTS

ALWAYS ensure that the vehicle is properly supported when raised off the ground. Don't work on, around, or underneath a raised vehicle unless axle stands are positioned under secure, load bearing underbody areas, or the vehicle is driven onto ramps.

DON'T suddenly remove the radiator or expansion tank filler cap when the cooling system is hot, or you may get scalded by escaping coolant. Let the system cool down first and even then, if the engine is not completely cold, cover the cap with a cloth and gradually release the pressure.

NEVER start the engine unless the gearbox is in neutral (or 'Park' in the case of automatic transmission) and the hand brake is fully applied.

NEVER drain oil, coolant or automatic transmission fluid when the engine is hot. Allow time for it to cool sufficiently to avoid scalding you.

TAKE CARE when parking vehicles fitted with catalytic converters. The 'cat' reaches extremely high temperatures and any combustible materials under the car, such as long dry grass, could ignite.

NEVER run catalytic converter equipped vehicles without the exhaust system heat shields in place.

NEVER attempt to loosen or tighten nuts that require a lot of force to turn (e.g. a tight oil drain plug) with the vehicle raised, unless it is properly supported and in a safe condition. Wherever possible, initially slacken tight fastenings before raising the car off the ground.

TAKE CARE to avoid touching any engine or exhaust system component unless it is cool enough so as not to burn you.

ALWAYS keep antifreeze, brake and clutch fluid away from vehicle paintwork. Wash off any spills immediately.

NEVER syphon fuel, antifreeze, brake fluid or other such toxic liquids by mouth, or allow prolonged contact with your skin. There is an increasing awareness that they can damage your health. Best of all, use a suitable hand pump and wear gloves.

ALWAYS work in a well ventilated area and don't inhale dust - it may contain asbestos or other poisonous substances.

WIPE UP any spilt oil, grease or water off the floor immediately, before there is an accident.

MAKE SURE that spanners and all other tools are the right size for the job and are not likely to slip. Never try to 'double-up' spanners to gain more leverage.

SEEK HELP if you need to lift something heavy which may be beyond your capability.

ALWAYS ensure that the safe working load rating of any jacks, hoists or lifting gear used is sufficient for the job, and is used only as recommended by the manufacturer.

NEVER take risky short-cuts or rush to finish a job. Plan ahead and allow plenty of time.

BE meticulous and keep the work area tidy - you'll avoid frustration, work better and loose less.

KEEP children and animals right away from the work area and from unattended vehicles.

ALWAYS wear eye protection when working under the vehicle or using any power tools.

BEFORE undertaking dirty jobs, use a barrier cream on your hands as a protection against infection. Preferably, wear thin gloves, available from DIY outlets.

DON'T lean over, or work on, a running engine unless strictly necessary, and keep long hair and loose clothing well out of the way of moving mechanical parts. Note that it is theoretically

possible for florescent striplighting to make an engine fan appear to be stationary - check! This is the sort of error that happens when you're dog tired and not thinking straight. So don't work on your car when you're overtired!

REMOVE your wrist watch, rings and all other jewellery before doing any work on the vehicle - especially the electrical system.

ALWAYS tell someone what you're doing and have them regularly check that all is well, especially when working alone on, or under, the vehicle.

ALWAYS seek specialist advice if you're in doubt about any job. The safety of your vehicle affects you, your passengers and other road users.

FIRE

Petrol (gasoline) is a dangerous and highly flammable liquid requiring special precautions. When working on the fuel system, disconnect the vehicle battery earth (ground) terminal whenever possible and always work outside, or in a very well ventilated area. Any form of spark, such as that caused by an electrical fault, by two metal surfaces striking against each other, by a central heating boiler in the garage 'firing up', or even by static electricity built up in your clothing can, in a confined space, ignite petrol vapour causing an explosion. Take great care not to spill petrol on to the engine or exhaust system, never alow any naked flame anywhere near the work area and, above all, don't smoke.

Invest in a workshop-sized fire extinguisher. Choose the carbon dioxide type or preferably, dry powder but never a water type extinguisher for workshop use. Water conducts electricity and can make worse an oil or petrol-based fire, in certain circumstances.

FUMES

In addition to the fire dangers described previously, petrol (gasoline) vapour and the vapour from many solvents, thinners, and adhesives is highly toxic and under certain conditions can lead to unconsciousness or even death, if inhaled. The risks are increased if such fluids are used in a confined space so always ensure adequate ventilation when handling materials of this nature. Treat all such substances with care, always read the instructions and follow them implicitly.

Always ensure that the car is outside the work place in open air if the engine is running. Exhaust fumes contain poisonous carbon monoxide - even if the car is fitted with a catalytic converter, since 'cats' sometimes fail and don't function with the engine cold.

Never have the engine running with the car in the garage or in any enclosed space.

Inspection pits are another source of danger from the build-up of fumes. Never drain petrol (gasoline) or use solvents, thinners adhesives or other toxic substances in an inspection pit as the extremely confined space allows the highly toxic fumes to concentrate. Running the engine with the vehicle over the pit can have the same results. It is also dangerous to park a vehicle for any length of time over an inspection pit. The fumes from even a slight fuel leak can cause an explosion when the engine is started.

MAINS ELECTRICITY

Best of all, use rechargeable tools and a DC inspection lamp, powered from a remote 12V battery - both are much safer! However, if you do use a mains-powered inspection lamp, power tool etc, ensure that the appliance is wired correctly to its plug, that where necessary it is properly earthed (grounded), and that the fuse is of the correct rating for the appliance concerned. Do not use any mains powered equipment in damp conditions or in the vicinity of fuel, fuel vapour or the vehicle battery.

Also, before using any mains powered electrical equipment, take one more simple precaution - use an RCD (Residual Current Device) circuit breaker. Then, if there is a short, the RCD circuit breaker minimises the risk of electrocution by instantly cutting the power supply. Buy one from any electrical store or DIY centre. RCDs fit simply into your electrical socket before plugging in your electrical equipment.

THE IGNITION SYSTEM

Extreme care must be taken when working on the ignition system with the ignition switched on or with the engine cranking or running.

Touching certain parts of the ignition system, such as the HT leads, distributor cap, ignition coil etc, can result in a severe electric shock. This is especially likely where the insulation on any of these components is weak, or if the components are dirty or damp. Note also that voltages produced by electronic ignition systems are much higher than conventional systems and could prove fatal, particularly to persons with cardiac pacemaker implants. Consult your handbook or main dealer if in any doubt. An additional risk of injury can arise while working on running engines, if the operator touches a high voltage lead and pulls his hand away on to a conductive or revolving part.

THE BATTERY

Don't smoke, or allow a naked light, or cause a spark near the vehicle's battery, even in a well ventilated area. A certain amount of highly explosive hydrogen gas will be given off as part of the normal charging process. Care should be taken to avoid sparking by switching off the power supply before charger leads are connected or disconnected. Battery terminals should be shielded, since a battery contains energy and a spark can be caused by any conductor which touches its terminals or exposed connecting straps.

Before working on the fuel or electrical systems, always disconnect the battery earth (ground) terminal.

When charging the battery from an external source, disconnect both battery leads before connecting the charger. If the battery is not of the

SAFETY FIRST!

'sealed-for-life' type, loosen the filler plugs or remove the cover before charging. For best results the battery should be given a low rate 'trickle' charge overnight. Do not charge at an excessive rate or the battery may burst.

Always wear gloves and goggles when carrying or when topping up the battery. Even in diluted form (as it is in the battery) the acid electrolyte is extremely corrosive and must not be allowed to contact the eyes, skin or clothes.

BRAKES AND ASBESTOS

Whenever you work on the braking system mechanical components, or remove front or rear brake pads or shoes:

i) wear an efficient particle mask,

ii) wipe off all brake dust from the work area (never blow it off with compressed air),

iii) dispose of brake dust and discarded shoes or pads in a sealed plastic bag,

iv) wash hands thoroughly after you have finished working on the brakes and certainly before you eat or smoke,

v) replace shoes and pads only with asbestos-free shoes or pads. Note that asbestos brake dust can cause cancer if inhaled.

Obviously, a car's brakes are among its most important safety related items. Do not dismantle your car's brakes unless you are fully competent to do so. If you have not been trained in this work, but wish to carry out the jobs described in this book, it is strongly recommend that you have a garage or qualified mechanic check your work before using the car on the road.

BRAKE FLUID

Brake fluid absorbs moisture rapidly from the air and can become dangerous resulting in brake failure. Castrol (U.K.) Ltd. recommend that you should have your brake fluid tested at least once a year by a properly equipped garage with test equipment and you should change the fluid in accordance with your vehicle manufacturer's recommendations or as advised in this book if we recommend a shorter interval than the manufacturers. Always buy no more brake fluid than you need. Never store an opened pack. Dispose of the remainder at your Local Authority Waste Disposal Site, in the designated disposal unit, **not** with general waste or with waste oil.

ENGINE OILS

Take care and observe the following precautions when working with used engine oil. Apart from the obvious risk of scalding when draining the oil from a hot engine, there is the danger from contaminates that are contained in all used oil.

Always wear disposable plastic or rubber gloves when draining the oil from your engine.

i) Note that the drain plug and the oil are often hotter than you expect! Wear gloves if the plug is too hot to touch and keep your hand to one side so that you are not scalded by the spurt of oil as the plug comes away.

ii) There are very real health hazards associated with used engine oil. In the words of Rover's MG RV8 handbook, "Prolonged and repeated contact may cause serious skin disorders, including dermatitis and cancer". Use a barrier cream on your hands and try not to get oil on them. Where practicable, wear gloves and wash your hands with hand cleaner soon after carrying out the work. Keep oil out of the reach of children.

iii) NEVER, EVER dispose of old engine oil into the ground or down a drain. In the UK, and in most EC countries, every local authority must provide a safe means of oil disposal. In the UK, try your local Environmental Health Department for advice on waste disposal facilities.

PLASTIC MATERIALS

Work with plastic materials brings additional hazards into workshops. Many of the materials used (polymers, resins, adhesives and materials acting as catalysts and accelerators) readily produce very dangerous situations in the form of poisonous fumes, skin irritants, risk of fire and explosions. Do not allow resin or 2-pack adhesive hardener, or that supplied with filler or 2-pack stopper to come into contact with skin or eyes. Read carefully the safety notes supplied on the can, tube or packaging.

JACK AND AXLE STANDS

Throughout this book you will see many references to the correct use of jacks, axle stands and similar equipment - and we make no apologies for being repetitive! This is one area where safety cannot be overstressed - your life could be at stake!

Special care must be taken when any type of lifting equipment is used. Jacks are made for lifting the vehicle only, not for supporting it. Never work under the car using only a jack to support the weight. Jacks must be supplemented by adequate additional means of support, such as axle stands, positioned under secure load-bearing parts of the frame or underbody. Drive-on ramps are limiting because of their design and size but they are simple to use, reliable and the most stable type of support, by far. We strongly recommend their use.

Full details on jacking and supporting the vehicle will be found in **Raising a car - Safely!** near the beginning of Chapter 3.

FLUOROELASTOMERS
MOST IMPORTANT! PLEASE READ THIS SECTION!

If you service your car in the normal way, none of the following may be relevant to you. Unless, for example, you encounter a car which has been on fire (even in a localised area), subject to heat in, say, a crash-damage repairer's shop or vehicle breaker's yard, or if any second-hand parts have been heated in any of these ways.

Many synthetic rubber-like materials used in motor cars contain a substance called fluorine. These materials are known as fluoroelastomers and are commonly used for oil seals, wiring and cabling, bearing surfaces, gaskets, diaphragms, hoses and 'O' rings. If they are subjected to temperatures greater than 315 degrees C, they will decompose and can be potentially hazardous. Fluoroelastomer materials will show physical signs of decomposition under such conditions in the form of charring of black sticky masses. Some decomposition may occur at temperatures above 200 degrees C, and it is obvious that when a car has been in a fire or has been dismantled with the assistance of a cutting torch or blow torch, the fluoroelastomers can decompose in the manner indicated above.

In the presence of any water or humidity, including atmospheric moisture, the by-products caused by the fluoroelastomers being heated can be extremely dangerous. According to the Health and Safety Executive, "Skin contact with this liquid or decomposition residues can cause painful and penetrating burns. Permanent irreversible skin and tissue damage can occur". Damage can also be caused to eyes or by the inhalation of fumes created as fluoroelastomers are burned or heated.

After fires or exposure to high temperatures observe the following precautions:

1   *Do not touch blackened or charred seals or equipment.*

2   *Allow all burnt or decomposed fluoroelastomer materials to cool down before inspection, investigations, tear-down or removal.*

3   *Preferably, don't handle parts containing decomposed fluoroelastomers, but if you must, wear goggles and PVC (polyvinyl chloride) or neoprene protective gloves whilst doing so. Never handle such parts unless they are completely cool.*

4   *Contaminated parts, residues, materials and clothing, including protective clothing and gloves, should be disposed of by an approved contractor to landfill or by incineration according to national or local regulations. Oil seals, gaskets and 'O ' rings, along with contaminated material, must not be burned locally.*

WORKSHOP SAFETY - GENERAL

1   *Always have a fire extinguisher of the correct type at arm's length when working on the fuel system - under the car, or under the bonnet.*

       If you do have a fire, DON'T PANIC! Use the extinguisher effectively by directing it at the base of the fire.

2   *NEVER use a naked flame near petrol or anywhere in the workplace.*

3   *KEEP your inspection lamp well away from any source of petrol (gasoline) such as when disconnecting a carburettor float bowl or fuel line.*

4   *NEVER use petrol (gasoline) to clean parts. Use paraffin (kerosene) or white spirits.*

5   *NO SMOKING! There's a risk of fire or transferring dangerous substances to your mouth and, in any case, ash falling into mechanical components is to be avoided!*

6   *BE METHODICAL in everything you do, use common sense, and think of safety at all times.*

SAFETY FIRST!

CHAPTER 2 – BUYING SPARES

Reliable though the MGB undoubtedly is, there are, of course, occasions when you need to buy spares in order to service it and keep it running. There are a number of sources of supply of the components necessary when servicing the car, the price and quality varying between suppliers. As with most things in life, cheapest is not necessarily best - as a general rule our advice is to put quality before price - this policy usually works out less expensive in the long run! But how can you identify 'quality'? It's sometimes difficult, so stick with parts from suppliers with a reputation, those recommended to you by others and parts produced by well-established brand names. But don't just pay through the nose! The same parts are often available at wildly different prices so, if you want to save money, invest your time in shopping around.

The MG RV8 VIN number plate location

In any event, when buying spares, take with you details of the date of registration of your car, also its chassis (or VIN) and engine numbers. These can be helpful where parts changed during production, and can be the key to a more helpful approach by some parts salespeople! You may, by now have entered this key information on the Auto-Biography pages at the front of this book, for ease of reference. The line drawings on page 14 show you where to find the relevant information on your car.

ROVER DEALERS

Always consider your local Rover dealership as a source of supply of spares. One benefit is that the spares obtained will be 'genuine' items. In addition, often the parts counter staff are familiar with the vehicles, and are only too pleased to help enthusiasts locate the spares required. Sometimes they will go to the trouble of contacting other dealers, on your behalf, in search of an elusive part, and this can usually be delivered within a day or so, if located at another dealer within the same group of companies, for example. Prices are occasionally reduced from the usual retail level - watch for special offers which are often listed at the parts counter. Try to avoid Saturday and Sunday mornings when buying - weekends are often very busy for parts counters, and you may find the staff have more time to help you if you visit early on a weekday morning, or in the evening, while on your way to or from work. At these times you are also less likely to have to queue for a long time! The biggest disadvantage - and it is a big one - is that there are an awful lot of MGB parts that either won't be in stock or that just aren't stocked by your Rover dealer.

PARTS FACTORS/MOTOR ACCESSORY SHOPS

Local parts factors and motor accessory shops can be extremely useful for obtaining servicing parts at short notice - many 'accessory' outlets open late in the evening, and on both days at weekends. Most servicing parts for the MGB are readily available, so, for example, requests for 'routine' items such as brake pads and shoes, spark plugs, contact breaker points, rocker cover gaskets, oil and air filters, are unlikely to draw a blank look from the sales assistant! Some outlets supply 'original equipment' spares, but in many cases the components are 'pattern' parts. In this case, if there is a choice, opt for well-known, respected names, even if the prices are a little higher than those required for possibly dubious 'cheap import' items. This is especially important when shopping for safety-related items such as brake pads. In this example, experience has shown that cheap pads can be subject to excessive brake fade under enthusiastic driving, and in any case such pads often wear rapidly.

Don't overlook the 'trade' motor factors outlets in the UK. One of the biggest (and a supplier of many of the parts used in this series of books) is Partco with branches all over the country - find them in Yellow Pages.

MG SPECIALISTS

There are a multitude of spares suppliers catering for the needs of MG owners, including, of course, those who run MGBs. They are particularly useful when buying components needed for restorations, but of course will also be pleased to help you with regard to servicing components. Most of the major suppliers run mail order services, and 'next day' deliveries are usually available. The spares supplied are often original specification items (this is not always the case, though, so enquire when buying), and prices are competitive. The only drawback is that you will have to pay postage and packing charges, in addition to the cost of the spares.

Many MG specialists advertise regularly in the many 'classic' car magazines. Many include lists of the parts they have on offer, and the prices they are asking. Again, watch out for special offers which can save you money. If you plan ahead, often you can buy spares now at a preferable rate, and keep them 'in stock' until needed.

The overwhelming advantage of buying from an MG Specialist (also, see 'Clubs', below) is that a good specialist will have the best stock of parts and the most useful fund of specialised knowledge to be found anywhere.

CLUBS

Members of the MG Car Club and the MG Owners' Club benefit from general spares information provided by the organisations, and the Club magazines often contain helpful pointers with regard to spares availability. The MG Owners' Club provides members with a handbook, on joining the Club, and this gives details of the various specialists. In addition, the Club runs its own spares service, and many special offers on components are made available to members.

BUYING SECONDHAND

We would strongly advise against buying secondhand brake, suspension, and steering components, unless you know the source of the parts, and really are sure that they are in first class condition. Even then, be sure that you see the vehicle they have been taken from, and avoid any such parts from accident-damaged cars. On the other hand, it might make sense to buy, say, a distributor, or carburettors which you know to be 'low mileage' units, to replace your worn out components. Such moves can help your car run more sweetly and less expensively! In every case, ensure that the components you are buying are compatible with your particular vehicle, and carry out basic checks to ensure that they too are not badly worn. In particular, in the case of distributors, ensure that the main spindle cannot be moved from side to side more than just perceptibly (if it can, the bearings are worn and properly setting the points gap/dwell angle and ignition timing will be impossible). With regard to carburettors, similarly check to make sure that there is minimal sideways play between the throttle spindle and the body of the unit. If there is excessive movement, the carburettor is worn, the result being air leaks and erratic running.

CHECKS ON RUNNING GEAR COMPONENTS

Although many outlets sell 'reconditioned' components on an 'exchange' basis, the quality of workmanship and the extent of the work carried out on such units can vary greatly. Therefore, if buying a rebuilt unit, always check particularly carefully when buying. It has to be said that, wherever possible, reconditioned units are best obtained from main agents, or from reputable specialist suppliers. Always talk to fellow owners before buying - they may be able to direct you to a supplier offering sound parts at reasonable prices. When buying, always enquire about the terms of the guarantee (if any!).

In any event, the following notes should help you make basic checks on some of the commonly required components:

BRAKES (NEW parts ONLY!): Look for boxes bearing genuine AP Lockheed or BMC/British Leyland/Austin Rover/Rover labels. If buying at an autojumble, inspect the contents of the box and reject any obviously rusty stock.

STEERING: Ball joints, king pins - buy new, again rejecting any moisture-damaged stock. Stub axles are available from almost all specialist suppliers on an 'exchange' basis. Ensure that the inner surfaces of the king pin bushes appear to have been properly reamed, and have uniform, smooth surfaces. With a new king pin inserted, the stub axle should rotate about the pin smoothly, without any undue slack or free play evident. Steering racks are available as exchange units. Ensure that you rotate the operating shaft fully from lock to lock, feeling for any undue free play, roughness, stiffness, or 'notchiness' as you do so. Reject any units showing signs of any of these problems, or - of course - oil leaks or split gaiters.

SUSPENSION: Lever arm shock absorbers, such as those used on the 'B', have relatively short working lives, and many have now been 'rebuilt' several times during their lifetime. In some cases, 'reconditioning' by less than scrupulous organisations can simply mean a quick clean-up and a new coat of paint... Therefore, it pays to buy from a reputable supplier. When buying, take a close look around the joints between the operating arm(s) and the body of the unit. If fluid seepage is evident, reject the shock absorber. In addition, with the shocker upright, work the operating arm(s) up and down several times by hand, throughout the full length of the stroke. After two or three strokes, the arm should move with a uniform, firm resistance throughout the length of the operating stroke. If resistance is 'patchy', or if the arm moves with little pressure needed, the unit is faulty. Again, look elsewhere. Indeed some owners prefer to pay more (usually, quite a lot more) to purchase new, unused shock absorbers, about which there are fewer doubts!

TYRES: For the ultimate in long life, roadholding and wet grip, brand new radial tyres from a reputable manufacturer offer the best solution, especially where the car is used all year round, on an 'everyday' basis. Remoulds are available at lower initial cost, but life expectancy is not as long as with new tyres. Cross-plies are still available, but apart from 'originality' considerations, they are less efficient in terms of handling qualities and life expectancy. They are also, these days, becoming expensive.

It is true that secondhand tyres can offer an inexpensive short-term solution to keeping a car on the road, but beware. Such tyres may have serious, hidden faults. If you purchase such covers, you are taking a risk in that you have no knowledge of the history of the tyres or what has happened to them, how they have been repaired, and so on. Our advice - very strongly given - is to stick to top quality, unused tyres from a reputable manufacturer. They may cost a little more, but at least you will have peace of mind, and should be able to rely on their performance in all road and weather situations. After all, your life - and those of other road users - could depend on it!

SAVING MONEY

Finally, if you want to buy quality and save money, you must be prepared to shop around. Ring each of your chosen suppliers with a shopping list to hand and your car's personal data from the Auto-Biography at the front of this book in front of you. Keep a written note of prices, whether the parts are proper 'brand name' parts or not and - most importantly! - whether or not the parts you want are in stock. Parts expected 'soon' have been known never to materialise. A swivel pin in the hand is worth two in the bush! (Bad pun!)

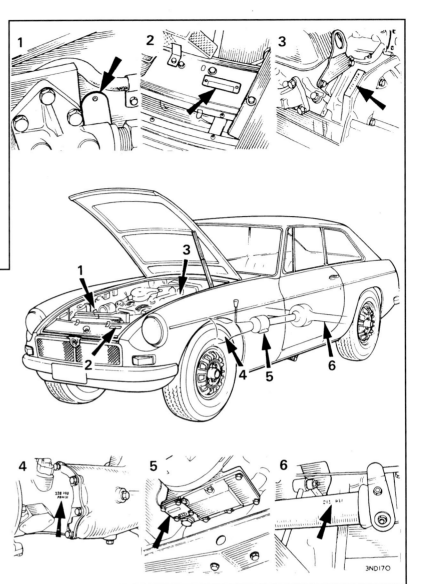

Here's where you find the MGB GT V8's identification numbers

1 **Car number.** Stamped on a plate secured to the right-hand valance.
2 **Commission number.** Stamped on a plate secured to the bonnet locking platform.
3 **Engine number.** Stamped on the left-hand side of the cylinder block directly behind the left-hand cylinder head.
4 **Gearbox number.** Stamped on the right-hand side of the gearbox casing.
5 **Overdrive unit number.** Stamped on a plate secured to the underside of the overdrive main casing.
6 **Rear axle number.** Stamped on the left-hand side of the rear axle tube near the spring seating.

The later model MGB's identification numbers are found in the locations shown here

1 **Car number.** Stamped on a plate secured to the right-hand valance.
2 **Engine number.** Stamped on a plate secured to the right-hand side of the cylinder block, or stamped directly onto the cylinder head.
3 **Gearbox number.** Stamped on the right-hand side of the gearbox casing.
4 **Overdrive unit number.** Stamped on a plate secured to the underside of the overdrive main casing.
5 **Rear axle number.** Stamped on the left-hand side of the rear axle tube near the spring seating.

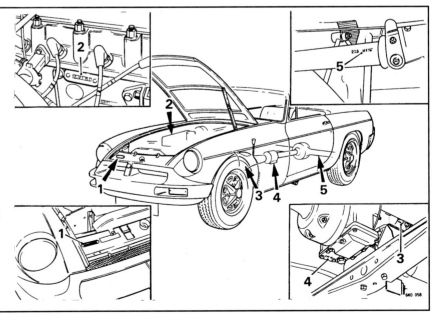

CHAPTER 3
SERVICE INTERVALS, STEP-BY-STEP

Everyone wants to own a car that starts first time, runs reliably and lasts longer than the average. And there's no magic about how to put your car into that category; it's all a question of thorough maintenance! If you follow the Service Jobs listed here - or have a garage or mechanic do it for you - you can almost guarantee that your car will still be going strong when others have fallen by the wayside... or the hard shoulder. Mind you, we would be among the first to acknowledge that this Service Schedule is just about as thorough as you can get: it's an amalgam of all the maker's recommended service items plus all the 'Inside Information' from the experts that we could find. If you want your car to be as well looked after as possible, you'll follow the Jobs shown here, but if you don't want to go all the way, you can pick and choose from the most essential items in the list. But do bear in mind that the Jobs we recommend are there for some very good reasons:

- ◆ body maintenance is rarely included in most service schedules. We believe it to be essential.
- ◆ preventative maintenance figures very high on our list of priorities. And that's why so many of our service jobs have the word "Check..." near the start!
- ◆ older cars need more jobs doing on them than new cars - it's as simple as that - so we list the jobs you will need to carry out in order to keep any car, older or new, in fine fettle.

USING THE SERVICE SCHEDULES

At the start of each Service Job, you'll see a heading in bold type, looking a bit like this:

☐ **Job 25. Adjust spark plugs.**

Following the heading will be all the information you will need to enable you to carry out that particular Job. Please note that different models of car might have different settings. Please check Chapter 8, Facts and Figures. Exactly the same Job number and heading will be found in Appendix 4, Service History at the back of this book, where you will want to keep a full record of all the work you have carried out. After you have finished servicing your car, you will be able to tick off all of the jobs that you have completed and so, service by service, build up a complete Service History of work completed on your car.

You will also find other key information immediately after each Job title and in most cases, there will be reference to an illustration - a photograph or line drawing, whichever is easier for you to follow - usually on the same page.

If the Job shown only applies to certain vehicles, the Job title will be followed by a description of the type of vehicle to which the Job title applies. For instance, Job 31 applies to "**US AND EXPORT CARS ONLY**" - and the information that follows tells you so.

Other special headings are also used. One reads **OPTIONAL**, which means that you may wish to use your own discretion as to whether to carry out this particular Job or whether to leave it until it crops up again in a later service. Another is *INSIDE INFORMATION*. This tells you that here is a Job or a special tip that you wouldn't normally get to hear about, other than through the experience and 'inside' knowledge of the experts at Bromsgrove MG Centre, who have helped in compiling this Service Guide. The third is **SPECIALIST SERVICE**, which means that we recommend you to have this work carried out by a specialist. Some jobs, such as setting the tracking or suspension are best done with the right measuring equipment while other jobs may demand the use of equipment such as an exhaust gas analyser. Where we think you are better off having the work done for you, we say so!

SAFETY FIRST!

The other special heading is the one that could be the most important one of all! SAFETY FIRST! information must always be read with care and always taken seriously. In addition, please read Chapter 1 Safety First! at the beginning of this book before carrying out any work on your car. There are many hazards associated with working on a car but all of them can be avoided by adhering strictly to the safety rules. Don't skimp on safety!

We are grateful to the MGB, C and V8 specialists at Bromsgrove MG Centre for their kind assistance with this chapter. Almost all of the work was photographed there.

Throughout the Service Schedule, each 'shorter' Service Interval is meant to be an important part of each of the next 'longer' Service Interval, too. For instance, under 1,500 Mile Mechanical and Electrical - Around the Car, Job 18, you are instructed to check the tyres for wear or damage. This Job also has to be carried out at 3,000 miles, 6,000 miles, 9,000 miles, and so on. It is therefore shown in the list of extra Jobs to be carried out in each of these 'longer' Service Intervals but only as a Job number, without the detailed instructions that were given the first time around!

The 'Catch-up' Service

When you first buy a used car, you never know for sure just how well it's been looked after. Even one with a full service history is unlikely to have been serviced as thoroughly as one with a Porter Publishing Service Guide history! So, if you want to catch-up on all the servicing that may have been neglected on your car, just work through the entire list of Service Jobs listed for the **36,000 miles - or Every Thirty Six Months** service, add on the **Longer Term Servicing** Jobs, and your car will be bang up to date and serviced as well as you could hope for. Do allow several days for all of this work, not least because it will almost certainly throw up a number of extra jobs - potential faults that have been lurking beneath the surface - all of which will need putting right before you can 'sign off' your car as being in tip-top condition.

The Service History

Those people fortunate enough to own a new car, or one that has been well maintained from new will have the opportunity to keep a service record, or 'Service History' of their car, usually filled in by a main dealer. Until now, it hasn't been possible for the owner of an older car to keep a formal record of servicing but now you can, using the complete tick list in **Appendix 4, Service History**. In fact, you can go one better than the owners of those new cars, because your car's Service History will be more complete and more detailed than any manufacturer's service record, with the extra bonus that there is space for you to keep a record of all of those extra items that crop up from time to time. New tyres; replacement exhaust; extra accessories; where can you show those on a regular service schedule? Now you can, so if your battery goes down only 11 months after buying it, you'll be able to look up where and when you bought it. All you'll have to do is remember to fill in your Service History in the first place!

RAISING A CAR - SAFELY!

You will often need to raise your car off the ground in order to carry out the Service Jobs shown here. To start off with, here's what you must never do: NEVER work beneath a car held on a jack, not even a trolley jack. Quite a number of deaths have been caused by a car slipping off a jack while someone has been working beneath. On the other hand, the safest way is by raising a car on a proprietary brand of ramps. Sometimes, there is no alternative but to use axle stands. Please read all of the following information and act upon it!

I

When using car ramps:

(**I**) Make absolutely certain that the ramps are parallel to the wheels of the car and that the wheels are exactly central on each ramp.

II

(**II**) Always have an assistant watch both sides of the car as you drive up. Drive up to the end 'stops' on the ramps but never over them! Apply the hand brake firmly, put the car in first or reverse gear, or 'Park', in the case of an automatic.

(**III**) Chock both wheels remaining on the ground, both in front and behind so that the car can't move in either direction. This also applies when the car is supported on axle stands.

III

INSIDE INFORMATION: wrap a strip of carpet into a loop around the first 'rung' of the ramps and drive over the doubled-up piece of carpet on the approach to the ramps. This prevents the ramps from skidding away, as they are inclined to do, as the car is driven on to them.

IV

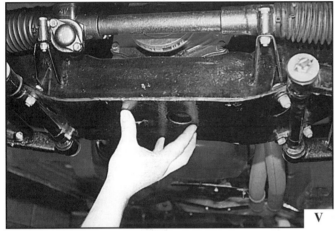

V

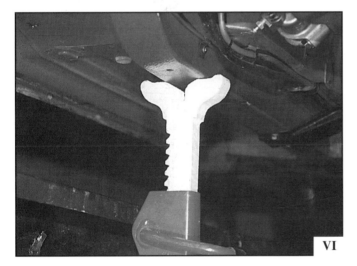

VI

VII

(**IV**) On other occasions, you might need to work on the car whilst it is supported on an axle stand or a pair of axle stands. These are inherently less stable than ramps and so you must take much greater care when working beneath them. In particular:
- ensure that the axle stand is on flat, stable ground, never on ground where one side can sink in to the ground.
- ensure that the car is on level ground and that the hand brake is off and the transmission in neutral.
- raise the car with a trolley jack - invest in one if you don't already own one; the car's wheel changing jack is often too unstable. Place a piece of cloth over the head of the jack if your car is nicely finished on the underside. Ensure that the floor is sufficiently clear and smooth for the trolley jack wheels to roll as the car is raised and lowered, otherwise it could slip off the jack.

(**V**) Place the jack beneath the front cross-member when raising the front of the car ...

(**VI**) ... and place the axle stands beneath the 'chassis' rails that run front-to-back, beneath the floor.

(**VII**) At the rear of the car, place the jack head securely beneath the differential casing, at the centre of the rear axle, and the axle stands beneath the spring shackle plates, where the axle is bolted to the springs. Take care not to let the axle stand perch on the head of one of the bolts sticking down, through the spring shackle. Settle it on a flat, level part of the surface of the shackle plate.

If, for any reason, you can't use the location points recommended here, take care to locate the top of the axle stand on a strong, level, stable part of the car's underside. A chassis member is ideal, but you should never use a movable suspension part because the part can move and allow the axle stand to slip, or use the floor of the car, which is just too weak.

Just as when using ramps - only even more importantly! - apply the hand brake firmly, put the car in first or reverse gear (or 'Park', in the case of an automatic) and chock both wheels remaining on the ground, both in front and behind.

Be especially careful when applying force to a spanner or when pulling hard on anything, when the car is supported off the ground. It is all too easy to move the car so far that it topples off the axle stand or stands. And remember that if a car falls on you, YOU COULD BE KILLED!

Whenever working beneath a car, have someone primed to keep an eye on you! If someone pops out to see how you are getting on every quarter of an hour or so, it could be enough to save your life! Do remember that, in general, a car will be more stable when only one wheel is removed and one axle stand used than if two wheels are removed in conjunction with two axle stands. You are strongly advised not to work on the car with all four wheels off the ground, on four axle stands. The car could then be very unstable and dangerous to work beneath.

When lowering the car to the ground, remember to remove the chocks, release the hand brake and place the transmission in neutral.

500 Miles, Weekly or Before Long Journeys, Whichever Comes First

These are the regular checks that you need to carry out to help keep your car safe and reliable. They don't include the major Service Jobs but they should be carried out as an integral part of every 'proper' service.

500 mile Mechanical and Electrical - The Engine Bay

☐ **Job 1. Engine oil level.**

Check the engine's oil level with the car on level ground.

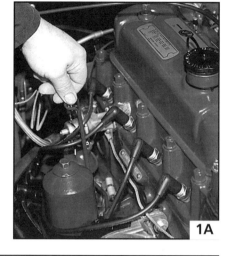

1A

1A. The MGB's and MGC's oil dipsticks are on the right hand side of the engine. Lift out the dipstick, wipe it clean with a clean cloth, push it back in and lift it out again. Take a look at the level of the oil on the dipstick. You might have to do it two or three times before you can see a clear reading - the oil on the stick sometimes 'smears' as the stick is pulled out.

1B. The oil level (1B.1) should be somewhere between the MAX and MIN levels. Make sure that the dipstick is pushed right back when replacing it and when 'dipping' it to discover the oil level.

The MGB's and MGC's filler caps (1B.2) are on the top of the rocker cover, on the top of the engine, although the MGC's is at the back. Both metal and plastic caps twist-and-lift off.

1C. The MGB GT V8's and MG RV8's dipsticks are on the left hand side of the engine, 'inside' the air cleaner assembly on the RV8, 'outside' it on the GT V8.

1D. The MG RV8's oil filler cap is on the left hand side, the earlier V8's is on the opposite side. V8 oil filler caps screw off. Don't force the cap down; just screw it down, by hand only, until you feel the seal grip.

Also, check the ground over which the car has been parked, for evidence of oil or other fluid leaks. (If any leaks are found, do not drive the car without first establishing where the leaks have come from - they could come from a major failure in the braking system.)

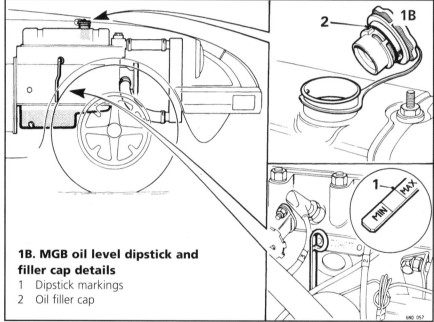

1B. MGB oil level dipstick and filler cap details
1 Dipstick markings
2 Oil filler cap

1C

1D

☐ Job 2. Clutch fluid level.

2. Check/top up clutch fluid reservoir. The level should be just at the bottom of the filler neck.

INSIDE INFORMATION: i) Check the ground on which the car has been parked, especially beneath the engine bay and inside each road wheel, for evidence of oil, clutch or brake fluid leaks. If any are found, investigate further before driving the car.
ii) Clutch fluid will damage painted surfaces if allowed to come into contact. Take care not to spill any, but if there is an accident, refit the master cylinder cap and wash off any accidental spillage immediately with hot soapy water.

SAFETY FIRST!
i) If brake/clutch fluid should come into contact with the skin or eyes, rinse immediately with plenty of water.
ii) The brake fluid level will fall slightly during normal use, but if it falls significantly below the bottom of the filler cap neck (or in the case of the MG RV8, below the bottom of the neck at all), stop using the car and seek specialist advice.
iii) If you get dirt into the hydraulic system it can cause brake failure. Wipe the filler cap clean before removing.
iv) Use only new brake fluid from an air-tight container. Old fluid will absorb moisture and this could cause the brakes to fail when carrying out an emergency stop or other heavy use of the brakes - just when you need them most and are least able to do anything about it, in fact!.

☐ Job 3. Brake fluid level.

3A. Check/top up brake fluid reservoir. The level should be just at the bottom of the filler neck.

3B. The MG RV8 has a transparent brake master cylinder. Be careful not to damage the wiring fitted to the cap when unscrewing - it's not easy!

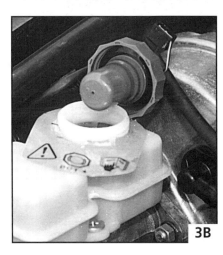

INSIDE INFORMATION: i) Check the ground on which the car has been parked, especially beneath the engine bay and inside each road wheel, for evidence of oil, clutch or brake fluid leaks. If any are found, investigate further before driving the car.
ii) Brake fluid will damage painted surfaces if allowed to come into contact. Take care not to spill any but if there is an accident, refit the master cylinder cap and wash off any accidental spillage immediately with hot soapy water.

US MODELS ONLY: Brake failure warning light. Press the switch on the dashboard to test the circuit. Do not drive the car if a fault is indicated, until the fault has been checked out and rectified.
MG RV8 ONLY: Test the brake fluid warning light and its circuit. Switch on the ignition and release the hand brake. When you press the flexible contact cover in the centre of the filler cap, the warning light should illuminate. If it does not, and the fluid level is satisfactory, consult your dealer.

SAFETY FIRST!

i) The gas given off by a battery is highly explosive. Never smoke, use a naked flame or allow a spark to occur in the battery compartment. Never disconnect the battery/ies (it can cause sparking) with the battery caps removed.

ii) Batteries contain sulphuric acid. If the acid comes into contact with the skin or eyes, wash immediately with copious amounts of cold water and seek medical advice.

iii) Do not check the battery levels within half an hour of the battery/ies being charged with a battery charger. The addition of fresh water could then cause the highly acid and corrosive electrolyte to flood out of the battery.

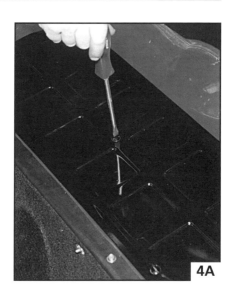
4A

☐ **Job 4. Battery electrolyte.**
INSIDE THE CAR

4A. The battery or batteries (depending upon model) can be found beneath a cover, under the carpet that fits over the parcel shelf, behind the seats. Release the cover by turning each screw half a turn, with a coin or screwdriver, which allows the cover to be lifted away.

4B. Unless the battery is a 'sealed for life' unit, remove the battery caps or cover and, with the car on level ground, check the level of the electrolyte - the fluid inside each battery cell. You often can't see it at first, use an inspection lamp or flashlight and tap the side of the battery to make the surface of the electrolyte ripple a little, so that you can see it. The plates inside the battery should just be covered with electrolyte. If the level has fallen, top up with distilled water,

4B

NEVER with tap water! Dry off the top of the battery. If the battery terminals are obviously furred, refer to Job 61.

4C. *INSIDE INFORMATION: i) Once water is mixed with the acid inside the battery, it won't freeze. So, in extremely cold weather, run the car (out of doors) so that you put a charge into the battery and this will mix the fresh water with the electrolyte, cutting out the risk of freezing and a cracked battery case.*

ii) Here's how to check the strength, or specific gravity, of the battery electrolyte. You place the end of a hydrometer into the battery electrolyte, squeeze and release the rubber bulb so that a little of the acid is drawn up into the transparent tube and the float, or floats, inside the tube (small coloured beads are sometimes used) give the specific gravity. If a battery goes flat because the car has been left standing for too long, use a small battery charger to re-charge the battery, following the maker's instructions and disconnecting the battery/ies on the car first. A battery that goes flat too rapidly can be checked by a garage - they may well check the specific gravity of the electrolyte in each cell in order to establish whether one or more has failed but since garages often tell you that you need a new battery anyway, it might be worth investing in a hydrometer and testing the cells yourself. Otherwise, you could try disconnecting the battery and seeing if it still goes flat. If not, suspect a wiring fault allowing the current to drain away but do be aware that some car alarms will drain a car battery in around a week. They are designed primarily for cars that are used almost every day, rather than classic or special interest cars that may not be used so often.

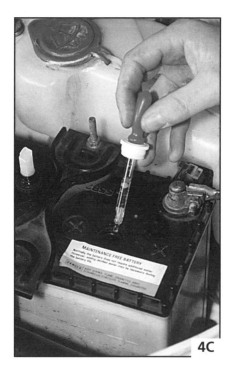
4C

5

☐ **Job 5. Washer reservoir.**
Check/top up the windscreen washer reservoir.

5. Remember that in cold weather a stronger concentration of washer fluid will help to prevent the washer system from freezing up. Check the recommended dilution on the package.

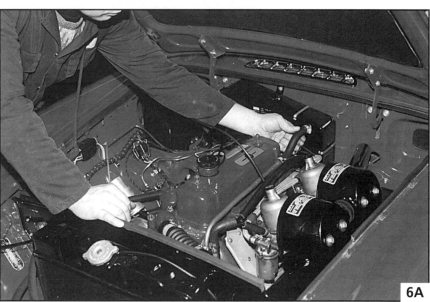

6A

☐ **Job 6. Coolant system**

6A. Carry out a visual check on all coolant system and other hoses in and around the engine bay for leaks.

6B. OLDER CARS: Top up with a mixture of 50% anti-freeze and water until the level is just beneath the filler neck on the radiator.

6C. NEWER CARS: (i.e. those cars with a separate expansion bottle).
Top up with a mixture of 50% anti-freeze and water to the 'coolant level' as indicated on the expansion bottle.

6B

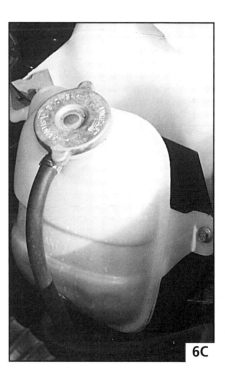

6C

SAFETY FIRST!
i) The coolant level should be checked WHEN THE SYSTEM IS COLD. If you remove the pressure cap when the engine is hot, the release of pressure can cause the water in the cooling system to boil and spurt several feet in the air with the risk of severe scalding. ii) Take precautions to prevent anti-freeze coming in contact with the skin or eyes. If this should happen, rinse immediately with plenty of water.

500 mile Mechanical and Electrical - Around the Car

☐ Job 7. Check horns.

Try the horn button. If the horns fail to work, examine the wiring to the horns, or the horns themselves.

SPECIALIST SERVICE: Horn wiring and connections can be more complex than they appear at first. For instance, on some models, both terminals at the horn should be 'live'! If there is no obvious problem with wiring connections, first check the fuses and if they are okay, have the horn, the circuitry and the switches checked over by a specialist.

☐ Job 8. Windscreen washers.

8. Check the operation of the windscreen washers. If one of them fails to work, check that the pipes have not come adrift and then check the jet; clear it with a pin. Some jets are adjustable by inserting a pin and twisting the jet inside its rubber housing; others are turned with a screwdriver, as shown.

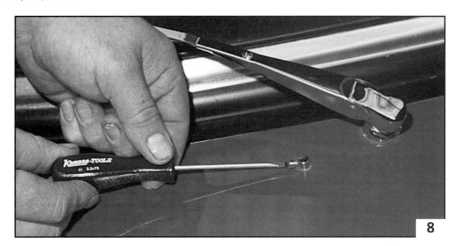

8

☐ Job 9. Windscreen wipers.

9A. Check that the wiper blades are not torn, worn or damaged in any way. Give each blade a wipe clean with methylated spirit (industrial alcohol). As you can see from ill. 9A.6, many wiper arms are held in place with a peg and spring. Lift the spring (9A.4) with your thumb nail and pull the sleeve of the wiper blade (9A.3) clear of the peg on the arm, sliding the blade free.

9B. With the later type of retainer, you must lift the wiper arm away from the windscreen and hold in the retaining button (9B.1), slide the wiper blade towards the screen for a little way (9B.2), then move the blade sideways and slide it free of the arm (9B.3).

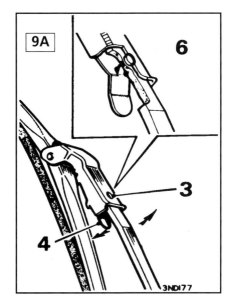

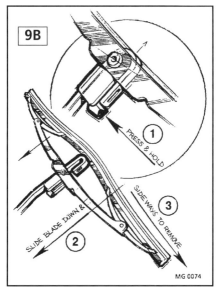

☐ Job 10. Tyre pressures.

10. Use a reliable tyre pressure gauge to check the tyre pressures on the car, but never after driving the car which warms up the tyres considerably and increases their pressures.

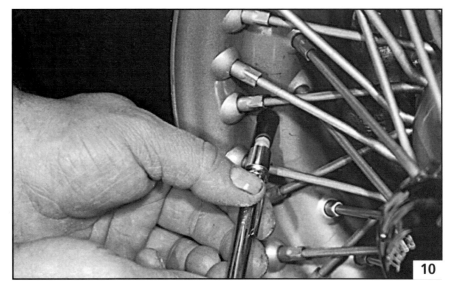

10

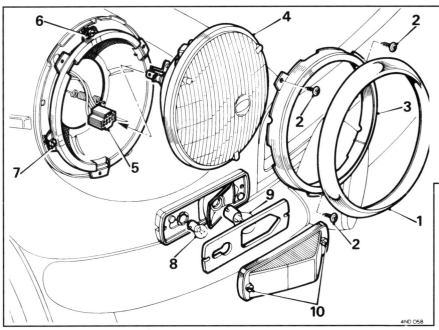

4ND OSB

11A. Sealed beam type headlamp unit and remote sidelamp assembly

1. Headlamp rim
2. Inner rim retaining screws
3. Inner rim
4. Headlamp unit
5. Wiring socket
6. Vertical beam adjustment screw
7. Horizontal beam adjustment screw
8. Sidelamp bulb
9. Direction indicator bulb
10. Lens retaining screws

INSIDE INFORMATION: if a complete 'set' of bulbs fails to operate (and especially if other electrical components fail at the same time) check fuses before suspecting any other fault.

☐ **Job 11. Check headlamps.**
SPECIALIST SERVICE: It is not possible to set headlamps accurately at home. In **Chapter 7, Getting Through the MoT**, we show how to trial-set your headlamps before going to the MoT Testing Station (in the UK). This method is only suitable if you are going to have the settings re-checked by a garage with proper beam checking equipment.

11A. The components for a sealed beam set-up are the simplest to deal with. The beam is set by turning in and out screws shown at numbers 11A.6 and 11A.7.

11B. Headlamp rims were never meant to be removed, it sometimes seems! Bromsgrove MG Centre do so by carefully levering between lamp and rim, taking enormous care not to crack the glass. You could lever at a similar point, between body and rim, with a piece of card to stop the screwdriver from damaging the body. Either method can go wrong, but the first is more straightforward.

11C. After removing the three screws (11A.2) holding the inner rim (11A.3), the unit inside will slip to the floor and break, if you're not careful! Sealed beam units just plug straight out and in again (11A.5).

11D. Latest, 'rubber bumper' MGBs have headlamps with integral sidelamps. When replacing a bulb, NEVER touch the bulb with your fingers. If you do so, wipe it clean with methylated spirit (industrial alcohol). Make sure that the spring holding the bulb in place fits over the bulb spigots and under the retaining spigots on the lamp unit (11D.10). Also, make sure that the seal (11D.6) is properly fitted before refitting the lamp unit to the car's body.

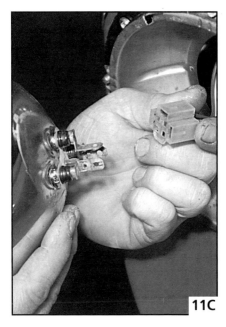

11B

11C

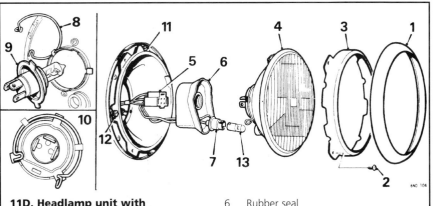

6ND 104

11D. Headlamp unit with integral sidelamp assembly

1. Headlamp rim
2. Inner rim retaining screws
3. Inner rim
4. Headlamp unit
5. Wiring socket

6. Rubber seal
7. Sidelamp bulb holder
8. Headlamp bulb retaining spring
9. Headlamp bulb
10. Bulb and spring correctly fitted
11. Vertical beam adjustment screw
12. Horizontal beam adjustment screw
13. Sidelamp bulb

11E. Inevitably, with a car that was in production for such a long time, there have been almost more types of bulb holder than you can shake a stick at. These are the earlier types.

Job 12. Check front sidelamps.

Check the front sidelamp, side marker lamp (where fitted) and indicator bulbs (and the direction indicator warning light) and replace if necessary. If you have to remove a lens (11A, 8 to 10), clean it inside and out by washing in soapy water - it makes a big difference! Bulbs are removed by pushing in, twisting anti-clockwise and pulling out - but there's precious little to grip!

INSIDE INFORMATION: If a bulb refuses to budge, try gripping with a piece of cloth - it provides a lot more grip and reduces the risk if the bulb glass breaks. If the bulb comes free of its brass ferrule, carefully break it away and push one side of the ferrule in with a screwdriver (lights/indicators turned off!). Spray releasing fluid behind the bulb base and leave for a while. Then work the base free by gripping the side that you have pushed in, using a pair of pliers.

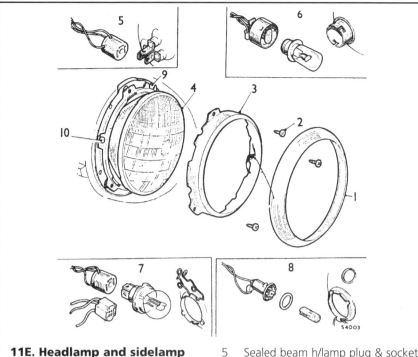

11E. Headlamp and sidelamp bulb assembly types

1 Headlamp rim	5 Sealed beam h/lamp plug & socket
2 Inner rim retaining screws	6 Early type headlamp bulb assembly
3 Inner rim	7 Later type headlamp bulb assembly
4 Headlamp unit	8 Early type sidelamp bulb assembly
	9 Vertical beam adjustment screw
	10 Horizontal beam adjustment screw

Job 13. Check rear sidelamps.

13A. Check/replace the rear sidelamp, side marker lamp (where fitted), stop lamp and indicator bulbs and clean the lenses. Earlier cars with more rounded lenses have one screw to hold the lens in place. Unscrew and lift the lens up and away. Later cars with squared-off lenses have two screws, one at the bottom and one half way up the lens. Corrosion is rarely a problem with any of these lamps, unlike the front lamps.

13B. Note that the rear tail lamp/stop lamp bulbs have a pair of offset pegs, so that they can't be fitted the wrong way round. This might explain why a new bulb won't go back in - but it's easy when you notice it!

Job 14. Number plate lamps.

14A. Check the rear number plate lamps, replace the bulbs if necessary and clean out the lenses. The type that bolt to the rear bumper have a nut behind each screw - not shown in some handbooks! These small nuts can be pigs to get at!

14B. Rubber bumper cars have a pair of bulbs each side of the number plate. A single screw - sometimes straight, sometimes cross-head - holds each cover in place.

13A

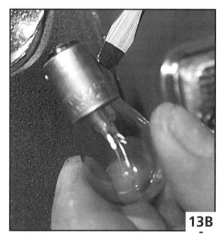
13B

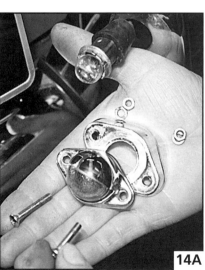
14A

14B

15

16

☐ Job 15. Reversing lamps.

15. Check the reversing lamps, replace the bulbs if necessary and clean the lenses. Also check any auxiliary lamps, such as fog lamps, that may have been fitted as original equipment (latest cars) or as accessories, in which case they are still supposed to function correctly, by law.

☐ Job 16. Check wheel spinners

WIRE WHEELED CARS ONLY:

16. Check the wheel spinners for tightness with the wheel raised from the ground, never with the weight of the car on the spinner, or it might seem tight when it is not, with the possibility of disastrous consequences. Note the instructions on each wheel spinner for the correct direction of tightening and removing. Use only the correct type of soft-faced mallet to avoid damaging the spinners, or use the correct spanner on later-type spinners with a hexagonal nut shape instead of ears.

INSIDE INFORMATION: Bromsgrove MG Centre advise that, in their great experience of servicing MGBs, wire wheels can and do come loose in use. This is a job that should not be avoided!

500 mile Bodywork and Interior - Around The Car

☐ Job 17. Valet bodywork.

Wash the soft-top, paintwork, chrome and glass with water and a suitable car wash detergent, taking care not to get 'wax-wash' on the glass. Finish by washing the wheels and tyre walls. Leather the paintwork dry and then polish. Use a separate leather on glass to avoid transferring polish from the paintwork. **SOFT-TOP CARS:** Use a soft brush to remove dust and flaking dirt prior to washing. Do not use any form of cleaning agents for cleaning the soft-top - ordinary car wash products will do the job.

INSIDE INFORMATION: If the weather is particularly wet or muddy, road dirt may collect beneath the leading edge of the soft-top where it fits against the windscreen surround. From time to time, open the soft-top and carefully wash this area.

1,500 Miles - or Every Month, Whichever Comes First

1,500 Mile Mechanical and Electrical - Around the Car

18A

☐ Job 18. Check tyres.

18A. Check the tyres for tread depth, using a tread depth gauge and note that in the UK, the minimum legal tread depth is 1.6 mm. However, tyres are not at their safest at that level and you might want to replace them earlier. Also check both sides of each tyre for uneven wear, cuts, bulges or other damage in the tyre walls. Raise each wheel off the ground, using an axle stand, otherwise you won't be able to see the inside of each tyre properly and nor will you be able to check that part of the tyre that is in contact with the ground.

☐ Job 19. Check spare tyre.

Check the tread depth, check for damage, check the wear pattern and the tyre pressure on the spare tyre, too. You should inflate the spare to the maximum recommended for high speed or high load running. Then, if you have a puncture whilst on a journey, you'll be OK. It's always easier to carry a tyre pressure gauge with you and let some air out than put some in!

SAFETY FIRST!

Tyres that show uneven wear tell their own story, if only you know how to speak the language! If any tyre is worn more on one side than another, consult your specialist MG centre or tyre specialist. It probably means that your suspension or steering is out of adjustment - probably a simple tracking job but conceivably symptomatic of suspension damage, so have it checked. If a tyre is worn more in the centre or on the edges, it could mean that your tyre pressures are wrong, but once again, have the car checked. Also see pages 94 and 95.

CHAPTER THREE

1,500 Mile Bodywork and Interior - Around the Car

☐ Job 20. Touch-up paintwork.
Treat stone chips or scratches to prevent or eliminate rust. Allow ample time for new paint to harden before applying polish.

☐ Job 21. Aerial/antenna.
Clean the sections of an extending, chrome plated aerial mast. Wipe a little releasing fluid (not oil - it will attract dirt) onto the surface and work the aerial in and out a few times.

☐ Job 22. Valet interior.
Use a vacuum cleaner to remove dust and grit from the interior trim and carpets. Those cheap 12 volt vacuum cleaners are generally a waste of money so if you can't get your domestic cleaner to the car, take the car to a garage with a self-service valeting facility. Proprietary upholstery cleaners can be surprisingly effective and well worthwhile if the interior has become particularly grubby. Very bad stains, caused by grease, chocolate or unidentified flying brown stuff are best loosened with white spirit or methylated spirit before bringing on the upholstery cleaner - but first test a bit of upholstery that you can't normally see, just in case either of the spirits removes upholstery colour.

Seat belts should be washed only with warm water and a non-detergent soap. Allow them to dry naturally and do not let them retract, if they're the inertia reel type, until completely dry.

☐ Job 23. Improve visibility!
Use a proprietary brand of windscreen cleaner to remove built-up traffic film and air-borne contaminants from the outside of the windscreen, and smears from the inside. Wipe wiper blades with methylated spirit to remove grease and contaminants.

20

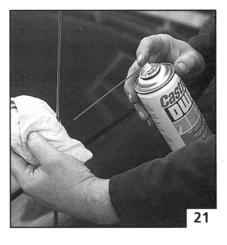
21

1,500 Mile Bodywork - Under the Car

> *SAFETY FIRST!*
> *Wear goggles when clearing the underside of the car. Read carefully the information at the start of this chapter on lifting and supporting the car.*

☐ Job 24. Clean mud traps.

24A. Hose the underside of the car (if particularly muddy) and allow to dry before putting it in the garage, or scrape off dry mud. Wear gloves because mud can force itself painfully behind finger nails!

24B. Clean out the main mud traps behind the head lamps and around the wheel arches. This shot shows a favourite gathering point for mud, which holds in moisture and salt and, of course, causes corrosion in a big way!

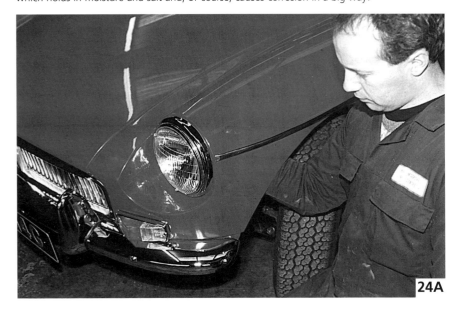
24A

24B

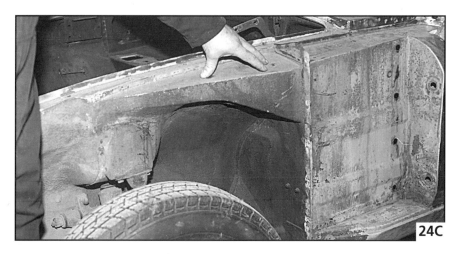

24C. A peculiarity to all models of MGB and MGC is this ledge beneath the wing. There's just the right size and shape of gap between the ledge and wing top for a mud poultice to do its worst! Always scrape it clear. Also, the vertical line, just to the rear, is where a mud shield (pause for ironical laughter!) is fitted. The seal between the mud shield and wing is notoriously poor, with the result that mud can penetrate. Try to keep it clear and replace the seal if it is missing. This, unfortunately, means having to unbolt a usually well rusted-in line of bolts...

3,000 Miles - or Every Three Months, Whichever Comes First.

3,000 mile Mechanical and Electrical - The Engine Bay

First carry out Jobs 2 to 6.

Job 25. Adjust spark plugs.

25A. Number the spark plug HT leads to avoid confusion when refitting, then carefully pull them off the plugs. Remove the spark plugs using a proper plug socket with a rubber insert. This prevents the plug from dropping on the floor and breaking, and also prevents the socket from leaning over and breaking the plug's insulator as it is unscrewed.

25B. Check the spark plugs to ensure that they are in acceptable condition (see colour illustrations on Page 65) and also check that i) the round terminal nut is tight - tighten with pliers - and ii) the gap is correct. Clean up the electrode end with a brass bristle wire brush applied vigorously! Check the gap with a feeler gauge - the end of the gauge should just go in, making contact and meeting just the smallest resistance from both sides, but without being forced in any way. Lever the longer earth (ground) electrode away to open the gap - but take great care not to move or damage the centre electrode or its insulation - and tap the electrode on a hard surface to close it up again. If in doubt, throw the plugs away and buy new. Running with damaged or worn out plugs is false economy - although having said that, don't just change them for the sake of it. Look for evidence of electrode erosion, insulator staining, damage - or just old age. Make sure that the threads are clean then screw the plugs back by hand. Finally tighten them to the torque setting given in **Chapter 8, Facts and Figures**. Carry out the next Job before refitting the HT leads.

Job 26. Check HT Circuit.

26A. Check the condition of the distributor cap and rotor arm and the security of the wiring connections to the distributor. Removing an MGB's and MGC's distributor cap is tricky because of its location, although the V8's is easy to get at. Try levering the tops of the cap clips with a screwdriver, but take care that the bottom of the clip doesn't jump off the distributor body, possibly losing the clip somewhere. Try to hold it on with your other hand as the screwdriver goes to work. Leave the plug HT leads in place on the distributor so that you can't confuse where they go. Disconnect the HT lead that comes from the coil if you want to take the cap away and into the daylight.

INSIDE INFORMATION: You're going to have to lean right over the car's wing, so cover it with a soft cloth or (Bromsgrove MG Centre's tip) 'bubble pack' plastic, held on with masking tape.

26B. Check the rotor arm tip for burning or brightness. If it's bright, it suggests that the distributor bushes have worn out and that means that reconditioning is needed. If the distributor rotor can move about, allowing its tip to brush against the contacts inside the distributor cap, the distributor accuracy will be way out too, which means that your car will run badly, uneconomically and may fail the emissions part of the MoT test. If this has been happening, the contacts will also be bright and you can expect to see quite a bit of brass or aluminium dust inside the distributor cap. Black dust in any quantity suggests that the top (carbon) contact has worn away - it should protrude from the centre of the cap and move in and out freely under light spring pressure. Also check for any signs of 'tracking' between the cap contacts. This will appear as a thin black line visible on the inside or outside of the cap between the contacts. These tracking lines are paths letting the spark run to earth instead of down the HT lead where it should be going. If you have any of these problems, fit a new cap. This is the MGB GT V8 distributor cap, complete with all those extra contacts in the cap.

If the cap looks OK, give it a good wipe inside and out with a clean cloth, and clean all the leads as well. Check each one for signs of corrosion at the end contacts and deterioration of the insulation. If in doubt fit a new set (not just one!).

☐ Job 27. Distributor.

27A. And this is where you'll find the distributor on the MGB: tricky to say the least!

27B. First remove the rotor arm (27B.1) by pulling it off the distributor shaft. You're not changing the contact breaker points at this stage, that comes later in the service schedule, but for now, with the ignition turned off, use a screwdriver to open the points up (27B.2) and see if they are badly pitted or burned. If there is any evidence of such marks, fit new points as shown in Job 65. and fit a new condenser as well because a faulty condenser will cause points burning.

27B. Distributor components

1. Rotor arm
2. Points gap
3. Distributor shaft cam
4. Pivot post
5. Distributor shaft felt pad
6. Distributor body lubrication point
7. Baseplate lubrication point
8. Fixing screw
9. Turn screwdriver anticlockwise to increase points gap
10. Turn screwdriver clockwise to decrease points gap
11. Fixing screw and washers
12. Contact breaker points assembly
13. Wiring connections
14. CB heel

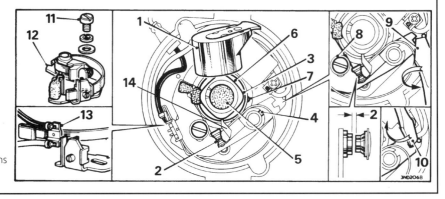

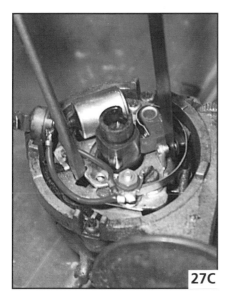

27C

27D

27E

Since the heel on the points can wear down, you'll have to adjust the points gap. Turn the engine over (either by pressing on the fan belt and turning the fan, or by using a spanner on the crankshaft pulley bolt) which will rotate the distributor shaft cam (27B.3). Stop turning when the heel on the points (27B.14) is at the top of the cam lobe. Now slacken the screw (27B.8).

27C. By inserting a screwdriver between the "V"-shape in the base plate and the "V" in the points (27B.10) you will be able to open and close the points gap (27B.2). Here you can see a feeler gauge inserted into the points gap. Adjust the gap until the feeler gauge just makes contact with both sides of the points at once - a tricky business because it's easy to close the points up too far so that they snap shut as you pull out the feeler gauge and it's equally easy to leave them too far apart because it's difficult to discern when the feeler gauge is actually in contact. Still, you have to persevere!

27D.The V8 distributor is far easier to get at, being situated on the front of the engine at the top, and the points gap is particularly easy to adjust. Use a spanner on the hexagonal nut sticking out of the side of the distributor body, shown here.

You should also take this opportunity to lubricate the distributor taking enormous care not to get grease or oil on to the distributor points or any other electrical components. Very lightly smear the cam (27B.3) with a very small amount of grease or petroleum jelly. Add a few drops of oil to the felt pad in the top of the distributor shaft, if there is one (27B.5), but do not oil the cam wiping pad. If you accidentally get any oil or grease onto the contact breaker points, wipe them clean with a cloth dampened with methylated spirits. Add another three or four drops between the contact plate and the distributor shaft (27B.6) so that the oil runs down into the body of the distributor beneath the base plate. If this hasn't been done for some time, it's a good idea to use a can of releasing fluid with an injector nozzle to spray a small quantity beneath the base plate and into the body of the distributor. The centrifugal weights inside the distributor can seize and this would cause the engine to lose power.

27E. The most accurate way of setting the points gap is by using a dwell meter - they can be bought quite inexpensively from motor accessory stores. See the instructions with the meter for its correct use.

Job 28. Generator belt.

28A. The generator belt should have about 1/2 inch (12 mm) of free movement on its longest length. This is an MGC with the radiator removed, just so that you can see more clearly without the use of X-ray specs.! The free movement you are looking for is towards and away from the pulley on the water pump, not backwards and forwards.

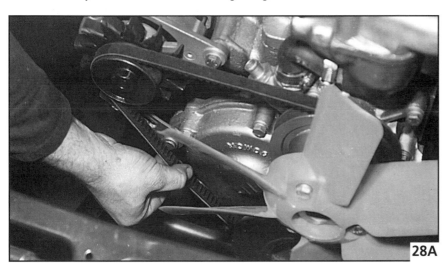

28A

28B. The generator belt should also be checked carefully for wear. If you see any signs of cracking or fraying, or if the driving surfaces of the belt look polished, renew it. Unfortunately, the modern type of toothed belt can only be properly checked by taking it off. Examine the inside of the belt all the way around, bending it back to front and looking for cracking.

INSIDE INFORMATION: Since this type of belt is so difficult to check without taking it off the car, and since the car is not drivable for very far without a belt fitted, it pays to always carry a spare with you. (And the tools to fit it!).

28C. There are slight differences in the mountings on different models and slight differences between alternators and dynamos, but the basic principles are the same. Slacken off all of the mounting bolts and the adjusting nut (28C.1 & 2). So that you don't cause any damage to an alternator, use a piece of wood rather than metal to lever the unit until the belt has the correct degree of tension. With this type of alternator, lever against the end bracket (28C.3) and not to any other part. Dynamos, with their steel casing, are not so susceptible to damage.

INSIDE INFORMATION: If you slacken off all of the bolts and nut just so far that the generator can move when levered, but not so far that it can twist on the top mounting bolts, you will be able to place a socket spanner on the adjuster nut (28C.2), holding it in place with one hand, while you lever on the piece of wood between the generator and engine block with the other. The socket spanner should stay in place while you loosen it in order to check the tension of the belt, and then you can rapidly tighten the adjuster nut, holding the generator in place. The three remaining bolts can then be tightened separately. DO NOT OVERTIGHTEN THE BELT because all that will do is cause the generator bearings and possibly the water pump bearing to fail prematurely and the belt will become stretched.

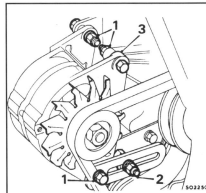

28C. Typical generator belt adjustment details
1   Mounting bolt and nuts
2   Adjuster nut
3   End bracket

☐ Job 29. SU carburettors.

OPTIONAL: SU carburettors can go out of tune quite rapidly, especially if they are past their first flush of youth! If you wish to adjust them, refer to Job 70 in the 6,000 mile service.

☐ Job 30. Check air filters.

If you ever wanted proof that the MGB was over-engineered and, in some respects, more complex than necessary, you'll find proof in those works of art, the air cleaners. Remove the air filter housing or housings, (dependent on model) and check the condition of the air cleaner elements. If they are lightly soiled at around the point where the air inlet is situated, rotate them. If they are more than very lightly soiled, replace with new. If the fibre washers holding the twin carburettor MGB's and MGC's air filter housings are split or missing, replace with new. If any gaskets are damaged or missing, renew them. The car will run badly if they're not in place and in good condition.

30A. Two long bolts pass through each air cleaner and screw into a horseshoe-shaped bracket behind each carburettor flange. One bracket has the choke cable fitted to it, the other will clang on to the floor or a chassis rail unless you put your hand on it as the bolts are undone.

30B.

30B. On the inside of each air filter housing is a cast aluminium plate - don't lose the rubber sealing ring that sits around the flange on it - and don't forget to fit a new paper gasket between the plate and the carburettor flange when refitting later on.

30C. This filter has done about 1,000 miles and is still perfectly usable. You get it out of the filter housing after taking the pressed steel plate off the bottom of the filter housing. Occasionally the base plate is difficult to remove, lever it out with a screwdriver in to the protruding lip that is pressed into both the filter housing and the base plate.

30D. By the time the MGC came along, the air filter housing was in one piece and held on with just two bolts. Make sure that the rubber seals around the carburettor mounting plates are in place

30E. The MGB GT V8 air filters are also somewhat simpler to work with.

30F. By the time the MG RV8 came along, this filtration system was both more efficient and sophisticated but also simpler to remove, each one being held on with a pair of over centre clips. This type of filter requires a minimal amount of maintenance and should not require replacement for tens of thousands of miles.

30C.

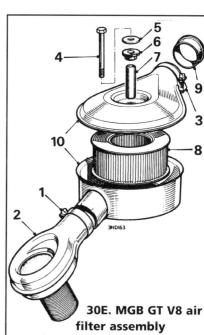

30E. MGB GT V8 air filter assembly

1 Clamp screw
2 Air temperature control assembly
3 Clamp screw
4 Retaining bolt
5 Flat washer
6 Sealing washer
7 Spacer tube
8 Air filter element
9 Rubber seal
10 Casing assembly

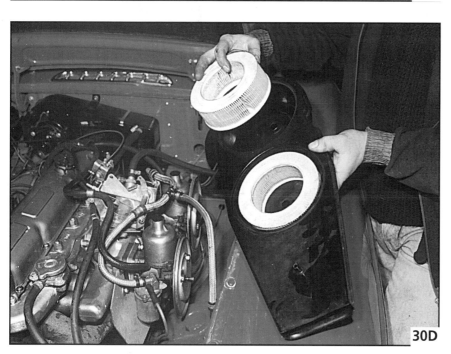

30D.

30F.

☐ Job 31. Check drive belts.

MG RV8, US AND EXPORT CARS ONLY

Check the condition and adjustment of the air conditioning pump belt (where fitted) and the air pump drive belt if your car is fitted with emission control equipment and an air pump. There should be 1/2 inch (12 mm) of movement at the longest section of drive belt visible between the pulleys but, depending on the air conditioning system fitted, check the maker's instructions.

Check the belts for cracking on their inner faces and for any signs of severe wear such as cords showing through the edges of the belt or polishing on the inner faces of the belt. Replace if any evidence of wear is found. For toothed belts, see the comments under Job 28B.

☐ Job 32. Pipes and hoses

Carry out a visual check on all flexible and rigid pipes and hoses in and around the engine bay for security, leaks or deterioration.

3,000 mile Mechanical and Electrical - Around the Car

First, carry out Jobs 7 to 16, then 18 and 19.

☐ Job 33. Hand brake travel.

INSIDE THE CAR, check the hand brake. It should be mounted securely, it should stay in the 'on' position - the ratchet can sometimes wear, allowing the brake to slip 'off', and the release mechanism can sometimes seize inside the lever, which prevents the ratchet from holding. Try lubricating with releasing fluid but if that fails, renew the ratchet or the mechanism. Seek specialist advice if necessary.

You should also check the hand brake to see if it has to be pulled too far before it operates correctly. Ideally, it should be fully on after three or four 'clicks' of the ratchet. If it's not, don't adjust the hand brake itself until the rear brakes are correctly adjusted - see Job 45 - and don't assume that MGC and MG RV8 brakes, with automatic adjusters will be correctly adjusted since the self-adjusters often don't work. See Job 136 for what to do about it. When the rear brakes are correctly adjusted, and with the rear of the car raised and securely supported, you may then adjust the hand brake cable.

> **SAFETY FIRST!**
> *Don't work beneath a car supported on axle stands with someone else sitting in the car trying the hand brake. It's too risky that their movements will cause the car to fall off the axle stands. Make sure that you are well clear of the raised car when someone's inside it. Read carefully the information at the start of this chapter on lifting and supporting the car.*

The adjuster is a brass nut on the bottom of the hand brake cable - but beneath the car, worse luck! Turn it half a turn at a time until the slack in the hand brake cable is such that the brake is on fully after three or four clicks. Also, make sure that with the handbrake released, both rear wheels are free to turn without binding. Lower the rear of the car to the ground on completion.

3,000 mile Mechanical and Electrical - Under the Car

> **SAFETY FIRST!**
> *Raise the front of the car off the ground after reading carefully the information at the start of this chapter on lifting and supporting the car.*

☐ Job 34. Steering rack.

34A. Turn the steering wheel fully to the left and check the right-hand steering rack gaiter for leaks or tears. Squeeze and pinch the gaiter hard and carefully check the recesses between the folds. Turn the steering to the right and check the left-hand gaiter in the same way. Replace both gaiters if any leaks, cracking or deterioration are found.

34A

34B

34C

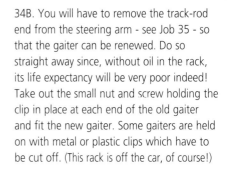

34B. You will have to remove the track-rod end from the steering arm - see Job 35 - so that the gaiter can be renewed. Do so straight away since, without oil in the rack, its life expectancy will be very poor indeed! Take out the small nut and screw holding the clip in place at each end of the old gaiter and fit the new gaiter. Some gaiters are held on with metal or plastic clips which have to be cut off. (This rack is off the car, of course!)

34C. Using an oil can, inject fresh oil into the gaiters to compensate for that lost. You can add more later on, as the oil feeds across the rack, by removing the clip once again. The capacity of the rack and the correct lubricant are given in *Appendix 1* and *Chapter 8, Facts and Figures*.

☐ **Job 35. Track rod ends.**

35A. Check the rubber boot on each track rod end. If torn, renew the complete track rod end. In theory, you can replace the boot but it's false economy for the following reasons: i) Chances are that the old TRE will be worn because the boot has split and because of the resulting absence of lubricant, and ii) the TRE has to be removed from the steering arm in any case. This can be such a pig of a job to carry out that you might as well get it over with and fit a relatively inexpensive, new track rod end whilst you're at it.

35A

Even if the rubber boot is OK, the track rod end balljoint may still be worn. Check it by holding the roadwheel at the 3 o'clock and 9 o'clock positions and moving it in and out. You will be able to feel and see movement in the track rod end if wear has taken place.

The tapered shank system gives a very positive location but it also makes the ball joint very difficult to remove. There are ball joint removal tools available from your local motorists' store and there is the traditional way of doing the job. With the latter, you hold one hammer against one side of the eye (on the end of the steering arm, fitted over the taper) and hit the other side sharply with another hammer. This deforms the eye enough to loosen it on the taper. Theoretically! In practice, you may have to use a removal tool and a pair of hammers - and to strike the eye repeatedly until a good, sharp blow shocks the joint free. You will probably cut the rubber boot on the ball joint as you hammer, so you will probably have to renew it even if you are just dismantling for another job.

Before you start, count the number of visible exposed threads on the steering arm up to the nut that locks the track rod end in place. You will have to remove this nut as well as the TRE if your doing this job to replace a steering rack gaiter, and it's very important that the nut goes back in the same position as before. Slacken this nut, remove the other nut holding the TRE to the steering arm, then remove the TRE as just described.

INSIDE INFORMATION: When you put it all back together and come to tighten the new locknut holding the track rod end to the steering arm, you'll probably find that the balljoint shank turns, making it impossible to tighten the nut. Try levering down on top of the TRE with a long bar engaged with the chassis rail. This will cause the tapered shank to lock in the steering arm allowing the nut to be tightened.

☐ **Job 36. Drain engine oil.**

If you're not draining the engine oil at this time, don't forget to carry out Job 1 instead, but wait until the car has been lowered to the ground, so that it's level for checking the oil.

SAFETY FIRST! Refer to the section on ENGINE OILS in Chapter 1 before carrying out the following work.

Warm the engine up just a little, but not so much that the oil becomes scalding hot - running the engine for just so long that it will idle off the choke should do it - so that the oil becomes warm and will therefore run more freely.

36A. Place an oil drain container in position beneath the sump with several sheets of newspaper beneath and protecting the surrounding area. Unscrew the oil drain plug with a ring spanner but beware! especially if the bolt is so tight that you have to use an extension on your spanner - an unsafe thing to do but something that is occasionally unavoidable.

*INSIDE INFORMATION: Note that for the MGC, you will need to use a container with a capacity of at least 12 pints (14.4 US pints or 6.8 litres) and for the V8, a capacity of 10.5 imperial pints, (12.6 US pints or 6 litres). For the MGB 1800, a 5 litre plastic oil can with one side cut out of it will be enough since the sump capacity with oil cooler is at most only 8.25 pints (9.6 US pints or 4.5 litres) and less for later engines - see **Chapter 8, Facts and Figures**.*

36A

SAFETY FIRST!

Oil drain plugs are often so tight that they seem to have been fitted by a gorilla with toothache. i) Take care that the spanner does not slip causing injury to hand or head. (Use a socket or ring spanner - never an open ended spanner - with as little offset as possible, so that the spanner is as near to the line of the bolt as possible.) ii) Ensure that your spanner is positioned so that you pull downwards, if at all possible. iii) Take even greater care that the effort needed does not cause the car to fall on you or to slip off the stands - remember those wheel chocks!

36B. Remove the oil drain plug and drain out the oil. Leave the car for several minutes for the oil to drain fully. Replace plug but be certain to use a new drain plug washer, available from your accessory shop or parts specialist

36B

☐ Job 37. Remove oil filter.

Before removing the oil filter, move the oil drain container so that it is situated beneath the oil filter. MG oil filters come in two broad types; the renewable element canister type with a steel casing, and the disposable type. Either type can be found facing either up or down, depending on model.

37A. A single bolt passes through the centre of the canister type of oil filter.

37B. If you wish, you can drain the filter by removing the plug (37B.1) although most people seem satisfied to let the oil run out through the bottom of the canister as the one method is only slightly less messy than the other, and both require a certain amount of wiping up afterwards. It is especially important that the various components go back together again in the right order. You should fit a new sealing ring on to the centre bolt (37B.3) and the rubber washer (37B.4) should be refitted between the large and small steel washers that go above the filter element. Take a careful note of the sealing washer (37B.5) since it appears later in a staring role.

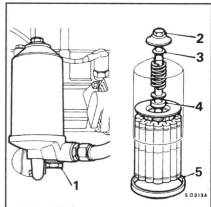

37B. Oil filter renewal details
1 Filter drain plug
2 Centre bolt
3 Sealing ring
4 Rubber washer
5 Sealing washer

37A

37C. The "pointing downwards" type of oil filter also has a sandwich plate from which the oil cooler is tapped. It's an idea to drain this type of filter by slackening off the centre bolt then pushing the filter body upwards along the bolt so that the oil runs out through the hole in the bottom of the body, between the body and the centre bolt. Alternatively, unscrew the bolt and body together, balancing them precariously together as they are lowered downwards between the engine and the chàssis rail. This will be a little bit tricky since the weight of the oil in the filter housing makes it somewhat more cumbersome, and the centre bolt will do its best to drop out at the worst possible moment.

37D. Here's the sealing ring referred to earlier. In fact, on the "pointing down" type of filter there are two of these rings, one on each side of the sandwich plate. Old rings can be stubborn to remove - a sharpened dart point is ideal! Scrape out any hardened or glued-in sealing ring that may remain.

37E. The MGB GT V8's oil filter is mounted on the front flitch panel. All of these disposable oil filters are best removed by using a special oil filter removing tool which attaches to your socket set. Be careful to turn it the right way, anti-clockwise to remove! Once you've drained the disposable oil filter, it can be safely discarded.

Job 38. New oil filter.
When fitting a disposable type of oil filter, wipe fresh oil around the oil seal to help prevent the oil filter from sticking. Do the same with the new rubber seals that you'll have to fit to the canister type of oil filter. Tighten the disposable type by hand only, don't use any tools

Job 39. Pour fresh oil.
Pour in fresh oil but note that later engines breath rather slowly and that it's easy to overfill the rocker cover, allowing oil to run down the engine in which case it invariably gets all over the exhaust manifold with horrendous results! Keep checking the oil level as the oil goes in to the rocker cover so that this does not happen.

Lower the car to the ground. Run the engine for a minute or so and then turn it off. While you're waiting for the oil to find its level, carry out Job 40, if your car is an automatic.

Job 40. Auto.-box park lock.
AUTOMATICS ONLY
Put the gear lever into 'Park' and release the hand brake. Get out of the car and try pushing the car, backwards and then forwards. The 'Park' brake should be locked and the car should only be able to rock a little against the locked gearbox. If the car rolls along, the 'Park' pawl is not engaging. The park brake pawl is fitted to the outside of the gearbox, on the left-hand side, just behind the bellhousing assembly. Check, free and lubricate it, but if it still fails to work perfectly, seek SPECIALIST SERVICE.

☐ **Job 41. Check oil level.**

Check the engine oil level and top up as necessary. See Job 1 if you need to understand the dipstick markings.

☐ **Job 42. Check for oil leaks.**

Check beneath the car and especially around the oil filter and drain plug for leaks.

> *SAFETY FIRST!*
> *Raise the front of the car off the ground once again, after reading carefully the information at the start of this chapter on lifting and supporting the car.*

☐ **Job 43. Check brake pads.**

43A

43A. You can check the condition of the front brake pads without carrying out any dismantling - but only if you know what you are looking for! That's why in this shot, we show a complete, new brake pad held in front of the brake calliper assembly. To examine the thickness of the pads, you'll have to look into the slot left by the springs that hold the pads in place. The friction part of the pad - the stuff that wears away - is the light coloured material with black edges, nearest to the camera. The Bromsgrove MG Centre mechanic is holding the metal backing plate and this is not, of course, the part that has to come into contact with the brake discs! The manufacturers recommend that the minimum permissible brake pad thickness before the pads are renewed should be 1/16 inch (1.6 mm) but you should allow for the fact that you won't be checking the brakes again for a further 3,000 miles or three months if the pads are approaching this limit. It's very common for one pad to wear down more quickly than the other and you should always take the thickness of the most worn-out pad as your guide. On the other hand, if one of the pads does not appear to be working at all (look for one pad very much thicker than the other or, possibly, one side of the disc shinier than the other), then it's SPECIALIST SERVICE time: have a garage check the calipers. One of the caliper pistons may have seized.

There is no facility for adjusting the front brakes since they adjust themselves automatically as the pads wear down, but the fact that the pads do wear accounts for the fact that the brake fluid level goes down whilst you're using the car. The significance of this fact will become apparent in Job 43C!

> *SAFETY FIRST! and SPECIALIST SERVICE:*
> *Obviously, a car's brakes are among its most important safety related items. Do not dismantle your car's brakes unless you are fully competent to do so. If you have not been trained in this work, but wish to carry out the work described here, we strongly recommend that a garage or qualified mechanic checks your work before using the car on the road. See the section on BRAKES AND ASBESTOS in Chapter 1, for further important information.*

43B. First step in removing the old brake pads, should they need it, is to pull out the two split pins that hold the two spring clips in place. Note that the ends of the split pins will have been opened out and that you need to squeeze them flat with your pliers before the split pin can be pulled out.

MGC ONLY: From the MGC calipers, pull out the two small retaining clips and tap out the pad retaining pins with a thin punch.

> *SAFETY FIRST!*
> *If the ends of the split pins show any signs of breaking off, which will happen after the split pins have been closed and reopened a number of times - fit new split pins. These are special items made specifically for your car's brakes so purchase them from your MG specialist or parts supplier.*

43B

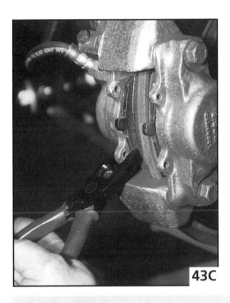

43C

43D

43C. It will be difficult to pull out the brake pads because the action of using the brakes will have kept them tight against the brake discs. Use pliers to squeeze the metal backing plate towards the caliper body to force the brake pads away from the disc.

43D. You can now pull out the pads quite easily. If you are fitting new pads, you'll probably have to push the round shaped pistons right the way back into the calliper, bearing in mind the information below about brake fluid being expelled from the top of the master cylinder. You should also clean out the inside of the caliper in which the friction pad assemblies lie, and scrape off any dirt or rust from the face of each piston.

SAFETY FIRST!
DO NOT use any other fluid or abrasive. Smear on a very light coating of brake grease around the piston before pushing the piston back in. You'll probably find a small sachet of this grease supplied with the new brake pads or you should be able to buy it from your parts supplier.

INSIDE INFORMATION: *Inside the brake calipers, as you will see when you pull out the pads, there is a piston on each side of the disc (two on each side in the case of the MG RV8) which pushes against the brake pad when you apply the brakes. The piston is itself pushed out by the hydraulic fluid which is forced down the brake pipe from the master cylinder. As you push the brake pads back against the piston, brake fluid will be pushed back up the pipe and into the master cylinder. Because you will need to push the pistons even further back into the caliper before fitting new pads; 1. Take a thin strip of lint-free cloth, moistened with brake fluid and clean all around the piston (clean around the back as if using dental floss). If the pistons are rusty or damaged,* **SPECIALIST SERVICE:** *have your garage fit replacement calipers if necessary. When pushing the pistons back in TAKE CARE NOT TO MARK OR DAMAGE THEM. 2. Note that, with the exception of the MGC and MG RV8, each piston has a cut away section, a recessed area covering about 1/3 of the part of the piston that pushes against the brake pad (in appearance, it looks like a tube but the end you can't see is, of course, solid so that the hydraulic fluid has something to push against). This recessed area should, and probably will be, facing the centre of the hub but if it isn't, turn the piston carefully so that it is correctly positioned. Chances are that brake fluid will now overflow from the master cylinder and make a terrible mess inside the engine bay - and do remember that brake fluid acts as a slow but efficient paint stripper. You could either siphon out some of the brake fluid from the master cylinder before pushing back the brake pads, or take off the master cylinder cap and stuff large amounts of soft, absorbent rags around the master cylinder so that any expelled fluid is quickly mopped up. You'll have to ensure that you don't have more fluid than the rags can cope with expelled from the master cylinder.*

43E

43E. Slide each new pad into the caliper just to make sure that each one moves freely, scraping out any corrosion on the insides of the callipers if necessary. If you are refitting previously fitted pads, it is permissible to use a file - lightly! - to remove any rust that may have built up on the edges of each steel backing plate. Now smear a little more of that brake grease - but only a very small amount - on to the back of the pad, in other words on the back of the metal backing plate NOT on the friction surface of the pad, which is the part that pushes against the brake disc. Now the new pads can be fitted into place and the springs seen in 43A. and 43B. held down against the pads while the split pins are slid back into place. Use a screwdriver to open up the ends of the "legs" on the split pins so that they cannot slip back out again.

SAFETY FIRST! Note carefully that new brake pads won't work as effectively as they should until they have "bedded in". Moreover, they can become glazed if the brakes are applied very hard within the first few hundred miles of running after fitting new brakes pads. AP Lockheed advise that for the first 150-200 miles (250-300 km), therefore, you should avoid braking hard unless you have to, such as in an emergency, and allow extra braking distance because of the fact that the brakes won't work quite as efficiently. You may also have noticed that the brake discs will have become scored and grooved and the new brake pads have to take the shape of the brake discs before they will work to maximum efficiency.

44

Job 44. Lubricate front suspension.
MGB AND MGC ONLY

The steering swivel or king pin is often neglected but desperately needs its regular quota of grease to prevent it from wearing out too quickly - and it's expensive to replace! This view, taken from the front of the car shows how easy it is to grease the king pin grease nipples with the wheel off the car. Some models have two grease nipples, one towards the top and one right at the bottom of the king pin; other models have three grease nipples, a third one being situated just above the bottom swivel pin. There's no grease nipple fitted in that position on this car, but the mechanic's finger points at the spot where it would be if there was one. Just to confuse matters further, sometimes this centre grease nipple is fitted on the same side as the other two but sometimes its on the back. It's sometimes difficult to get grease to go through the grease nipples. Push the grease gun firmly onto the grease nipple - the nozzle on the end of the grease gun is spring loaded so it should clip into place - and hold the grease gun in alignment with the grease nipple to give the grease the best chance of going into the suspension swivel.

INSIDE INFORMATION: If you find it impossible to get grease through the grease nipple, try unscrewing it and with the grease nipple held in a vice or a self-grip wrench - grip the spanner flats, not the thread - see if you can persuade grease to go through it. If not, fit a new grease nipple and try again. New ones will be available from your parts supplier although high street stores may not stock them.

WIRE WHEEL CARS ONLY:

INSIDE INFORMATION: Wire wheel splines wear out quickly. Every time you remove the wheels, wipe a thin smear of grease onto the conical surfaces on the hub and the spinner as well as the splines themselves. If you haven't had to remove the rear wheels as part of this service schedule, do so after greasing and refitting the front wheels, after Job 44 and before carrying out Job 45. See Job 143 for more information on where to apply grease.

Now refit the front wheels, tighten the spinners if wire wheels are fitted and lower the car to the ground. If bolt-on wheels are fitted, tighten the wheel nuts fully once the car is on the ground.

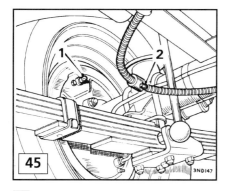

45

SAFETY FIRST!
Raise the rear of the car off the ground after carefully reading the information at the start of this chapter on lifting and supporting the car. SPECIALIST SERVICE: Obviously, a car's brakes are among its most important safety related items. Do not dismantle your car's brakes unless you are fully competent to do so. If you have not been trained in this work, but wish to carry out the work described here, we strongly recommend that you have a garage or qualified mechanic check your work before using the car on the road. See also the section on BRAKES AND ASBESTOS in Chapter 1, for further important information.

Job 45. Adjust rear brakes.
MGB ONLY

45. The brake adjuster for each rear brake is situated on the inside of each brake back plate (136A). The adjuster is operated by a square shaft and it's well worth while buying a proper brake adjusting tool rather than relying on a spanner which will probably slip and round off the adjuster. Before starting to check the brake adjustment, spray a little releasing fluid on to the back of the brake adjuster and wipe off any loose dirt. Bear in mind that to carry out the rest of this job, the wheel on which you will be working needs to be off the ground and the hand brake in the "off" position with the gearbox is in neutral. Check first of all that the wheel can be rotated by hand - it won't be all that easy because of the drag of the differential and gearbox but it will turn freely, bearing in mind all the mechanical stuff that is having to be rotated at the same time.

Try turning the brake adjuster (45.1) a notch or two at a time in a clockwise direction (when looking at the brake back plate) until a little resistance is found. Continue turning the adjuster until the wheel is locked up and can't be turned by hand but DON'T force the adjuster. Once the wheel is locked, apply the footbrake firmly to centralise the brake shoes. Now turn the adjuster in an anti-clockwise direction until the road-wheel can just be rotated freely without any sense that the brakes are binding. You may need, at first and until you are more experienced, to tighten and untighten the adjuster two or three times until you get the feel of things. Before leaving the brakes, grease the threads on the back of the adjuster (136.J).

INSIDE INFORMATION: MGB brake adjusters are notorious for seizing solid, unfortunately! They're also notorious for the squared adjuster shaft being rounded off by ham-fisted mechanics who use the wrong tools on an adjuster that has become stiff and arthritic. If the brake adjuster on your car has become rounded off, there may be nothing for it but to renew it - see Job 136 where the operation of the adjuster can be more clearly seen. The adjuster is very simply bolted to the brake back plate and can be removed once the brakes have been stripped down. If you are a novice at mechanical work, either regard this job as a SPECIALIST SERVICE *item, or have a trained mechanic check the work over before the car is used again on the road.*

When you've adjusted both sides, lower the car to the ground.

3,000 mile Mechanical and Electrical - Road Test

☐ Job 46. Clean controls.

Clean the door handles, controls and steering wheel, since they may well have become greasy from your hands while you were carrying out the rest of the service work on your car. Start up the engine while you are sitting in the driver's seat.

☐ Job 47. Check instruments.

Before pulling away, and with the engine running, check the correct function of all instruments and switches.

MG RV8 ONLY: Check that all of the system warning indicators are giving safe readings and are functioning correctly.

☐ Job 48. Throttle pedal.

48. Check the throttle pedal for smooth operation. If the throttle does not operate smoothly, turn off the engine and check the cable itself for a cracked or broken casing, kinks in the casing, or fraying at the cable ends, especially where the ends of the cable 'disappear' into the cable 'outer'. If you find any of these faults, replace the throttle cable.

48

☐ Job 49. Hand brake function.

Check the function of hand brake as described under Job 33. But this time, add a further check. An experienced mechanic will be able to engage first gear and let in the clutch just a little at a time until the clutch 'bites' and strains against the hand brake - not too much - just enough to let him know that the brakes are working, and without travelling more than three or four feet (1 metre) or so. If you're not an experienced driver or mechanic and there's some risk that you might strain the car's mechanical components, try turning the engine off, pulling the hand brake on, putting the gearbox in neutral, getting out of the car - only do this on level ground! - and see if you can push the car with the hand brake on. If, in the first test, the car moves blithely away, unhindered by the effect of the hand brake, or in the second, if the car moves at all, you've got major problems with the rear brakes, *but note that this will identify a handbrake that is totally useless!* The most likely reason for handbrake failure is that the brakes are oiled with rear axle oil, because of a failed oil seal, or because the brake hydraulic wheel cylinder is leaking brake fluid onto the brake shoes. Both require SPECIALIST SERVICE, unless you are an experienced mechanic and in both cases THE CAR SHOULD NOT BE DRIVEN until repairs have been carried out.

☐ Job 50. Brakes and steering.

SAFETY FIRST!
ONLY CARRY OUT THE FOLLOWING TESTS IN DAYLIGHT, IN CLEAR DRY CONDITIONS WHEN THERE ARE NO OTHER ROAD USERS ABOUT AND NO PEDESTRIANS. USE YOUR MIRRORS AND MAKE SURE THAT THERE IS NO TRAFFIC FOLLOWING YOU WHEN CARRYING OUT THE FOLLOWING BRAKE TESTS.

Only a proper brake tester at an MoT testing station will be able to check the operation of the brakes accurately enough for the MoT test, but you can rule out some of the most obvious braking problems in the following way. Drive along a clear stretch of road and, gripping the steering wheel fairly lightly between the thumb and fingers of each hand, brake gently from a speed of about 40 mph. Ideally, the car should pull up in

3,000 MILE SERVICE

a dead straight line without pulling to one side or the other. If the car pulls to the left (when being driven on the left-hand side of the road) or to the right (when being driven on the right-hand side of the road, such as in the USA), it might be that there is no problem with your brakes, but that the camber on the road is causing the car to pull over. If you can find a stretch of road with no camber whatsoever, you may be able to try the brake test again or failing that, find a one-way street where you can drive on the "wrong" side of the road and see if the pulling to one side happens in the opposite direction. If it does not, then you've got a problem with your brakes. Before assuming the worst, check your tyre pressures and try switching the front wheels and tyres from one side of the car to the other. If the problem doesn't go away, seek SPECIALIST SERVICE.

The second test, which is only partially applicable in the case of the MG RV8, is to ensure that the self-centring effect of the steering works correctly. If the steering stiffens up over a period of time, you can easily get used to it so that you don't notice that it doesn't operate as it should. After going round a sharp bend, the steering should tend to move back to the straight-ahead position all by itself without having to be positively steered back again by the driver. This is because the king pins are set slightly ahead of the centre line of the wheels so that the front wheels behave rather like those on a supermarket trolley - or at least those few that work properly! If the king pins have become stiff internally because of rust or if new ones have been fitted badly, the steering will be stiff and no self-centring will be evident. Alternatively, the steering rack could be dry due to loss of oil caused by a split gaiter (see Job 34). Whichever the case, you've got a problem with the steering and should seek a little more of that SPECIALIST SERVICE, unless you're experienced enough to feel capable of diagnosing an rectifying these problems yourself, using your workshop manual.

Now, if you're ready to begin the road test proper, you can check the function of the brakes and the self-centring effect of the steering.

3,000 mile Bodywork and Interior - Around the Car

First carry out Jobs 17, and 20 to 23.

☐ Job 51. Wiper blades and arms.
51. Check the operation of the windscreen wipers and correct position of 'sweep'. The wiper arms push onto the splines (51.2) but on some models are additionally locked in place by a small screw. The MGB handbook recommends that the spring clip is depressed (51.1) but in practice, it is usually enough to fold back the arm, grasp in near the splines and pull off with a slight rocking movement (slacken the locking screw first, where fitted). Put on a smear of grease before refitting to prevent seizing up

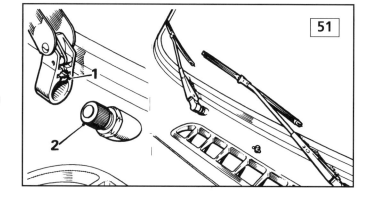

☐ Job 52. Check windscreen.
Check the windscreen for chips, cracks or other damage - see **Chapter 7, Getting Through the MoT** for what is, and is not, acceptable according to UK regulations.

☐ Job 53. Rear view mirrors.
Check your rear view mirrors, both inside and outside the car, for cracks and crazing. Also ensure that the interior rear view mirror is soundly fixed in place since they can come loose and when they do, the vibration can get so bad that you can't tell whether you're being followed by a long distance truck or one of the boys in blue!

☐ Job 54. Check floors.
Lift the carpets to check for water accumulation beneath them, (including the boot and spare wheel well). Find and eliminate sources of water leaks before the smell of rotting carpet drives you to it - by which time the problem of rotting steel will have joined the list. Look at windscreen seals, tailgate seals on GTs and boot lid seals on roadsters, look at door seals and look for - and hope you don't find - rust holes in the floor. Leaks are best found with the inside of the car dry and, if necessary, the carpets taken out. Have someone play a hose on one area of the car at a time whilst you go leak hunting. Take care not to spray water through the horrendous gaps that are always apparent between the door glass and the soft-top.

MG RV8: The soft-tops on some RV8s can leak around the front and rear of each door glass. The solution would seem to be to consult your dealer if the car is new enough, or even to consider having a custom-made soft-top made if the problem persists. Alternatively, try applying a brush-on waterproofing agent, specially made for cloth soft-tops. Try specialist vintage car suppliers, advertising in collectors' car magazines.

INSIDE INFORMATION: A common but hard to track down source of water coming in is the drain tube for the fresh air vent just ahead of the windscreen. See Job 99, for more details.

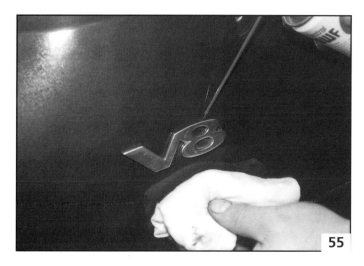

☐ Job 55. Chrome trim and badges.

55. Rust can easily start to form behind badges and in the holes where badges are mounted. Apply a water dispersant behind the chrome trim and badges.

3,000 mile Bodywork - Under the Car

SAFETY FIRST! Only raise the car off the ground after carefully reading the information at the start of this chapter on lifting and supporting the car.

First, carry out Job 24.

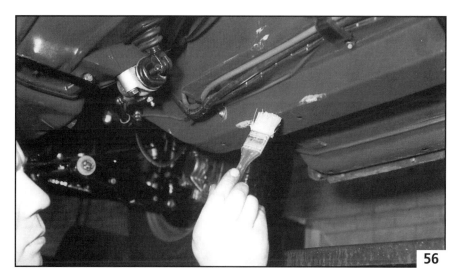

☐ Job 56. Inspect underside.

56. When dry, inspect the underside of the car for rust and damage. Renew paint, underbody sealant and wax coating locally as necessary. Most cars are somewhat dirtier underneath than the one photographed here! Look for loose underseal in particular, especially that of the old-fashioned bitumen type. It goes brittle and comes loose, allowing water to get behind it and form a breeding ground for corrosion. Scrape off any such loose underseal and paint on wax coating in its place, when dry.

6,000 Miles – or Every Six Months, Whichever Comes First.

6,000 mile Mechanical and Electrical - The Engine Bay

First, carry out Jobs 2 to 6, then 26, 28, 30, 31, 32.

The first part of this section is to be carried out with the engine cold, partly for safety reasons (the risks involved in handling hot components, in spilling fuel when changing the fuel filter, and partly for comfort and ease of working.

☐ Job 57. Cooling system.

SAFETY FIRST! Only work on the cooling system when the engine - and thus the coolant - is cold.

Check the cooling and heating systems for leaks and all hoses for condition and tightness. Look at the ends of hoses for leaks, check the clamps for tightness and pinch the hoses to ensure that they are not starting to crack and deteriorate. If you don't want a hose to burst and let you down in the worst possible place, change any hoses that seem at all suspicious.

57. INSIDE INFORMATION: i) Heater hose connections can often leak invisibly on the inside of the heater casing if the pipes have been pushed hard up against the casing before the clamps are tightened. Look for coolant dribbles and staining down the front of the heater casing - and when reconnecting such hoses, try to remember to leave a small gap between the end of the hose and the heater casing - a Bromsgrove MG Centre special tip!

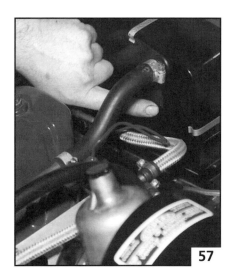

57

ii) When you have to replace hoses, don't bother trying to take them off in the conventional way. If the hose clamps unscrew, fine - but they probably won't. And if the hose pulls off the stub, fine - but it's probably been firmly glued on by the heat. So, use a junior hacksaw to cut through the hose, just away from the stub. Cut carefully through the clamp, pulling it away with pliers and/or gloved hands - it will be sharp! Then cut carefully through the hose at a 45 degree angle to the end of the stub TAKING GREAT CARE ALL THE WHILE NOT TO CUT INTO THE STUB! When you've gone through, peel the hose remnant off the stub and away - you could save hours, prevent bleeding knuckles and reduce the risk of damaging the heater core through too much pulling.

Job 58. Coolant check.
58. Use a hydrometer to check the specific gravity of the coolant. If below the level recommended on the tester - most have a system of coloured balls, some of which may float and some may not, to determine whether there is sufficient anti-freeze present - top up with anti-freeze, until the correct specific gravity is obtained.

V8 ENGINES: Rover recommend that the proportion of anti-freeze to water should be around 50% and never more than 60%. These aluminium engines are more critical in this respect than cast-iron units.

58

INSIDE INFORMATION: Some owners think that there is little to be gained by using anti-freeze in their cast-iron block MGB or MGC all the year round, particularly in those parts of the world where frost is not a problem. Wrong! Anti-freeze to a concentration of 25% not only gives protection against around -13 degrees Celsius (9 degrees Fahrenheit) of frost, it also helps to stop the radiator from clogging and so helps to keep the car running cooler in hot weather. Owners also forget that there is aluminium in, or rather on, MGB and MGC engines and that it does corrode items such as the heater valves. Use anti-freeze and cut down on the common problems with heater valve corrosion, seizure and failure. A 50% mix, by the way, gives protection down to -36 degrees Celsius (-33 degrees Fahrenheit).

Job 59. Heater valve.
59. Talking of which (Job 58), check the heater control valve for correct operation and lubricate, with releasing fluid if seized, with thin oil if working. Ditto the control cable, adding oil or fluid to the ends before working the heater control open and shut a good few times.

Job 60. Check water pump.
60. Check the water pump for leaks - the first sign of failure - by looking for water leaks or stains around the spindle. Look especially along the top of the timing chain cover on the MGB and MGC, where leaking will appear as a brown stain on the top of the cover. (This MGC's radiator and bottom hose are removed, making it easier to see where we are pointing at!)

59

60

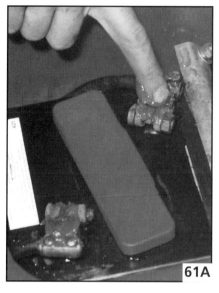

61A

61B

☐ **Job 61. Battery terminals.**

> *SAFETY FIRST!*
> *Refer to the information in Chapter 1, Safety First! for safe working practice in connection with working on the battery or batteries.*

61A. Clean and grease the battery connections. Better still, use petroleum jelly or copper-impregnated grease.

Drive the car out of doors before carrying out the next Job.

61B. INSIDE INFORMATION: Despite what any manual tells you, the best way of cleaning old grease and corrosion from battery terminals is a kettle full of water that has just boiled. Pour it slowly over each terminal and you'll see a bright, shiny surface appear from underneath the fur. Make sure that the battery caps or cover are firmly in place first and pour a second jug full of water down the sides of the battery, over the battery carrier so that nothing lodges on the metal battery carrier, causing corrosion. If the battery terminals are badly furred, it is likely that some corrosion will have taken place inside the battery clamps. Indeed, it has been known for the clamps to be almost completely eaten away inside, while appearing sound from the outside. Disconnect the clamps, wash off any furring with hot water and clean both the inside of the clamps and the outside of the terminals with a medium grit sandpaper. Apply petroleum jelly or copper-impregnated grease to the bottom of the clamp but it's best to leave the electrical connection dry, and never apply ordinary grease to this area.

62A

62B

☐ **Job 62. Accelerator controls.**

62A Lubricate the accelerator control linkage at the carburettors...

62B ...and the throttle pedal pivot, deep down in the recesses of the footwell. Use spray-on lubricant or use white silicone grease, so as not to spoil your shoes with dripping oil - it stains leather!

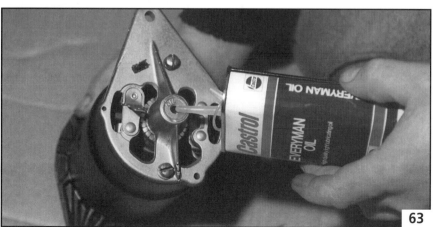

63

☐ **Job 63. Dynamo bearings.**
Lubricate the dynamo bearings with a few drops of oil (early models). Here, the dynamo is seen off the car so that you can see the oil hole more clearly. Take care not to over oil or to get oil inside the body of the dynamo.

☐ **Job 64. Fit new spark plugs.**

OPTIONAL: Fit new spark plugs, with correct gaps. Some owners leave spark plugs in place for longer, but there is always the risk that the insulation will break down and lower the performance of the plug, even though it may appear perfect in every other way. Never leave them in place for longer than 12,000 miles, even with regular cleaning and adjustment as described elsewhere in the schedule.

When fitting new spark plugs, ensure that the threads in the cylinder head are free enough for you to screw the plugs in as far as their seats - engine cold - by hand. If there are any obstructions, have your Rover dealer chase out the threads with a proper spark plug thread chasing tool. This is especially important with the V8 engines with aluminium heads. Take GREAT CARE not to cross thread the spark plugs when fitting, and make sure that they are tightened to the torque setting given in *Chapter 8, Facts and Figures*.

☐ **Job 65. Renew cb points.**

In normal use, contact breaker points invariably deteriorate causing a steady and indiscernible drop off in performance. They're such inexpensive items that it is best to renew them at 6,000 miles, although not necessarily at six months, since it is purely the usage that causes them to deteriorate. Jobs 26 and 27 showed how to remove the distributor cap and rotor arm and also illustrated the later Lucas type 45D distributor. The earlier 25D distributor shown in the line drawing 65A only has minor differences from the later type.

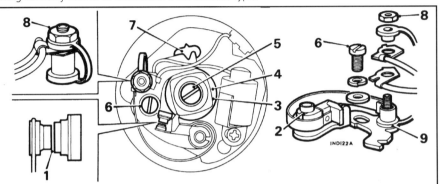

65A. Contact breaker points renewal
1. Points gap
2. Pivot post
3. Distributor shaft cam
4. Baseplate lubrication point
5. Distributor shaft retaining screw
6. Fixing screw
7. Adjustment "V" slot
8. Wiring connections retaining nut
9. Insulating bush

65A. You can see here the correct order in which the various connections have to be made to the new distributor points as they are fitted. Note that the fixing screw (65A.6) and its two washers are not supplied with the new points but are part of the distributor fittings, so be careful not to lose this screw!

65B. Another inexpensive item and one that is well worth fitting every time the points are renewed, is the condenser. Note that the fixing screw that holds the condenser in place is even smaller and easier to lose than the screw for fixing the points in place. If you have straight-point and cross-point magnetic screwdrivers, use them for removing these screws, but do take care not to drop the washers. Alternatively, unscrew the nut holding the wiring connections to the contact breaker points and remove those connections. Then undo the screw with your screwdriver whilst lifting the old contact breaker points, and take off the points, screw and washers all in one piece. Similarly, when removing the condenser, lift the condenser as you remove the screw and take the screw out of the hole in the end of the condenser when you've got it safely out of the engine bay.

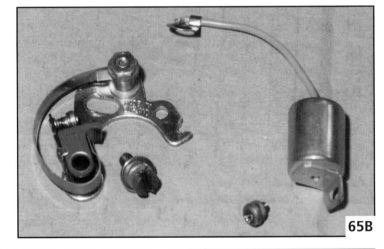
65B

65C. Before offering up the new points, remember to lubricate the distributor as shown in Job 27, and in addition, put a very small amount of grease on the pivot post shown in Job 27 (27B.4).

65D. The only significant difference when fitting points to the later Lucas 45D distributor is the simpler method of connecting the internal wiring. There's no tiny nut and washers to lose since the connections just clip together.

Follow the instructions under Job 27 for setting the points gap correctly.

65C

65D

SPECIALIST SERVICE: Have a specialist with the appropriate equipment check the voltage drop between the coil CB terminal and earth

Job 66. Ignition timing.

With the contact breaker points correctly adjusted it's necessary to make sure that the spark plugs are firing at just the right time, that is just before the piston on the firing stroke reaches the top of its travel.

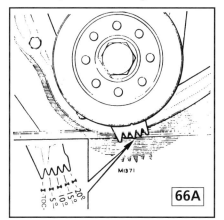

66A. Note the position of the Number 1 spark plug HT lead on the distributor cap, then remove the cap. Turn the engine over in the correct direction of rotation (either by pressing on the fan belt and turning the fan, or by using a spanner on the crankshaft pulley bolt) until the distributor rotor arm is approaching the position of the Number 1 spark plug lead contact in the cap. Now look down at the timing scale, which is located on the engine timing chain cover, either below or above the crankshaft pulley, and turn the engine further, until the notch on the crankshaft pulley is aligned with the appropriate timing mark on the timing scale. Refer to *Chapter 8, Facts and Figures* for the correct static ignition timing setting for your car. With the engine in this position, the contact breaker points should just be opening. It's a bit tricky to determine the exact moment when the points open and the best way to do this is to connect a 12 volt test lamp between the LT wiring connection on the distributor and a good earth (ground) - any unpainted metal part of the engine will do for the earth connection. Now, with the ignition switched on, the bulb will light when the points open.

If the bulb is already illuminated, then the points have opened too soon meaning that the timing is too far advanced; if the bulb isn't illuminated, the points haven't opened yet, so the timing's too far retarded. If your distributor has a small knurled vernier adjustment wheel opposite the vacuum unit, turn this wheel in one direction or the other until the points just open and the test lamp lights. If no vernier adjustment wheel is fitted, it will be necessary to slacken the clamp bolt securing the distributor to the engine, and turn the actual distributor body to achieve the same effect. Tighten the clamp bolt when you've finished. Once the timing has been set, turn the engine over again, until the rotor arm is once more approaching the same position as before, check the timing marks and make sure the bulb lights up when it should. When everything's okay, switch off the ignition and disconnect the test lamp.

66B. With the static timing set, this is a good time to see if the distributor vacuum advance is working properly. Disconnect the vacuum advance pipe from its connection on the carburettor or manifold and wipe clean the end of the pipe. Suck on the pipe, while you watch the contact breaker points. If the vacuum unit is in good condition you'll feel resistance when you suck, and also see the distributor baseplate and points move slightly. If nothing happens, the rubber diaphragm inside the vacuum unit is likely to be punctured (a common occurrence) and a new vacuum unit will be needed. Refit the vacuum pipe and distributor cap after making this check.

The most accurate way of setting the ignition timing is dynamically using a stroboscopic timing light (this is also the only way to do it if your car has an electronic ignition distributor). Timing lights can be bought from motor accessory stores and then used as instructed or, SPECIALIST SERVICE: have your dealer or local garage check the ignition timing for you when you've finished the service.

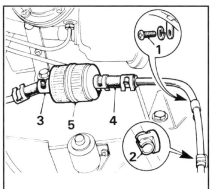

67. In-line fuel filter connections
1 Fuel pipe retaining screw
2 Pipe retaining clip
3 Hose clip
4 Fuel hose
5 Filter

Job 67. Fit fuel filter.

SAFETY FIRST! Disconnect the battery and read the precautions given in Chapter 1, Safety First! before doing any work on the fuel system.

OPTIONAL: If your car, or its fuel tank is more than a few years old, carry out this job at the 6,000 mile interval. Otherwise, fitting a new filter at 12,000 miles will be sufficient.

67. Fit a new in-line fuel filter. If one wasn't fitted to your model of car as standard, you are strongly recommended to fit one now. In-line fuel filters are easily obtainable from car accessory stores - follow the fitting instructions on the pack. When replacing a fuel filter fitted as standard, you must first disconnect the fuel pipe from the engine bay by taking out the fixings on the engine-side of the filter. On rubber bumper MGBs, for instance, this involves taking out the screw (67.1) and pulling the pipe out of the clip (67.2) taking care that you don't break the clip or pull it off the bodywork. The clips holding the filter to the inlet and outlet hoses (67.3 and 67.4) are disconnected by pinching the sticking-out tags on each clip with a pair of pliers. This releases the tension on the clip - which is left in place for re-use later - enabling you to pull the pipe (67.4) off the filter and the filter off the car. Note that some filters are meant to be fitted so that the petrol flows through in one direction only. Some are marked with 'IN' and 'OUT' on the ends of the filter; some have a direction arrow on the body.

Job 68. Fuel connections.

Check the fuel filter, carburettor connections and fuel pipes at the front of the car, in the engine bay, for chafing, leaks and corrosion.

Job 69. Top-up dashpots.

69. Top up the SU carburettor dashpots with the correct grade of oil. Unscrew the dashpot cap and pull out the plunger. The dashpot contains a damper which prevents the fuel flow needle in the carburettor from fluttering and allows more petrol to come through when you accelerate hard - performance and fuel economy will be better if the dash pots are not allowed to run dry. Use ordinary engine oil, nothing thicker. Very thin oil tends to disappear too quickly! Top up until the level is just above the hollow piston rod.

INSIDE INFORMATION: Some SU carburettors tend to consume oil very quickly for a variety of reasons; some to do with driving style, some to do with general wear. If your carburettors are like this, check the oil more frequently than every 6,000 miles.

Now run the engine, partly to ensure that the ignition has been reassembled correctly. If it hasn't the car probably won't start at all or will run very badly - if so, check that the plug leads are in the correct order, that the points are gapped correctly and are opening correctly and that the electrical connections to the points are correct - it's all too easy to fit one of the wires to the insulator on the points incorrectly! The running engine will also enable you to make further checks for petrol leaks around the fuel filter.

69

Job 70. Set carburettors.

SAFETY FIRST!
Please read the information contained in Chapter 1, Safety First! especially that relating to the safety hazards surrounding petrol (gasoline). In addition, note that you will have to run the car with the air filters removed. There is the slight risk of a flashback through the carburettors, so don't get your face or clothing too close. Also, have a suitable workshop-sized fire extinguisher to hand, in case the worst should happen. If a fire should break out, turn off the ignition - and thus the engine and fuel pump - immediately, so that no more petrol can be pumped through. Because of the fire risk, however slight, and because of the very strong danger from exhaust fumes, carry out this next part of the work out of doors.

CARS WITHOUT US EMISSION CONTROL EQUIPMENT ONLY
Many owners shy away from the idea of adjusting their own carburettors and, while they certainly look complicated, it's a job that can be carried out at home with the simplest of tools, although a couple of inexpensive special tools will make all the difference. It's important that the contact breaker points and plugs are in good shape and that the ignition timing and valve clearances are set correctly. (See Job 120, if valve clearance adjustment has not been carried out as part of your regular maintenance schedule.) You should also check that your carburettors are not too badly worn. With the air filters removed, turn the butterfly until it is open and try moving the spindle on which it turns. If there is a lot of play in the spindle, consider swapping your carburettors for a reconditioned pair - they are available from MG specialists, both reconditioned and new. See Job 113 for an illustration of a carburettor butterfly being opened, although for a different reason.

70A. These two drawings of the earlier SU HS4 carburettor will be referred to later in the text. An almost identical type of carburettor was fitted to the MGC.

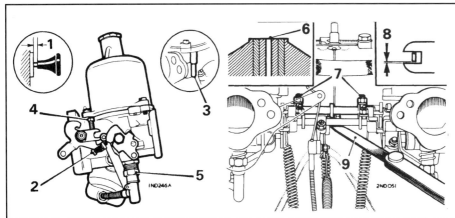

70A. SU HS4 carburettor details
1 Choke control free movement
2 Fast idle adjustment screw
3 Piston lifting pin
4 Idle speed screw
5 Jet adjusting nut
6 Brass jet top surface flush with carburettor bridge
7 Throttle cross-shaft pinch bolts
8 Throttle lever pin-to-operating fork clearance
9 Feeler gauge for choke cross-shaft clearance adjustment

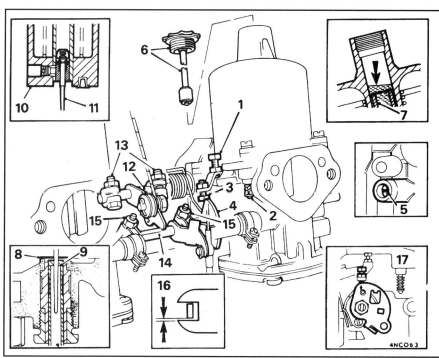

70B. SU HIF4 carburettor details
1. Idle speed screw
2. Piston lifting pin
3. Fast idle adjustment screw
4. Fast idle cam
5. Jet adjuster screw
6. Piston damper
7. Piston damper oil level
8. Carburettor bridge
9. Brass jet top surface
10. Piston
11. Jet needle
12. Throttle cross-shaft
13. Throttle cross-shaft pinch bolts
14. Choke cross-shaft
15. Choke cross-shaft pinch bolts
16. Throttle lever pin-to-operating fork clearance
17. Fast idle cam positioned for fast idle speed adjustment

70B. This is the later, SU HIF4 type of carburettor which will also be mentioned later. The MGB GT V8's carburettor is very similar but the RV8, of course, is fitted with a fuel injection system in place of carburettors - very much a **SPECIALIST SERVICE** item.

70C

In a nutshell, the procedure for adjusting twin SU carburettors is as follows: i) disconnect the linkages joining the two carbs together so that setting one does not disturb the other, ii) setting the jet inside each carburettor to a reasonable starting point, just in case someone has been 'fiddling' and the instrument is miles out and iii) adjusting the two settings - idle speed and mixture and finally, iv) setting the choke fast-running - not critical but it's nice to have it set properly. Of course, if this is a routine adjustment, you will even be able to skip stage ii), which will save a bit of dismantling.

Use a felt pen to mark the position of the dashpot on the body of the carburettor so that when you come to replace it, the dashpot goes back on in the same place - most important if the piston is to slide smoothly up and down the dashpot, which it must!

Try yours, pushing your finger inside the mouth of the carburettor and lifting the piston as far as it will go. When you release the piston, it should slide down smoothly and end with a slight 'clunk'. If it doesn't, try turning the dashpot from its original position - screw it down properly before trying again - and raise and lower the piston once more. It could be that someone else has fitted the dashpot in the wrong position!

70C. Note that as you lift the dashpot off the carburettor, the piston will come out with it only to slide out slowly - there's a big, lazy spring in there - and oil may go everywhere. Take great care not to damage the needle fitted to the base of the piston.

INSIDE INFORMATION: If your carburettor piston doesn't slide down with a smooth movement, ending in a small 'clunk', it could also be that the jet in the base of the carburettor is not centred correctly. This probably won't be a problem on HIF carburettors (as they have what is known as a 'fully-floating' jet needle) but it certainly can be on the HS unit. In that case, you will have to centre the jet. Fortunately, this is NOT a standard service item, more what you might have to do just once in order to be able to carry out the rest of this Service Job satisfactorily. So, to do it, unscrew the fuel pipe from the float bowl and remove the screw holding the jet to the linkage arm. Unscrew and remove the (bottom) adjuster nut (70A.5) and take off the spring above it. Slacken the (top) locknut (above 70A.5) so that the jet bearing, the threaded tube that sticks out of the bottom of the carburettor can just be moved by hand. Put the jet and the adjuster nut, without the spring, back in place. Now look at the bottom of the piston (70C, in mechanics left-hand) and make sure that the shoulder on the brass needle is level with the bottom of the piston (70B.10 and 70B.11) - a single screw holds it in place. You can now insert the piston back into the carburettor body and push it right down - it should push the jet into its correct position (70B.8 and 70B.9). You can now tighten the (top) nut that holds the jet bearing in position. Check that the piston does now slide up and down and end its fall with a slight 'clunk' if not, try centring the jet again - then put the jet assembly back together.

70D. Note that 70D and 70E do not need to be carried out at every service - only if you don't know whether previous settings have been close or miles away! Screw the jet adjuster nut or screw (see 70A.5, for earlier carburettors; 70B.5 for later carburettors) ...

70E. ...so that the top surface of the brass jet is flush with the bridge - the flat area being pointed out here and in illutration 70A.6. This gives a good, average starting point from which to make later adjustments.

For the next operations the engine needs to be at normal operating temperature so warm it up first before proceeding.

Slacken the pinch bolts connecting the choke and throttle cross-shafts to each carburettor, so that each can be adjusted independently.

INSIDE INFORMATION: a simple but invaluable tool is a 12 inch (300 mm) length of small bore hose, such as heater hose, to enable you to carry out the next Job – balancing the flow of air through each carburettor. You hold one end of the hose over the carburettor intake, with the other end close to your ear and listen to the 'hiss' made by the air flow through each carburettor. At this stage you'll probably notice that one sounds different to the other, so to get them both the same ...

70F. ... turn the idle speed screw on one carburettor in or out as necessary, until the 'hiss' in both units is about equal. Once they're balanced, turn the idle speed screws on both carburettors by the same amount so that the idle speed is as specified in **Chapter 8, Facts and Figures**. Turning both the screws by equal amounts alters the tickover while keeping the carburettors in balance.

INSIDE INFORMATION: i) When listening to the 'hiss' made by the air flow through the carburettors, what you're really listening for is more like a change in tone, or pitch, rather than loudness. Try it a few times and you'll soon get an 'ear' for it.

70G. If you can't seem to get it right, use a carburettor balancer available from motor accessory stores. These simple devices are placed over the carburettor intake and the 'suction' created causes a ball to rise up a scale. Note the level and adjust the other carburettor until it matches the first.

70D

70E

70F

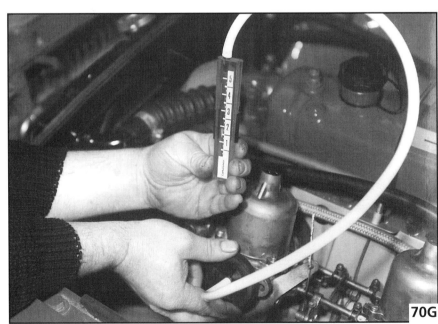
70G

With the engine idling and the carburettors balanced, the mixture can be adjusted. Screw the jet adjuster nut, or screw, on each carburettor (70A.5 and 70D for earlier units; 70B.5 for later units) up or down, or in or out (according to type) until the mixture is right. Knowing when it is right is the hard part. You should notice as you turn the adjuster, that the engine will eventually start to run roughly, accompanied by a drop in engine speed. Now, if you turn the adjuster the other way, the engine will smooth out, the speed will increase, and then it will all go off again. Where you want to be, is midway between those two extremes of rich and weak - when the speed is highest and the engine smoothest. And you have to do it on each carburettor! You may find that this part becomes a **SPECIALIST SERVICE** operation if you just can't get it right, so do the best for now and take it to a dealer or garage later. Once it's as good as you can get it, remember to re-adjust the idle speed because it will have altered during the mixture adjustment.

INSIDE INFORMATION: Motor accessory stores sell an excellent tool called a Colortune. It screws into the cylinder head in place of a spark plug. You run the engine and the Colortune provides its own spark. The glass insulator on the Colortune enables you to see the colour of the ignition - blue for too weak; yellow for too rich, like a school lab Bunsen burner. Use it first in cylinder one to check the front carburettor, then in 4 to check the back one. Have a properly equipped garage check your settings later, if you wish.

70i

70i. Reconnect the cross shafts, ensuring that the pins that engage on the throttle lever, have an equal clearance on each side of the operating forks (70A.8 and 70B.16). Insert a feeler gauge of 0.060 inch (1.5 mm) for manual gearbox cars, 0.028 inch (0.7 mm) for automatics, between the choke cross-shaft and the throttle lever (70A.9). Check the clearances referred to above and tighten the pinch bolts. Finally, adjust the fast idle cam, so that when the choke knob is pulled out about 1/4 inch (6.0 mm), the cam (70B.17) opens up the throttle to a speed of about 1,000 rpm. Check that there is a small clearance between the adjuster screw and the cam when the choke is pushed right in. Note that this screw is NOT to be confused with the idle speed screw (70A.4 and 70B.1)

US CARS WITH ZENITH/STROMBERG CARBURETTORS:
These carbs require the use of special tools, making them a **SPECIALIST SERVICE** item.

☐ Job 71. Exhaust emissions.

SPECIALIST SERVICE: Have a properly equipped garage carry out an exhaust emissions check, especially for carbon monoxide (CO) and unburned hydrocarbons. But note the comments in **Chapter 7, Getting Through the MoT** regarding the difficulty of persuading SU carburettors to pass the UK's emissions regulations.

72

6,000 mile Mechanical and Electrical - Around the Car

First, carry out Jobs 7 to 16, then 18, 19 and 33.

☐ Job 72. Top-up gearbox oil.

The gearbox oil level is checked in one of two ways. One of them is mounted on the gearbox casing, accessed beneath the car; the other is via a dipstick reached from inside the car. Believe it or not, the external one is by far the easier to get at!

72. **EARLIER CARS:** Lift the carpet flap behind the centre console and over the gearbox tunnel. Remove the rubber plug in the tunnel. Feel down in the depths and you will find a metal loop on the top of a dipstick.

INSIDE INFORMATION: Use a hook of some sort to pull out the dipstick - it can be very difficult to move. Once out, try tying a nylon wiring tie through the metal loop - it will give you more to pull on next time!

Topping up the gearbox is no less difficult. Use a funnel pushed through the hole in the gearbox cover or a plastic oil container with a long spout. Top up with the correct grade of oil (see **Chapter 8, Facts and Figures**) until the level is up to the upper mark on the dipstick.

LATER CARS:
Beneath the car, on the right-hand side of the gearbox, there is a filler/level plug. Remove the plug and top up the oil to the level of the plug orifice. Wipe around the plug before removing so that no dirt can get into the gearbox.

> **SAFETY FIRST!**
> **If you don't have access to an inspection pit or hoist, refer to the safety information at the start of this chapter on lifting and supporting the car.**

AUTOMATIC GEARBOX CARS:
The oil level dipstick is sensibly located in a tube, which also acts as the filler tube, situated inside the engine bay. The level of the Automatic Transmission Fluid - never ordinary engine/gearbox oil - must be checked with the engine fully warmed up, such as after a run, and with the engine running and the gear selector in 'P' (Park). The gearbox level should be maintained at 'MAX' - the difference between 'MAX' and 'MIN' is 1 pint (1.2 US pints; 0.57 litre).

INSIDE INFORMATION: Only wipe the dipstick with paper or an old pair of tights, never cloth, since any cloth lint getting into the automatic gearbox could damage it.

☐ Job 73. Adjust headlamps.
SPECIALIST SERVICE: It is possible to adjust your own headlamps, but not with sufficient accuracy. Badly adjusted headlamps can be dangerous if they don't provide you, the driver, with a proper view of the road ahead, or they dazzle oncoming drivers. Older drivers and those with poor eyesight, can become disorientated when confronted with maladjusted head lights. Have the work carried out for you by a garage with beam measuring equipment. Any MoT testing station in the UK will be properly equipped.

☐ Job 74. Fuel filler pipe.
74. Check the fuel filler pipe connections for leaks and tightness.

☐ Job 75. Front wheel alignment.
SPECIALIST SERVICE: Have the front wheel alignment checked and tested. Wheel alignment will go 'out' through regular use and especially if you go over a pothole or a kerb. The car will become less stable and tyres will wear out much more quickly. This is not work that can be carried out at home, special alignment equipment is required.

74

☐ Job 76. Rear ride height.
76. *INSIDE INFORMATION: Measure the rear ride height, between the ground and the underside of the body, comparing one side with the other. If they are different, look for broken or soft leaf springs, and also check for faulty front springs - different levels there will throw out the rear ride height, too.*

☐ Job 77. Front ride height.
77. Measure the front ride height, as described above.

MGC ONLY:
The MGC's front right height can be adjusted (See workshop manual or - **SPECIALIST SERVICE**). Measure the front ride height, both sides.

77

78

☐ **Job 78. Check tyre clearance.**

78. INSIDE INFORMATION: Look for evidence of tyres rubbing on wheel arches and in particular, examine the tyre side walls for evidence of rubbing. It could be that axle-to-spring bolts have come a little loose, over-size tyres, or non-standard wheels with a greater offset have been fitted, or a wire wheel conversion kit has been fitted. If you see evidence of rubbing, listen for aural evidence when cornering, especially with the boot loaded. Check to see if the clearance is greater one side than the other, in which case the axle may have shifted over, requiring attention to the axle mountings, or the springs.

79

☐ **Job 79. Check wheel nuts.**

79. Check tightness of the road wheel nuts using, preferably, a torque wrench, at least until you have tried it once to gain an idea of the amount of tightness required. (But do make sure that the nuts run freely up and down each stud.) See **Chapter 8, Facts and Figures** for the correct torque settings - many people over-tighten wheel nuts which, in extreme cases, can be dangerous.

6,000 mile Mechanical and Electrical - Under the Car

First carry out Jobs 34 to 45.

SAFETY FIRST! Raise the front of the car off the ground after carefully reading the information at the start of this chapter on lifting and supporting the car.

80

☐ **Job 80. Front fuel lines.**

80. Check the fuel lines beneath the front end of the car, taking note that on MGCs the pipes run right across the front of the car, ahead of the engine.

INSIDE INFORMATION: Most corrosion takes place beneath the pipe clips where it cannot easily be seen. Examine carefully.

☐ Job 81. Front brake lines.

81A. Check all brake lines beneath the front end of the car for corrosion - once again, especially behind pipe clips where most corrosion takes place - and check all flexible pipes for chaffing and perishing.

81B. *INSIDE INFORMATION: i) bend each flexible hose back on itself, especially near the unions. This will show up perishing and cracking in the pipe. ii) have an assistant press hard on the brake pedal while you look out for bulges in the flexible hoses. If you see ANY signs of weakness or deterioration in any of the pipes, stop using the car until they have been replaced.*

☐ Job 82. Brake pedal adjust.

82. Adjust the free movement at the brake pedal. There should be 1/8 inch (3.0 mm) of free movement, measured at the pedal. To adjust, slacken the locknut (82.1) and screw the stoplight switch (82.2) in or out, to increase or decrease the free movement. Take care not to damage the stoplight switch wiring.

81A

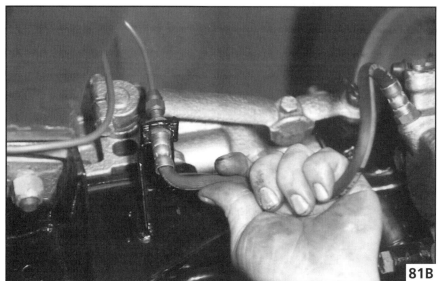

81B

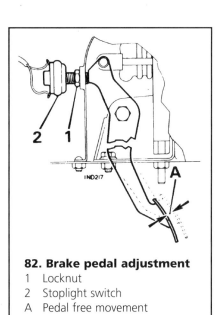

82. Brake pedal adjustment
1   Locknut
2   Stoplight switch
A   Pedal free movement

☐ Job 83. Exhaust manifold.

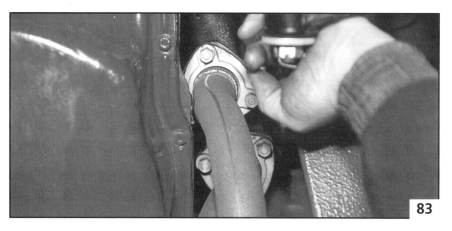

83

83. Check the exhaust manifold and the front of the exhaust system for leaks and security of the mountings. If any manifold bolts are missing, or the flange is broken, it will be extremely difficult to obtain a correct seal between the exhaust pipes and the manifold - the gaskets will quickly blow. Broken studs should be replaced, drilling out if necessary and replacing with separate long bolts if all else fails. Otherwise, a new manifold will be required.

INSIDE INFORMATION: An excellent way of spotting leaks in the exhaust system is to hold a rag over the end of the exhaust pipe, while the engine is running on tickover. You'll hear any leaks, loud and clear, as gases are forced through them. Do so only out of doors.

☐ Job 84. Front dampers.

84. Check for fluid leaks from the front dampers, especially where the wishbones pivot at the dampers, and also check the condition of the damper bushes. If they appear soft, spreading - or non-existent! - fit new ones. Leaking dampers must be replaced but exchange dampers are not too expensive. Always replace dampers in pairs.

84

☐ Job 85. Clutch hydraulics.

85. Check all clutch pipes for corrosion or perishing of the flexible pipe, and check the clutch slave cylinder for leaking fluid. You often won't be able to spot a failing clutch because the rubber boot is too efficient to let out escaping fluid. Peel back the boot from the slave cylinder and take a look for fluid leaks.

SAFETY FIRST!
Lower the front of the car, then raise the rear of the car off the ground after carefully reading the information at the start of this chapter on lifting and supporting the car.

☐ Job 86. Rear brake lines.

Check all brake lines beneath the back end of the car for corrosion - once again, especially behind pipe clips where most corrosion takes place - and check all flexible pipes for chaffing and perishing.

INSIDE INFORMATION: i) bend each flexible hose back on itself, especially near the unions. This will show up perishing and cracking in the pipe. ii) have an assistant press hard on the brake pedal while you look out for bulges in the flexible hoses. If you see ANY signs of weakness or deterioration in any of the pipes, stop using the car until they have been replaced.

85

☐ Job 87. Rear fuel lines.

SAFETY FIRST!
Keep sparks, naked lights and all sources of ignition away from the fuel system. See Chapter 1, Safety First! for further information.

Check the fuel pump and fuel pipes at the rear of the car for chafing, leaks and corrosion, and the fuel tank for dark staining from the top of the tank, which probably indicates that the top of the tank has corroded and is leaking, requiring replacement.

☐ Job 88. Exhaust system.

Check the rear of the exhaust system for leaks and security of the mountings.

☐ Job 89. Rear dampers.

89. Check for fluid leaks from each rear damper, especially where the damper arm pivots on the body, and check the condition of the damper bushes. If they appear soft, spreading - or non-existent! - fit new ones. Leaking dampers must be replaced but exchange, reconditioned dampers are not too expensive. Always replace dampers in pairs.

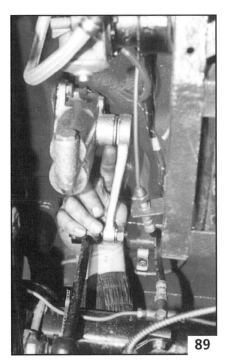

89

6,000 MILE SERVICE

☐ Job 90. Hand brake mechanism.

90. Lubricate the hand brake mechanical linkage and the cable. There is a grease nipple on the outer cable - give it the grease gun treatment! (See Job 45, illustration 45.2).

☐ Job 91. Universal joints.

91. Lubricate the propshaft universal joints. Earliest cars had a grease nipple on each universal joint. Some survive, which shows how much better it can be to add grease instead of just waiting for a 'sealed-until-death' UJ to fail! All have a grease nipple on the sliding spline on the propshaft. Add three or four shots of grease.

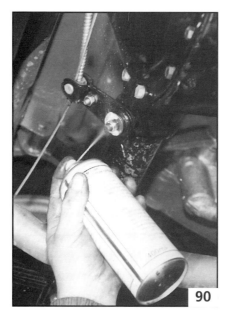

☐ Job 92. Rear axle oil.

92. You will need a large Allen key to remove the plug from the rear of the differential casing. Wire brush and wipe with a rag around the plug so that no dirt can drop in to the differential casing. With the plug removed, use a plastic container with a spout to inject the correct grade of rear axle oil into the differential casing until it just starts to dribble out of the drain plug aperture. See **Chapter 8, Facts and Figures** for the correct grade of rear axle oil. Refit the plug and wipe the differential casing.

☐ Job 93. Rear springs.

93. Spray or brush oil - or better still, wax underbody treatment - over the edges of the leaf springs. This allows the leaves to slide against each other as they should, improving the ride and cutting out squeaks, but keep oil off rubber bushes.

Lower the car to the ground.

6,000 mile Mechanical and Electrical - Road Test

Carry out Jobs 46 to 50.

6,000 mile Bodywork and Interior - Around the Car

First, carry out Jobs 17, 20 to 23 and 51 to 55.

☐ Job 94. Bonnet release.

94. Lubricate the bonnet release safety catch using clean silicone grease so that you won't damage clothes when leaning into the engine bay.

INSIDE INFORMATION: Put a large dab of grease the onto the end of the cable, to stop water driving down the cable, something which it is very prone to doing, making the bonnet release catch stiff and difficult to pull. Lubricate the bonnet hinges, too.

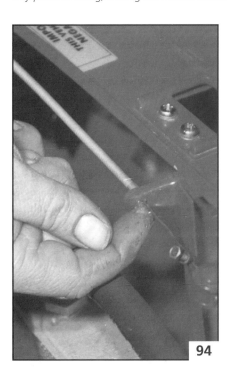

94

95A

☐ Job 95. Door locks.

95A. Lubricate the door locks with silicone releasing fluid, using an extension tube to direct the spray.

95B. Also lubricate the door latches, using silicone grease where they can come into contact with clothes.

95C. Note that the door hinges have a special oiling channel into which thin lubricating oil can be run, from where it reaches the hinge pins inside the bodywork.

☐ Job 96. Boot lock.

Lubricate the boot lock, latch and hinges.

NB Do not lubricate the steering lock, except with a drop of oil on the end of a key, to prevent the lock barrel from seizing.

☐ Job 97. Seats and seat belts.

Check the condition and security of seats and seat belts. Shake each seat to check its security, pull hard on each length of belt webbing near where each section is fitted to the car, test each buckle. Check inertia reel belts. With most types, you can test by tugging; if you pull hard and quickly on the belt the reel should lock, with others the lock may only work under braking. Carry out a careful road test, in the daylight, under dry road conditions and with no other traffic or pedestrians about.

95B

95C

CHAPTER THREE

6,000 miles Bodywork - Under the Car

First, carry out Jobs 24 and 56.

SAFETY FIRST!
Only raise the car off the ground after carefully reading the information at the start of this chapter on lifting and supporting the car.

☐ **Job 98. Rustproof underbody.**

Renew wax treatment to wheel arches and underbody areas. Refer to **Chapter 5, Rustproofing**, for full details.

☐ **Job 99. Clear drain holes.**

99. Check and clear the drain holes in the sills, doors, boot and scuttle.

INSIDE INFORMATION: This last drain hole is not mentioned in the 'official' list of drain checks, but it is most important. Beneath the air intake, but right under the body, is a drain pipe - a black rubber tube with a bulge or ball on the end. When this clogs (and it does!) water will get inside the car. Use a stick or length of steel to open the bottom of the drain pipe, and keep it open while you flush water through from above. Much poking and flushing may be necessary, if this has not been done before!

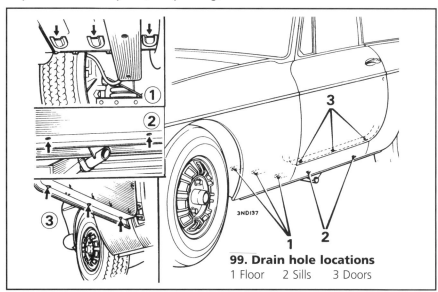

99. Drain hole locations
1 Floor   2 Sills   3 Doors

12,000 Miles - or Every Twelve Months, Whichever Comes First

12,000 mile Mechanical and Electrical - Emission Control Equipment

The first emission control equipment was fitted shortly after the launch of the MGB and there are many different variations fitted to MGBs, MGCs and the V8 models with most modifications being fitted to US MGBs.

SPECIALIST SERVICE: Very many emission control components are not serviceable without the correct specialist equipment such as a vacuum gauge, pressure gauge, exhaust gas analyser, distributor advance tester, carburettor piston loading tool, and an engine oscilloscope, depending upon model of car. Without describing every type of emission control system in detail, the following Job numbers list the components that can be tested or serviced at home. All should be carried out at the 12,000 miles/twelve months service interval.

CERTAIN US CARS ONLY:
Those fitted with a Crankcase Emission Valve System with Air Pump. Please note that this system will only work properly if the engine is generally kept in a proper state of tune.

☐ **Job 100. Crankcase breather.**

EARLIER CARS:
100. Take off the spring clip (100.2) and remove the cover plate, diaphragm (100.3), metering valve (100.4) and valve spring. Clean the rubber diaphragm in methylated spirit (denatured alcohol) and the metal parts with white spirit (mineral spirit).

INSIDE INFORMATION: i) If there are stuck-on deposits, try boiling the metal parts in an old saucepan first. If any parts are damaged, or if the diaphragm looks perished, replace it. Reassemble, taking care that the metering valve fits correctly in its guides and that the diaphragm seats correctly. ii) If the breather pipes have become blocked, it is certain that the breather connections on the engine block will also be congested. The early type is part of the tappet chest, behind the exhaust manifold; later ones are part of the timing chain cover (104.5). Either type will have to be removed, boiled clean and washed out. Fit new gaskets when reassembling.

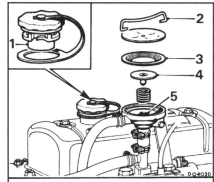

100. Crankcase breather assembly
1   Oil filler cap
2   Spring clip
3   Diaphragm
4   Metering valve
5   Valve body

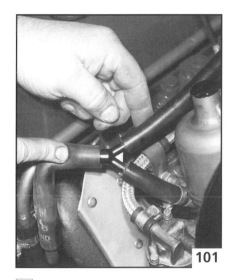

101

Job 101. Hoses and connectors.

101. On all models, the hose can come loose at either end, can deteriorate externally, or can collapse and clog up internally. Replace hose and/or hose clips, as necessary. On later models, the crankcase breather connects to the carburettors via a plastic 'Y'-piece in the breather hose, as shown in this illustration. The plastic is prone to breaking - check and replace if necessary.

Job 102. Oil filler cap.

Most models, including all UK cars with plastic oil filler caps, take in their air through the oil filler cap, which contains an integral filter, in which case the filler cap should now be replaced (100.1). A blocked filler/filter cap will cause the car to burn oil, put out smoke and display several symptoms of a worn-out engine. A new cap comes a lot less expensive!

US CARS:

Take careful note that some models, identified by the adsorption canister fitted approximately above the distributor, have a sealed oil filler cap which appears similar at first sight (104.4). In the latter case, no replacement is normally necessary. DO NOT FIT THE WRONG TYPE OF CAP!

Job 103. Air valve filter.

Some latest cars, in order to comply with European emission regulations, are fitted with an air control valve to the underside of the carburettor air cleaner. It consists of a short length of pipe on the end of which is a small filter. Remove the air cleaner and hoses, (Push-on type): pull off the old filter and throw away; (Cap-type): remove the screw and washer, pull off the cap, discard the renewable filter element found beneath and fit a new one.

Job 104. Adsorption canister.
US CARS ONLY:

104. You have to take out the canister (104.2) in order to renew the filter. Disconnect the three pipes at the top and one at the bottom of the canister, unscrew the clip that holds the canister in place and lift it away. Remove the screw that holds the bottom of the canister in place and take out the air filter pad secured by the end cap of the canister. Fit a new filter pad. When refitting the canister, make sure that the purge pipe that runs from the engine rocker cover (104.3) is connected to the centre connection on the top of the canister.

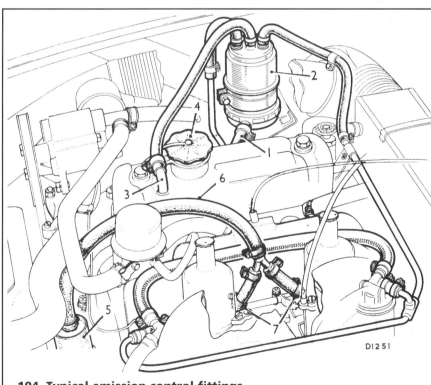

DI251

104. Typical emission control fittings

1	Lower hose connection	5	Oil separator
2	Adsorption canister	6	Breather hose
3	Rocker cover connection	7	Breather hose-to-carburettor connections
4	Oil filler cap		

Job 105. Second fuel filter.
US CARS ONLY:

Some cars fitted with an evaporative loss control system are equipped with two in-line fuel filters in order to ensure that no residue can enter and damage the system. Ensure that both are changed at 12,000 miles/twelve months. After changing the filter/s, turn on the ignition and ensure that there are no fuel leaks.

Job 106. Air pump belt.
US CARS ONLY:

Change the air pump drive belt. When correctly tensioned, the belt should deflect by about ½ inch (12 mm) half way along the longest part of the belt between the pulleys. Retighten the mounting bolts to a torque of 10 lb ft (1.38 kg m). Check all pipes and connections for soundness. Replace if necessary. Faulty air pumps usually become excessively noisy.

INSIDE INFORMATION: Try disconnecting the air pump belt then running the engine again, to see if the noise is actually coming from the pump.

SPECIALIST SERVICE: If you suspect the air pump of any other fault, seek specialist advice for diagnosis, rebuild or for the cost of a replacement.

☐ **Job 107. Air pump filter.**

US CARS ONLY:

Some systems fitted with an air pump have a renewable type of paper air filter. Replace it.

☐ **Job 108. Test check valve.**

US CARS ONLY:

Some systems fitted with an air pump have a check valve on the inlet side. Check it by removing, then trying to blow through from one end and then the other. The valve should only allow air to pass from the 'inlet' end, not the air pump end. If it does so, discard and replace.

☐ **Job 109. Fuel filler cap.**

US CARS ONLY:

Check the condition of the fuel filler cap seal. Replace the seal if it appears damaged.

☐ **Job 110. Emission system.**

SPECIALIST SERVICE: Have a specialist run a check over the emission control and evaporative loss control systems for leaks and correct operation of all the valves and components that cannot be checked without specialist equipment.

12,000 mile Mechanical and Electrical - The Engine Bay

First, carry out Jobs 2 to 6, 26, 27, 28, 30, 32, and Jobs 57 to 71.

☐ **Job 111. Zenith/Stromberg carbs.**

US CARS ONLY:

Check the rubber diaphragms on Zenith/Stromberg carburettors for perishing and replace if necessary. Take out the dashpot damper (very similar to that on SU carbs.), take out the four screws holding the top cover in place (after marking its position) and beneath it you will see the rubber diaphragm, held in place with a plate and four more small screws. In general, work on Zenith/Stromberg carburettors requires the use of special tools so little more than this can be accomplished without **SPECIALIST SERVICE**.

☐ **Job 112. Check heat shields.**

MGBs ONLY:

112. Check the heat shields beneath the carburettors and above the exhaust manifolds. Held over the engine bay is what a complete heat shield, later type, should look like. The car is fitted with the correct earlier type. Check for breakage and replace if necessary.

☐ **Job 113. Carb. poppet valves.**

112

SPECIALIST SERVICE: The carburettors must be removed from the engine for this check. If you feel this is beyond your capabilities, seek specialist advice. If, however you are competent in this work, proceed as follows.

LATER MODELS ONLY:

113. Check the spring-loaded poppet valves in the throttle butterflies of later carburettors. If the valve is seized open, free the valve or see *INSIDE INFORMATION* below. Alternatively, if you want to retain the anti-run-on property provided by the poppet valves, fit new butterflies. They are easily replaced by taking out the two screws holding the butterfly into the shaft. But first, close up the ends of the bifurcated screws (i.e. split and turned open, like split-pins) with pliers.

INSIDE INFORMATION: These valves proved so troublesome in service, that many BL mechanics soldered them shut! If you are experiencing difficulty with engine idle speed setting, or getting the engine to slow down when the throttle is released, these valves may be the cause.

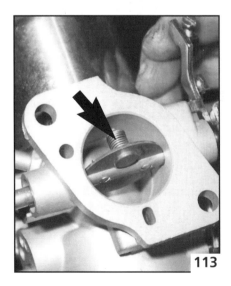

113

114

☐ Job 114. V8 flame traps.

V8 ENGINES ONLY:

114. Remove the engine flame traps and replace with new.

☐ Job 115. Oil leaks.

Check for engine oil leaks, especially around the bottom of the sump (check the sump flanges), around the back of the engine and the bottom of the gearbox bellhousing (could be an engine rear oil seal or gearbox oil seal, although all very early 3-main bearing engines, with prefix No. 18G and 18GA, leak through the rear bearing - no separate oil seal is fitted). Check the tappet covers, check behind the exhaust manifold and the timing chain cover at the front of the engine, both around the flanges and behind the pulley, where the front oil seal is situated. Especially check the rocker cover at the top of the engine - oil can run all the way down, of course! In general, leaks call for gasket or oil seal renewal. Rear oil seal renewal is a very major, engine-out job. Check for oil cooler leaks, from the unions at the top of the oil cooler and the cooler itself, and check the cooler pipes for perishing, leaking and rubbing on the steering column universal joint, something they are prone to do when they become old and droopy.

☐ Job 116. Clean radiators.

Carefully clean the front surface of the radiator and oil cooler fins, taking care not to damage the radiator. Use a soft brush on the front and blast from the rear with an ordinary garden hose. You could easily do this with the air line at your local garage when you fill up with petrol.

117

☐ Job 117. Grease water pump.

EARLY MODELS ONLY:

117. Lubricate the water pump by taking out the screw, shown here on this stripped-down engine, fitting a grease nipple, and adding a just a little grease.

☐ Job 118. Remote brake servo filter.

MGB ONLY:

118. Clean the brake servo filter. Carefully prise off the cover with a screwdriver, take out the filter and blow it clean with compressed air. You could also carry out this job with the air line at your local garage when you fill up with petrol.

> **SAFETY FIRST!**
> **Wear goggles when using compressed air!.**

☐ Job 119. In-line brake servo filter

MGB ONLY, LATER MODELS:

SPECIALIST SERVICE: Some later models were fitted with an in-line brake servo and this type has the filter located where the brake pedal push-rod enters the servo unit. Access is difficult, and ideally the servo should be removed for this work, so seek specialist advice from your dealer or garage.

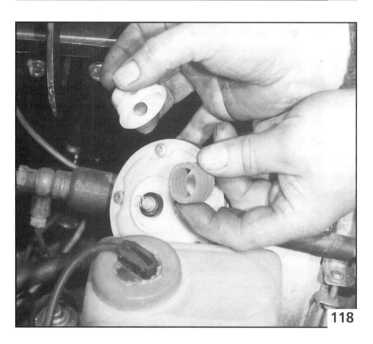

118

☐ Job 120. Valve clearances.
NOT MGB GT V8, OR MG RV8.
Please note that V8s have hydraulic tappets and no adjustment is necessary or possible. The following adjustments apply to 4- and 6-cylinder engines only.

Adjust the valve clearances, with the engine hot or cold but not in-between (although it will be jolly uncomfortable to work on when hot!). It is best to remove the spark plugs when carrying out this work since the engine will have to be turned over several times. Turn the engine over (either by pressing on the fan belt and turning the fan, or by using a spanner on the crankshaft pulley bolt). Valve clearances are checked when each valve is in the fully closed position. The only way of being sure of this is to follow a mechanic's rule that says that each valve will be shut when another particular valve is fully open - and you can see that they are open because the rocker arm will have 'rocked', pushing the valve right down. Try it; it's easy!

INSIDE INFORMATION: Mechanics know which valves relate to which by the 'rule of nine' for 4-cylinder engines and the 'rule of thirteen' for 6-cylinder engines. Here's how it works: The engine has two valves per cylinder making eight - or twelve, for the larger engines - in all. Start counting from the front. When No. 1 is open, No. 8 will be closed (1+8=9). When No. 2 is open, No. 7 will be closed (and 2+7=9 again, of course). Follow the rule right through and you can identify which 'open' valve relates to which 'fully closed' one, each time. It's exactly the same for the MGC, except that the valves concerned are No. 1 and No. 12, making 13; then on to No. 2 and No. 11, also making 13, and so on.

120

120. Setting valve clearances (tappets) is easy! Undo the locknut, which allows the centre screw to be turned in and out, thus changing the valve clearance. Use a feeler gauge to establish when the gap is exactly 15 'thou', or 0.015 inch (0.38 mm) - it should be a tight sliding fit - and tighten the locknut as the screw is held tight. You will probably find that the last turn of the locknut also tightens the screw further, no matter how hard you hold the screwdriver. Try edging the gap open a touch to allow for the fact, but check carefully with the feeler gauge when the locknut is tight to ensure that the gap is correct.

☐ Job 121. Rocker cover gasket.

121. Fit a new gasket and grommets to the rocker cover and refit the cover. Don't make the common mistake of over-tightening the cover - it causes leaks - just 'nip' the nuts down on to the top of the cover.

Drive the car for several miles until it reaches its normal operating temperature. Check the rocker cover again for leaks.

121

122

☐ Job 122. Check cylinder compressions.

SAFETY FIRST!
Take off the HT lead that runs from the coil to the distributor at the coil end so that there is no risk of sparks or an electric shock. Carry out this work outside, and make sure that the gearbox is in neutral.

SPECIALIST SERVICE: If your car is fitted with electronic ignition (MG RV8 and later MGBs), do not disconnect any of the coil wiring without first ascertaining that damage will not be caused to the electronic ignition circuitry – check your handbook; if in doubt, use **SPECIALIST SERVICE**.

Ensure that the engine oil is up to the recommended level and that the engine is at running temperature. Remove the spark plugs.

122. Screw the tester or hold it against the first spark plug port. Have an assistant hold the throttle fully open while the engine is spun over on the starter motor and make a note of the maximum reading on the gauge. Repeat the operation on each cylinder. If the engine is in good condition, there should not be a variation of more than five to six p.s.i. (or at the very most ten p.s.i.) between each cylinder.

INSIDE INFORMATION: i) Low similar readings on two adjacent cylinders suggests a faulty head gasket between the two cylinders. ii) If one cylinder shows a higher reading than the others, check the spark plug from that cylinder for oil or excessive carbon. Worn or broken piston rings could allow oil to be forced passed the rings to create a better seal - paradoxically, an indication that the engine is very heavily worn. iii) If you suspect worn or broken rings, pour a teaspoon full of engine oil through the spark plug hole and carry out the check again. If there is a temporary increase in the p.s.i. reading, suspect the piston rings. If there is no increase, then the valves in the cylinder head are probably badly burnt.

☐ Job 123. Exhaust manifold bolts.
MG RV8 ONLY:
Check the exhaust manifold bolts to ensure that they are tightened up to the correct torque.

12,000 mile Mechanical and Electrical - Around the Car

First, carry out jobs 7 to 19, 33, and 72 to 79.

☐ Job 124. Test dampers.
'Bounce' test each corner of the car in turn in order to check the efficiency of the dampers. If the car 'bounces' at all, the dampers have had it. They should be replaced in pairs as an axle set. Efficient dampers can make an enormous difference to your car's safety and handling.

☐ Job 125. Alarm remote units.
Replace the battery in each alarm sender unit (if fitted). Otherwise, as the author once found, it is all too easy to be banished from your own car, if the battery 'dies' at an inopportune moment. Like in France. With the shops shut...

12,000 mile Mechanical and Electrical - Under the Car

First carry out Jobs 34 and 35, 43 and 44, then 80 to 85.

126

SAFETY FIRST!
Raise the front of the car off the ground after reading carefully the information at the start of this chapter on lifting and supporting the car.

☐ Job 126. Wishbone bushes.

126. Check the front suspension wishbone bushes for wear.

INSIDE INFORMATION: If front suspension bushes are worn, replace with the far longer lasting V8 type, shown here.

☐ Job 127. Damper pivots

Check the damper pivots for wear. See if there is any play in them when you attempt to move them up and down.

☐ Job 128. Kingpins.

128. Check the kingpins for wear. Place a jack up beneath the wishbone pans and just raise them slightly. It is important that the jack compresses the suspension, but don't go beneath the car! Use a lever to lift and lower the road wheel and look for movement in the top and bottom of the kingpin.

☐ Job 129. Check front hubs.

129. Check the front hubs for excessive play. Have an assistant look behind the wheel to see if there is any movement in the hub when you push and pull, top and bottom. Don't go beneath the car! Have the hubs adjusted if necessary - SPECIALIST SERVICE.

☐ Job 130. Front brake calipers.

Examine the front brake calipers for fluid leakage. Overhaul the calipers or fit new calipers if any is found.

SAFETY FIRST! and SPECIALIST SERVICE: Obviously, a car's brakes are among its most important safety related items. Do not dismantle your car's brakes unless you are fully competent to do so. If you have not been trained in this work, but wish to carry out the work described here, we strongly recommend that you have a garage or qualified mechanic check your work before using the car on the road. See also the section on BRAKES AND ASBESTOS in Chapter 1, for further important information.

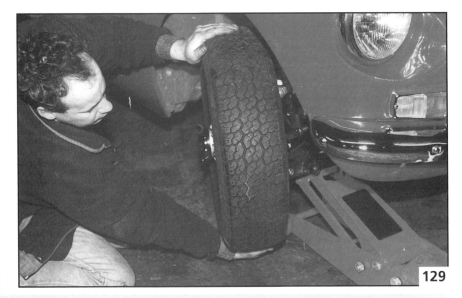

128

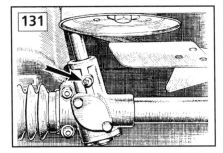

129

131

☐ Job 131. Lubricate Steering.

EARLY CARS ONLY:

131. Give ten strokes maximum of the correct grade of oil (not grease) to the grease nipple on the steering rack of early cars. See **Lubrication Chart** on page 108 for the correct oil type.

☐ Job 132. Steering Mountings.

132. Check that the steering rack mounting bolts are tight. The rear bolt goes down into a captive nut and should be fitted with a spring or lock washer. The front bolt's nut is gripped by the rack bracket so once again, the lock washer should be beneath the bolt head. The nut should be a nyloc nut.

132

134

Job 133. Check Free Play.

Check for excessive free play at the steering wheel, and if present, find out why. See Chapter 7, Getting Through The MoT for details of what is, and is not, acceptable.

Job 134. Check Ball Joints.

134. Check for excessive free play in all ball joints, especially those at the inner ends of the steering rack, and check the (outer) track rod ends.

Job 135. Adjust dampers.
MGB RV8 ONLY:
SPECIALIST SERVICE: Check and adjust all four dampers. This is a complicated operation requiring removal of each damper from the car. Have the work carried out by your Dealer.

Now carry out Jobs 36 to 42.

Lower the front of the car to the ground, and raise the rear.

SAFETY FIRST!
Only raise the rear of the car off the ground after carefully reading the information at the start of this chapter on lifting and supporting the car.

First carry out Jobs 86 to 93.

Job 136. Rear brake inspection.

SAFETY FIRST! and SPECIALIST SERVICE:
Obviously, a car's brakes are among its most important safety related items. Do not dismantle your car's brakes unless you are fully competent to do so. If you have not been trained in this work, but wish to carry out the work described here, we strongly recommend a garage or qualified mechanic checks your work before using the car on the road. See the section on BRAKES AND ASBESTOS in Chapter 1, for further important information.

When fitting new brake shoes, Lockheed, the suppliers of much MG 'original equipment', recommend that you avoid heavy braking - except in an emergency - for the first 150-200 miles (250-300 km).

136A. Remove the brake drums by taking off the four bolts (wire wheel cars) or the two cross-head screws (bolt-on wheeled cars). First slacken off the brake adjuster on the back plate as far as it will go (also see 136D.)

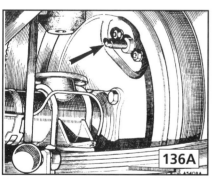

136A

136B

136B. The brake drum will probably not slide straight off as it should. Hammer quite firmly around the outer edge of the brake drum but ONLY: i) with a soft faced mallet and ii) hitting the drum right on its edge, as shown. The brake drum can now be pulled and wriggled off its studs.

MGC AND MG RV8 ONLY:
If necessary, back off the automatic adjusters to allow removal of the brake drum (see Job 161).

136C. Use a proprietary brand of brake cleaner. Spray large quantities all over the brakes. The cleaner will kill the dust and wash a good deal of it away, reducing the risk of brake squeal later on, and allowing the parts to work more efficiently. Wipe out any residue and be sure to throw away any rags you have used in a sealed plastic bag.

136D. This is the brake adjuster with a proper brake adjusting tool held near the back of the back plate where it has to be used. Adjusters, as mentioned earlier, are prone to seizure. It's a good idea to add a small dab of brake grease to the inside of the brake adjuster, through the front as shown here.

If the brake shoes are worn down close to the rivets, replace them with new ones. Use only asbestos-free items, for safety's sake. With the exception of hydraulic parts, metal to metal contact points such as the tips of the shoes, the areas of the backplate where contacted by the shoe platforms, the wheel cylinder and the abutment slots should be lubricated sparingly with brake grease (not ordinary grease!).

The threads of the adjuster screws should be coated with brake grease, but take care not to get grease on the shoe linings, the rubber parts or the friction surface of the drum.

136E. You can fit the brake shoe springs to the brake shoes whilst they are off the car. Note how the bottom spring is fitted to the back of the brake shoe. Check for broken or missing springs and renew if necessary.

136C

136D

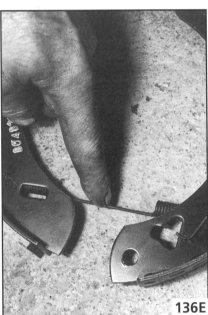

136E

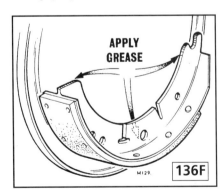

APPLY GREASE

136F

136F. The brake shoes are first fitted to the adjuster and then pulled apart at the bottom and fitted to the wheel cylinder. Only the smallest amount of brake grease should be used. (Courtesy AP Lockheed)

136G

136G. Ensure that as you push the brake shoes into place, both ends of the hand brake lever protrude through the brake shoes, one end through the bottom of each shoe. You can then fit the pull-off spring, hooking it through one of the lever ends and using a screwdriver to stretch it over to the other lever end.

You can learn a lot about the condition of an engine from looking at the spark plugs. The following information and photographs, reproduced here with grateful thanks to NGK, show you what to look out for.

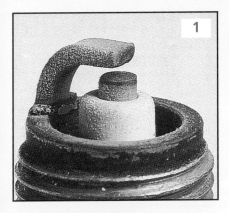

1. Good Condition

If the firing end of a spark plug is brown or light grey, the condition can be judged to be good and the spark plug is functioning at its best.

4. Overheating

When having been overheated, the insulator tip can become glazed or glossy, and deposits which have accumulated on the insulator tip may have melted. Sometimes these deposits have blistered on the insulator's tip.

6. Abnormal Wear

Abnormal electrode erosion is caused by the effects of corrosion, oxidation, reaction with lead, all resulting in abnormal gap growth.

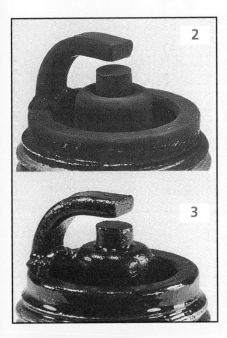

2. Carbon Fouling

Black, dry, sooty deposits, which will eventually cause misfiring and can be caused by an over-rich fuel mixture. Check all carburettor settings, choke operation and air filter cleanliness. Clean plugs vigorously with a brass bristled wire brush.

3. Oil Fouling

Oily, wet-looking deposits. This is particularly prone to causing poor starting and even misfiring. Caused by a severely worn engine but do not confuse with wet plugs removed from the engine when it won't start. If the "wetness" evaporates away, it's not oil fouling.

5. Normal Wear

A worn spark plug not only wastes fuel but also strains the whole ignition system because the expanded gap requires higher voltage. As a result, a worn spark plug will result in damage to the engine itself, and will also increase air pollution. The normal rate of gap growth is usually around 'half-a-thou.' or 0.0006 in. every 5,000 miles (0.01 mm. every 5,000 km.).

7. Breakage

Insulator damage is self-evident and can be caused by rapid heating or cooling of the plug whilst out of the car or by clumsy use of gap setting tools. Burned away electrodes are indicative of an ignition system that is grossly out of adjustment. Do not use the car until this has been put right.

136H. The brake shoe steady pin washer. To remove/refit:
(1) Push in
(2) Turn washer with pliers

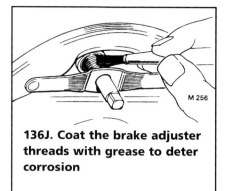

136J. Coat the brake adjuster threads with grease to deter corrosion

136H. Two steady pins - one for each brake shoe - are pushed through the back of the back plate and through the hole in the middle of the brake shoe. The spring and steady washer can then be fitted. You hold the steady pin tight against the back plate (from the back of it), push the steady washer over the pin and against the force of the spring and twist through 90 degrees. (But then you found this out earlier, when you removed them, didn't you ...). (Courtesy AP Lockheed)

Inspect the rear wheel cylinders (Job. 137) before refitting the brake drum.

136J. Adjust the brakes correctly as shown in Job 45. Apply the brakes firmly using the foot pedal to centralise the shoes, before backing off the adjuster so that the wheel will just turn freely. Coat the threads on the back of the adjuster with grease to deter future corrosion. (Courtesy AP Lockheed)

Job 137. Rear wheel cylinders.

137. Peel back the rubber dust cover on each rear brake wheel cylinders and examine for fluid leakage. Replace the wheel cylinder if any is found. Check that the wheel cylinder pistons aren't seized by trying to turn them with a screwdriver in the slotted ends. Also check for swollen rubber seals - evidence of contamination from oil, grease, or the wrong type of brake fluid. If any of these problems are found: **SPECIALIST SERVICE**, so consult a properly qualified garage. Brake fluid might need draining, flushing and renewing; brake wheel cylinders or seals might require replacement.

137

Refit the brake drum and roadwheels then adjust the brakes.

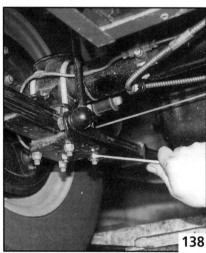

138

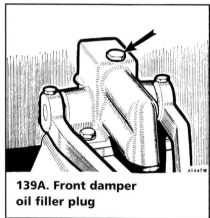

139A. Front damper oil filler plug

Job 138. 'U'-bolt tightness.

138. Check the tightness of rear springs/axle 'U'-bolts. They can come loose, periodically!

Job 139. Top up dampers.

139A. Top up the hydraulic dampers, front and rear, using special hydraulic damper fluid. Clean around each damper top before removing the plugs, so that no dirt can fall into the dampers. Note that MGCs with telescopic front dampers are sealed. If they show signs of fluid leakage, they should be replaced with new units, replacing them only as a set of two.

139B. The rear dampers are located beneath prise-off caps, either side of the rear parcel shelf.

Job 140. Universal joint flanges.

140. Check the universal joint flange nuts for tightness.

Lower the car to the ground.

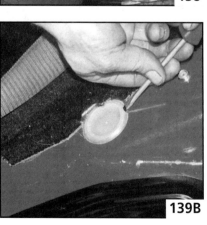

139B

140

12,000 mile Mechanical and Electrical - Road Test.

Carry out jobs 46 to 50.

12,000 mile Bodywork and Interior - Around the Car

First, carry out Jobs 17 to 23, 51 to 55 and 94 to 97.

☐ Job 141. Seat runners.

141. Carefully lubricate the seat runners, preferably using non-staining silicone grease, taking care not to get grease onto the carpet or rubber mats.

☐ Job 142. Toolkit and jack.

142. Inspect the toolkit, wipe the tools with an oily rag to stop them rusting and lubricate the jack, checking that it works smoothly. Also, check that the spare wheel retaining bolt hasn't rusted in. Remove it and lubricate the threads with a little grease.

141

142

☐ Job 143. Wire wheel splines.
WIRE WHEELED CARS ONLY:

143A. Remove each wire wheel in turn and wash dirt and grease from the splines, cones and spinners using engine degreaser. Examine the splines for wear: 'sharp' splines are worn out and should be replaced. If they fail - and in extremis they can fail, you will be left without brakes, in effect, on that particular wheel - extremely dangerous!

143B. Lubricate them with fresh grease, paying special attention to the tapering cones, in addition to the splines.

143A

143B

☐ Job 144. Wire wheel spokes.

144. *INSIDE INFORMATION: With each wheel off the car, tap each spoke with the handle end of a screwdriver, so as not to chip the finish. Each spoke should strike approximately the same note. If not, some spokes have gone out of tension. If you hear large differences,* **SPECIALIST SERVICE:** *Have a specialist check the wheels for spoke tension and true running; you might need the wheels rebuilding.*

144

CHAPTER THREE

12,000 mile Bodywork - Under the Car

First, carry out jobs 24 and 56, bearing in mind that Job 145 entails a more thorough wax coating treatment.

Job 145. Top-up rustproofing.

Renew the wax rust treatment to the underside of the car, the box sections, sills (both sides of diaphragm), insides of doors and other hidden areas such as between inner and outer front and rear wings. See **Chapter 5, Rustproofing** for full details.

> **SAFETY FIRST!**
> **Only raise the car off the ground after carefully reading the information at the start of this chapter on lifting and supporting the car.**

24,000 Miles - or Every Twenty Four Months, Whichever Comes First

The Service Jobs mentioned below should be carried out in addition to the regular 12,000 mile/twelve month Service Jobs shown previously. They cover the sort of areas that experience has shown can give trouble in the longer term or, in some cases, they cover areas that may prevent trouble from starting in the first place. Most of them don't appear on manufacturers' service schedules - but these are the sort of jobs which make all the difference between a car that is reliable, and one that gives problems out of the blue.

24,000 mile Mechanical and Electrical - The Engine Bay

Job 146. Engine mountings.

Check the engine mountings, especially the round type used on later models. Also on rubber bumper cars, check the steel mounting brackets themselves since they can sometimes fracture.

Job 147. Refill cooling system.

> **SAFETY FIRST!**
> **Only work on the cooling system when the engine is cold. If you try to drain a hot engine, the water inside can boil up as the pressure is removed, releasing spurting, scalding steam and water.**

Every two years, the coolant should be drained from the cooling system and discarded and then refilled with fresh. This is to ensure that the anti-corrosion properties of the coolant are retained and you should also take the opportunity to flush out the cooling system, getting rid of any debris that may have built up in there. Before draining down the cooling system, turn the heater tap on to the fully open position and remove the filler caps. On the MGC this means taking off the expansion tank cap (147B.1) and the filler neck cap (147B.2); on later MGBs the filler plug on top of the cylinder head has to be removed (147A.1) on the MGB GT V8 it's a matter of removing the expansion tank cap and the plug from the top of the radiator (147C.2), and for the MG RV8 remove the expansion tank cap and the plug from the filler pipe on top of the engine.

147A. On later cars there is a drain plug on the block (147A.4) whereas on earlier cars you will find a drain tap situated there. Also on later cars, the only way of draining down the radiator is by removing the bottom hose from the radiator stub (147A.3). On earlier cars there is a tap on the bottom of the radiator similar to that shown for the MGC in 147B.3.

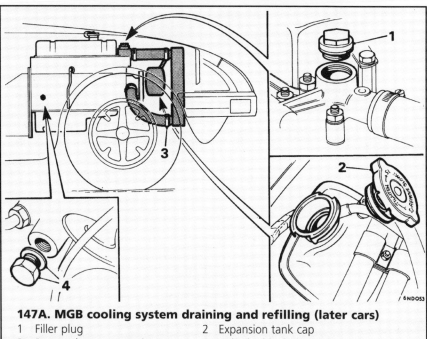

147A. MGB cooling system draining and refilling (later cars)
1 Filler plug	2 Expansion tank cap
3 Bottom hose connection	4 Cylinder block drain plug

147B. The MGC's system is similar to that of the MGB with a drain plug or tap on the engine block, although on the opposite side (147B.4) and with a drain plug rather than a tap on the bottom of the radiator (147B.3).

147C. With the MGB GT V8, the drain tap on the bottom of the block (147C.3) must be opened and the bottom hose must be disconnected from the bottom of the radiator in order to drain the system. On the MG RV8 only the bottom hose needs to be disconnected.

Before refilling the system flush it through. With all filler caps and plugs still disconnected, put a garden hose into the car's bottom hose and plug the gap between the small bore of the garden hose and the larger bore of the bottom hose with a rag. Turn on the tap and run the water until no more sediment comes out of the filler cap or filler plug. Try turning the heater tap on and off so that the flow through the heater surges through it and helps to clear sediment from the heater itself. If you suspect the heater of being badly clogged, disconnect the two heater hoses and flush the heater radiator separately. Now take the garden hose and insert it into the bottom stub of the radiator and flush that out in the same way.

In order to refill the system, look in **Chapter 8, Facts and Figures** and establish the capacity of the cooling system of your car. Mix water and anti-freeze in a 50/50 solution. After reconnecting the hoses and closing all drain taps, refill with the prepared coolant - in the case of later engines with a filler plug or the MGC with a filler cap on the block, top up the engine until full, then top

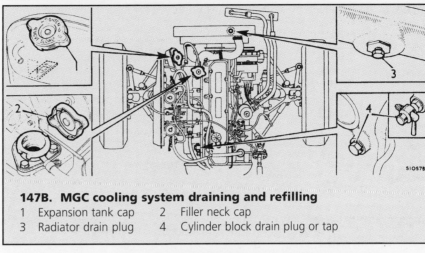

147B. MGC cooling system draining and refilling
1   Expansion tank cap   2   Filler neck cap
3   Radiator drain plug   4   Cylinder block drain plug or tap

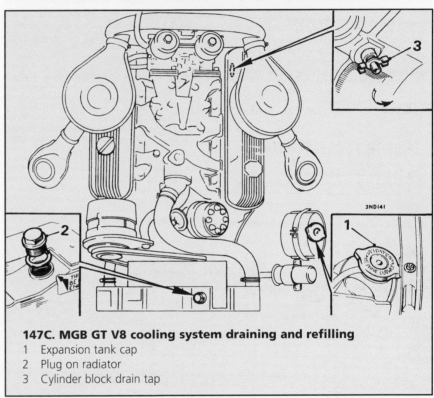

147C. MGB GT V8 cooling system draining and refilling
1   Expansion tank cap
2   Plug on radiator
3   Cylinder block drain tap

up the expansion tank until it is half full. Replace plugs and caps and run the engine until the top of the radiator begins to feel warm. Stop the engine and carefully remove the expansion tank cap, or the cap on the top of the radiator in the case of earlier models or the cap at (147B.1) in the case of the MGC. Remove the filler plug or filler cap on the MGC (147B.2) or the radiator cap on earlier cars and top up once again. For cars fitted with an expansion bottle, refill it to half full. Now you should run the car, getting it up to full operating temperature and revving the engine rapidly on several occasions so that the water pump pushes the water quickly round the system and removes any air locks. Wait for the water to cool down fully and then check the levels once again. Take care to check the water levels after the first time you use the car on the road, allowing the water to cool down fully before taking off the pressure cap.

INSIDE INFORMATION: Fill the system slowly and squeeze the bottom hose a few times during filling to help expel any trapped air.

SAFETY FIRST!
Keep your hands away from the cooling fan and belts when the engine is running.

☐ **Job 148. Radiator pressure cap.**

Renew the radiator pressure cap - the spring weakens over time and the rubber seal perishes which reduces the pressure in the system which, in turn, allows the coolant to boil at a lower temperature.

☐ Job 149. Drive belts.

Renew all drive belts (normally only one - the 'fan belt', unless the car has an air pump or air conditioning).

150

☐ Job 150. V8 engine breather.
V8 ENGINES ONLY:
150. Remove the engine breather filter, found out of the way, between the back of the carburettors and the heater box, and replace with new. The filter is held to the back of the air filter box with a clamp, held down with a nut and two washers. Slacken the nut - take care not to remove and drop it - and pull the filter off the pipe beneath. Remove the top, curved pipe and fit it to the new filter before fixing back into place.

☐ Job 151. Renew adsorption canister.
US CARS ONLY:
With adsorption canister in emission/evaporative loss control system.

See Job 104 under 12,000 miles/twelve months service for full details of how to remove or replace. Note that it is not possible to 'recover' or restore the absorption canister - it contains charcoal granules which have a finite life.

24,000 mile Mechanical and Electrical - Under the Car

SAFETY FIRST!
Raise the car off the ground as necessary after carefully reading the information at the start of this chapter on lifting and supporting the car.

☐ Job 152B. Engine Flushing Oil

On older engines, whose service history may be doubtful or unknown it's a good idea to clean out all the accumulated sludge that will have gathered in the sump over the years, using flushing oil. On later cars, and those that have had the benefit of regular oil changes, this operation probably won't be necessary. After draining the engine oil in the normal way, leave the oil filter in place and refill the sump with engine flushing oil. Follow the instructions which come with the oil but in general, run the engine for a little while to allow the flushing oil to clean out the engine's oil passages. Drain off the flushing oil - don't run the car with the flushing oil in the sump; that's not what it's for! - and then carry out the remainder of **Job 36, Drain Engine Oil**, in the normal way for a regular 3,000 mile Service.

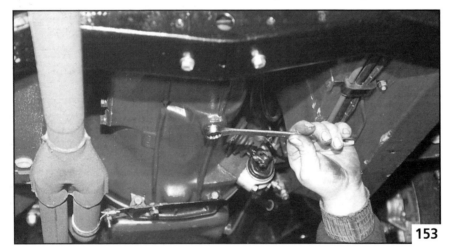
153

☐ Job 153. Gearbox oil.
153. Drain and replace the gearbox oil. The drain plug is shown here; refilling is described in Job 72. If an overdrive gearbox is fitted, carry out Job 154 before refilling with fresh oil. Run the engine for a few minutes, switch off, then check the gearbox level and top up as necessary.

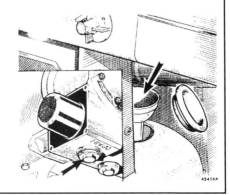

154A. Overdrive unit drain plug (arrowed in inset) and using a funnel (arrowed) for refilling

☐ Job 154. Service overdrive.
OVERDRIVE GEARBOXES ONLY:
154A. EARLY D-TYPE OVERDRIVE: fitted only to cars with three- speed synchromesh gearboxes i.e. no synchro on bottom gear. Drain the oil from the overdrive by removing the drain plug shown. Remove the filter cover plate, shown here, and the gasket (on the left-hand side of the unit) and withdraw the filter gauze seal and magnetic rings. Wash off in white spirit (or turpentine substitute), cleaning out any metal swarf and replace.

154B. Transmission and overdrive service points

1 Gearbox filler plug/dipstick (early type)
2 Transmission tunnel rubber access plug
3 Overdrive unit oil drain plug
4 Overdrive cover plate
5 Gasket and filter assembly
6 Relief valve plug
7 Relief valve filter
8 Automatic transmission dipstick

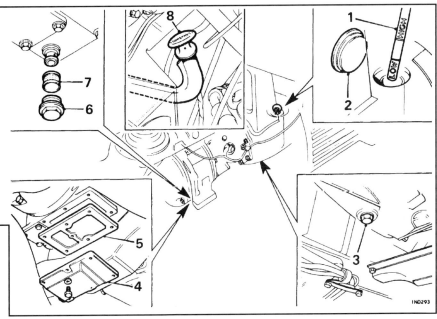

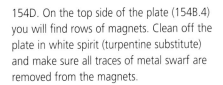

154B. ALL LATER OVERDRIVE UNITS: Now remove the six screws and washers holding the sump cover plate (154B.5) in place taking careful note that ...

154C ... a quantity of oil will run out from the sump. Have a drain tray and plenty of newspapers at the ready. Behind the plate will be a thick gasket with in-built filter (154B.5). It may have to be prized from the overdrive sump with a screwdriver. Renew the filter if it tears. If it looks sound but seems reluctant to come away, go with the flow and leave it in place!

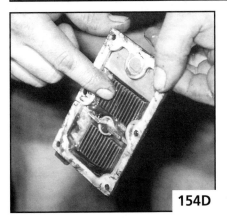

154C

154D. On the top side of the plate (154B.4) you will find rows of magnets. Clean off the plate in white spirit (turpentine substitute) and make sure all traces of metal swarf are removed from the magnets.

154E. Remove the relief valve filter (154B.7) by unscrewing the plug (154B.6) that holds it in place. The filter assembly may be tricky to remove; or it might not. If it is, insert a screwdriver and tease it out.

154D

154E

154F. The filter assembly is different on different models. This is a complex one and it is important that the parts are maintained in their correct order. Wash in white spirit (turpentine substitute) and refit.

INSIDE INFORMATION: Never use gasket compound on any of the parts being fitted to the overdrive unit. Ant bits of compound that come away and get into the overdrive unit could cause damage.

154F

24,000 MILE SERVICE

155

Job 155. Suspension mountings.

155. Check that all suspension and steering rack mountings are secure and all fastenings tight.

Job 156. Check brake discs.

Use a micrometer to measure the thickness of the brake discs. If below the minimum thicknesses shown for each model in *Chapter 8, Facts and Figures*, replace with new discs. SPECIALIST SERVICE: If the discs are thick enough but badly scored, you may be able to have an engineering shop skim them down for you. (Provide them with the minimum permissible thickness and ask them to check that the discs run true before spending money on them.) But you will probably find it less expensive, in the UK at least, to buy new replacement discs.

Job 157. Brake calipers.

157

SAFETY FIRST! and SPECIALIST SERVICE:
Obviously, a car's brakes are among its most important safety related items. Do not dismantle your car's brakes unless you are fully competent to do so. If you have not been trained in this work, but wish to carry out the work described here, we strongly recommend that you have a garage or qualified mechanic check your work before using the car on the road. See also the section on BRAKES AND ASBESTOS in Chapter 1, for further important information.

157. *INSIDE INFORMATION: See Job 43 for information on removing and replacing brake pads. When it is time to check the front pads, remove them and wash and scrape out the brake calipers, with proprietary brake cleaner, to reduce the risk of brake squeal and seizure.*

Job 158. Renew brake fluid.

First read the *SAFETY FIRST! and SPECIALIST SERVICE* note in the previous Job. If this work is carried out in an unskilled manner, the car's braking system could fail totally. If the work is not carried out at all, the system could also fail. Brake fluid deteriorates over a period of time - it absorbs moisture from the air and then, under heavy braking, the water can turn to vapour, creating a vapour lock in the braking system and leaving the car without brakes. The brake fluid renewal procedures vary considerably between models, especially with later cars, and can be quite complex. Do not attempt to carry out this work without a workshop manual and a thorough understanding of what is involved. It may be best to invest in the cost of having this work carried out by a qualified MG specialist or Rover dealership.

159A

159B

Job 159. Rear axle oil.

159A. Drain the differential and fill with new oil. You will need a special square-headed removal tool to remove the drain plug, such as the multi-sized drain plug remover by Kamasa, available inexpensively from car accessory stores.

159B. Use only the correct grade of oil as specified in *Chapter 8, Facts and Figures* to top up the differential. A 'squeezy' plastic bottle makes the job easier.

INSIDE INFORMATION: In winter, the thick oil will be time-consuming to squeeze out. Stand the bottle (sealed) in hot water for several minutes before using.

☐ **Job 160. Check brake drums.**

First read the SAFETY FIRST! and SPECIALIST SERVICE note at the beginning of Job 157.

Examine thickness and depth of wear of rear brake drums. If excessively scored or worn thin or if any sign of cracking is found, replace. If you don't have sufficient experience to know whether the drums are excessively worn or not, take professional advice from a fully trained mechanic.

INSIDE INFORMATION: Tap the drum, suspended on a piece of string or a hook, to see if it rings true. If it produces a flat note, the drum is cracked and must be replaced: don't use the car until you have done so.

☐ **Job 161. Brake back plates.**

Strip and clean the rear brake back plates using brake cleaner (to reduce risk of brake squeal and seizure) and clean out and lubricate the brake adjuster.

First read the SAFETY FIRST! and SPECIALIST SERVICE note at the beginning of Job 157.

MGC ONLY:
(i) Lubricate the slot in which the rear wheel cylinder moves using only the smallest smear of special brake grease. Note that this is the automatic adjuster inside the MGC's rear brake drum. Lubricate and if necessary, remove from the car and free off with releasing fluid (keep it off the brakes!).

161A and 161B: To adjust or release the brakes manually, turn the cog (by mechanic's thumb) with a screwdriver through the access hole in the brake drum.

(ii) The correct functioning of the Lockheed type automatic adjusters may be checked by operating the footbrake gently when the drum is off; after a short movement the ratchet will be heard to click. (Take care not to allow the wheel cylinder pistons to move too far out of the bores when doing this). Depress the small adjuster plate to fully de-adjust the mechanism before re-fitting the drum.

MG RV8 ONLY:
The self-adjusting mechanism used on the RV8 rear brakes is part of the trailing brake shoe assembly. Operation can be checked in the same way as described for the MGC, but the serrated adjuster pawl must be released to fully de-adjust the mechanism before refitting the drum. To release the mechanism with the drum in place, remove the rubber plug on the rear of the backplate and depress the adjuster mechanism with a screwdriver inserted through the backplate access slot.

24,000 mile Bodywork and Interior - Around the Car

☐ **Job 162. Maintain window mechanism.**

Lubricate the window control mechanism. Take off the door interior trim and lubricate with grease the window winder gear and in particular the channel in which the window runners move and the toothed quadrant arm on which the winder handle operates.

☐ Job 163. Maintain door gear.

With the door trim still off, lubricate, with a dab of grease on each pivot point, the door lock and latch release gear, inside the door frame.

☐ Job 164. Lamp seals.

Remove the side lamp/indicator lenses, particularly the fronts, and ensure that the seals are effective. If water has been getting in to the lamps, remove the bulbs and smear a light coating of petroleum jelly inside the bulb holder to help prevent rust. Renew the seal.

36,000 Miles - or Every Thirty Six Months, Whichever Comes First

Carry out all of the jobs listed under the earlier service headings before undertaking these additional tasks.

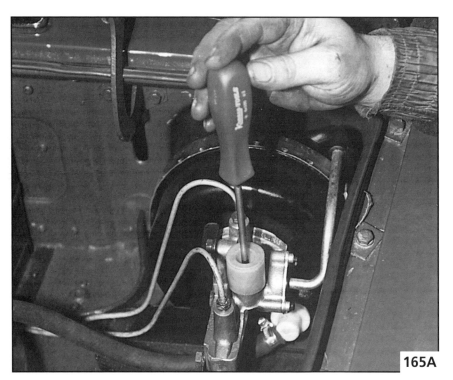

165A

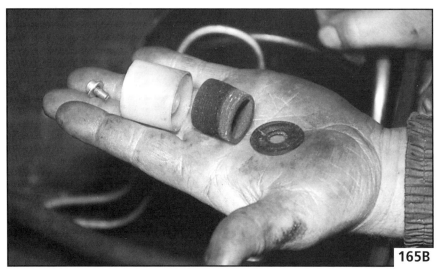

165B

☐ Job 165. MGC brake servo.
MGC ONLY:
165A. Clean around the brake filter area. Remove the centre fixing screw, filter cover, filter and seal...

165B. ...and after wiping the seat clean, fit a new filter. Unlike the MGB and V8's filters, it cannot be cleaned but must be replaced. If left to become clogged with dirt, the efficiency of the servo will suffer.

☐ Job 166. Overhaul ignition.

Renew the distributor cap, high tension leads and condenser. Faulty leads and cap may look perfect but can be major contributors to poor starting in damp weather. Replace them before they start to go wrong and let you down! Take great care not to confuse the order in which the leads are fitted. Fold a piece of masking tape around each lead as you remove it and number it 1, 2, 3, 4, and so on depending on engine. Make a diagram of the distributor cap and write down the correct lead positions. You can now match the new to the old.

Job 167. Clean float bowls.

167. Remove the carburettor float bowls and clean out sediment if any is found to be present, before it gets into the carburettor jet.

Job 168. Steering rack oil.

Drain the old oil from the steering rack - lift one side of the car and support it on axle stands. Disconnect the track-rod end of the side nearest the ground, take off the rack gaiter and let the oil drain into a drain tank. Refill the rack, with the oil specified in *Chapter 8, Facts and Figures* either

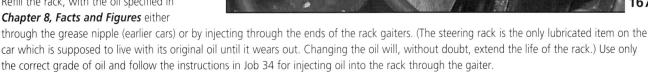

167

through the grease nipple (earlier cars) or by injecting through the ends of the rack gaiters. (The steering rack is the only lubricated item on the car which is supposed to live with its original oil until it wears out. Changing the oil will, without doubt, extend the life of the rack.) Use only the correct grade of oil and follow the instructions in Job 34 for injecting oil into the rack through the gaiter.

Job 169. Hub lubrication.

169. Take out the grease retainer cap from the front hub. On wire wheeled cars, it is inside the spline tube, there being a stud on the end of the cover for you to take hold of; on bolt-on wheel cars, the cover levers off. Pack the retainer with fresh high-melting point grease and put the retainer back in place.

SPECIALIST SERVICE: Don't be tempted to strip, clean and regrease the hub yourself. The strip down and refit process is not difficult, but the hub free-play needs to be set by a garage with a dial gauge for measuring end float - worth remembering when bearings need replacing.

169

Longer Term Servicing

48,000 miles

Job 170. Fit new filters.
MG RV8 ONLY:
Renew the main fuel filter and PCV intake filter.

60,000 miles

Job 171. Auxiliary drive belts.

Renew all auxiliary drive belts such as the fan belt and the air pump belt and air conditioning belt.

CHAPTER 4
REPAIRING BODYWORK BLEMISHES

However well you look after your car, there will always be the risk of car park accident damage - or even worse! The smallest paint chips are best touched up with paint purchased from your local auto. accessory shop. If your colour of paint is not available, some auto. accessory shops offer a mixing scheme or you could look for a local paint factor in Yellow Pages. Take your car along to the paint factor and have them match the colour and mix the smallest quantity of cellulose paint that they will supply you with.

Larger body blemishes will need the use of body filler. You should only use a filler with a reputable name behind it, such as Isopon P38 Easy Sand and that's what we used to carry out this repair.

SAFETY FIRST!
Always wear plastic gloves when working with any make of filler, before it has set. Always wear a face mask when sanding filler and wear goggles when using a power sander.

4.1

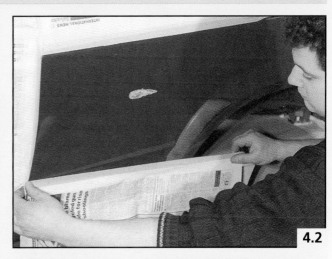

4.2

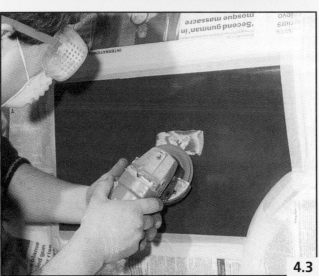

4.3

4.1 The rear of this car has sustained a nasty gash - the sort of damage for which you will certainly need to use body filler.

4.2 The first stage is to mask off. Try to find "natural" edges such as body mouldings or styling stripes and wherever you can, mask off body trim rather than having to remove it.

4.3 Isopon recommend that you remove all paint from the damaged area and for about 1 in. around the damaged area. Roughen the bare metal or surface with coarse abrasive paper - a power sander is best - and wipe away any loose particles. If you have access to professional spirit wipe, so much the better and the whole area should now be wiped down. If not, wipe over the area with white spirit (mineral spirit) and then wash off with washing-up liquid in water - not car wash detergent.

4.4 Use a piece of plastic on which to mix the filler and hardener, following the instructions on the can.

4.4

4.5 Mix the filler and hardener thoroughly until the colour is consistent and no traces of hardener can be discerned. It's best to use a piece of plastic or metal rather than cardboard because otherwise, the filler will pick up fibres from the surface of the card.

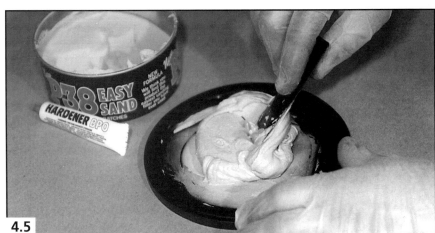

4.5

4.6 You can now spread the filler evenly over the repair.

4.7 If the damage is particularly deep, apply the paste in two or more layers, allowing the filler to harden before adding the next layer. The final layer should be just proud of the level required, but do not overfill as this wastes paste and will require more time to sand down. (Courtesy Isopon)

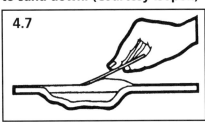

4.7

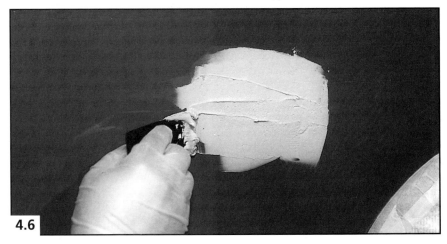

4.6

4.8 It is essential when sanding down that you wrap the sanding paper around a flat block. You can see from the scratch marks that the repair has been sanded diagonally in alternate directions until the filler is level with the surrounding panel but take care not to go deeply into the edges of the paint around the repair.

4.8

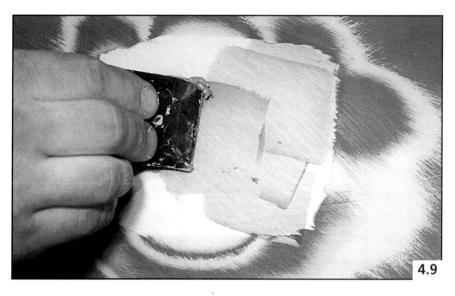

4.9 There will invariably be small pin holes even if, as in this case, the right amount of filler was applied first time. Use a tiny amount of filler scraped very thinly over the whole repair, filling in deep scratches and pin holes and then sanding off with a fine grade of sand paper - preferably dry paper rather than wet-or-dry because you don't want to get water on to the bare filler - until all of the core scratches from the earlier rougher sanding have been removed.

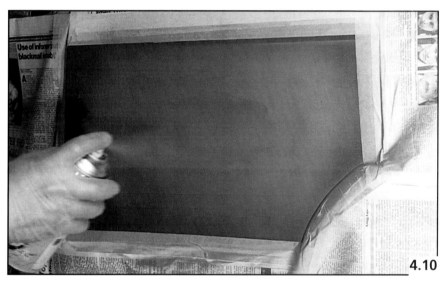

4.10 You can now use an aerosol primer to spray over the whole area of the repair but preferably not right up to the edges of the masking tape...

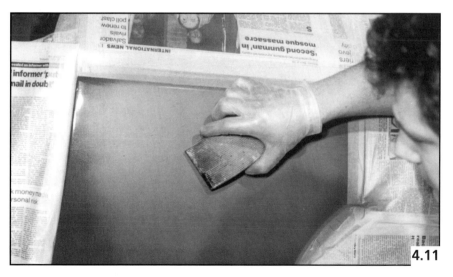

4.11 ...and you can now use wet-or-dry paper, again on a sanding block, to sand the primer paint since the Isopon is now protected from the water by the paint. If you do apply paint right up to the edge of the tape, be sure to 'feather' the edges of the paint, once it has dried off thoroughly (usually next day) so that the edges blend in smoothly to the surrounding surface, with no ridges.

SAFETY FIRST!
Always wear an efficient mask when spraying aerosol paint and only work in a well-ventilated area, well away from any source of ignition, since spray paint vapour, even that given off by an aerosol, is highly flammable. Ensure that you have doors and windows open to the outside when using aerosol paint but in cooler weather, close them when the vapour has dispersed otherwise the surface of the paint will "bloom", or take on a milky appearance. In fact, you may find it difficult to obtain a satisfactory finish in cold and damp weather.

4.12 Before starting to spray, ensure that the nozzle is clear. Note that the can must be held with the index finger well back on the aerosol button. If you let your finger overhang the front of the button, a paint drip can form and throw itself on to the work area as a paint blob. This is most annoying and means that you will have to let the paint dry, sand it down and start again.

4.13 One of the secrets of getting a decent coat of paint which doesn't run badly is to put a very light coat of spray paint on to the panel first, followed by several more coats, allowing time between each coat for the bulk of the solvent to evaporate. Alternate coats should go horizontally, followed by vertical coats as shown on the inset diagram.

4.14 If carried out with great care and skill, this type of repair can be virtually invisible. After allowing about a week for the paint to dry, you will be able to polish it with a light cutting compound, blending the edges of the repair into the surrounding paintwork.

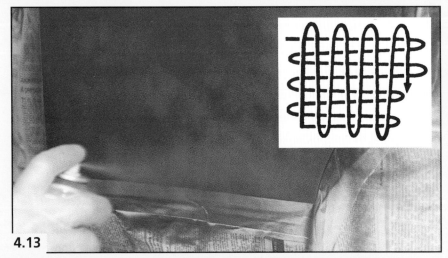

4.12

Do note that if your repairs don't work out first time and you have to apply more paint on top of the fresh paint that you have already used, allow a week to elapse otherwise there is a strong risk of pickling or other reactions taking place. Also note that a prime cause of paint failure is the existence of silicone on the surface of the old paint before you start work. These come from most types of polish and are not all that easy to remove. Thoroughly wipe the panel down with white spirit before starting work and wash off with warm water and washing-up liquid to remove any further traces of the polish and the white spirit - but don't use the sponge or bucket that you normally use for washing the car otherwise you will simply introduce more silicones onto the surface!

4.13

4.15 We are grateful to W. David & Sons Ltd, the makers of Isopon for their assistance with this section of the book and to CarPlan for their supply of the aerosol paints featured here. Isopon P38 is available in several different sizes of container and can easily be matched to the size of the repair that you have to carry out and all of the products shown here are readily available from high street motorists' stores.

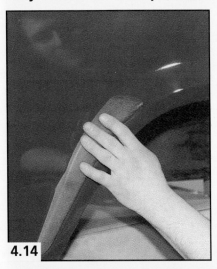

4.14

4.15

CHAPTER 5 - RUSTPROOFING

When mechanical components deteriorate, they can cost you a lot of money to replace. But when your MGB's bodywork deteriorates it can cost you the car, if the deterioration goes beyond the point where the car is economic to repair. All right, so there are Heritage bodyshells available and a godsend they are too, but it just goes to show that time and money spent on servicing and maintaining your car's bodywork will save you even more money in the long run than that spent on its mechanical components. You may have noticed several places in *Chapter 3, Service Intervals Step-by-Step* where checking the cars underbody and topping up its rust preventative treatment is called for. Here's how to carry out that preventative treatment in the first place and, of course, how to reapply it when the time comes. Please remember, however, that different models of MGB have 'access' holes (they weren't put there for that, of course) in different places, so it isn't possible to be specific about which cars have to be drilled and which can use existing holes.

Do take note of the fact that in Britain, the Automobile Association has carried out research into rustproofing materials and has found that inadequately applied materials do more harm than good. A car's body panels are forever in the process of rusting unless there is a barrier in place to keep out the air and moisture which are necessary to help the rusting process along. However, if that barrier is inefficiently applied, the rusting process seems to concentrate itself on the areas where the rustproofing is missing which speeds up the rusting and makes it worse in those areas. So do take great care that you apply the rustproofing materials used on your car as thoroughly as possible. It's not a question of quantity; more a question of quality of application - reaching every part of the car with a type of rustproofing fluid that "creeps" into each of the seams, into any rust that may have already formed on the surface and using an applicator that applies the fluid in a mist rather than in streams or blobs which unfortunately is all that some of the hand applicators we have seen seem to do.

Also, you should note that the best time to apply rustproofing materials to your car is in the summer when the warmer weather will allow the materials to flow better inside the hidden areas of the car's bodywork and, just as importantly, the underside of the car and the insides of the box sections will be completely dried out. In spite of what some makers say, you are better off applying rust preventative materials when the car is dry than when it is wet.

SAFETY FIRST!
Wear gloves, a face mask and goggles when applying rustproofing materials. Keep such materials away from your eyes but if you do get any into your eyes, wash out with copious amount of cold water and, if necessary, seek medical advice. All rustproofing materials are flammable and should be kept well away from all sources of ignition, especially when applying the them. All such materials are volatile and in vaporised form are more likely to catch fire or explode. Do bear in mind that, if any welding has to be carried out on the car within a few months of rustproofing materials being injected into it, you must inform those who are carrying out the welding because of the fire risk. Cover all brake components with plastic bags so that none of the rustproofing material can get on to the brake friction materials and keep well away from the clutch bellhousing and from exhaust manifold and exhaust system. Always carry out this work out of doors since the vapour can be dangerous in a confined space.

*INSIDE INFORMATION: i) All electric motors should be covered up with plastic bags so that none of the rustproofing fluids get into the motors (these include power windows and power aerials) and all windows should be fully wound up when injecting fluid inside the door panels. ii) Ensure that all drain channels are clear (see Job 99 in **Chapter 3, Service Intervals Step-by-Step**) so that any excess rustproofing fluid can drain out and also check once again that they are clear after you have finished carrying out the work to ensure that your application of the fluid has not caused them to be clogged up, otherwise water will get trapped in there, negating much of the good work you have carried out.*

Job 1. Wash Underbody

You will need to wash off the underside of the car before commencing work, scraping off any thick deposits of mud with a wooden scraper and also remove any loose paint or underseal beneath the car. Here you can see a power washer being used - very efficient, but you'll have to leave the car for about a week in warm dry weather so that it dries out properly underneath. Some garages have car washing equipment on the forecourt that enables you to wash underneath the wheel arches where, of course, most of the heavy mud resides.

All of the better rustproofing materials manufacturers make at least two types: one which is "thinner" and which is for applying to box sections and another one which is tougher and is for applying to the undersides of wheel arches and anywhere that is susceptible to blasting from debris thrown up by the wheels.

1

Job 2. Equipment

Gather together all the materials and equipment you will need to carry out the work. Bear in mind the safety equipment you will need - referred to in Safety First! - see above. You will also need lifting equipment and axle stands - see **Chapter 1, Safety First!** for information on raising and supporting a car above the ground and also the Introduction to **Chapter 3, Service Intervals Step-by-Step**, for the correct procedures to follow when raising your car with a trolley jack. You will need copious amounts of newspaper to spread on the floor because quite a lot of the fluid will run out of the car and you may need to park your car over newspaper for a couple of days after carrying out this treatment. Do remember that the vapour given off will continue for several days and you would be best parking the car out of doors for about a week after carrying out the work shown here. Probably the best known makes of rust preventative fluid in the UK are Waxoyl and Dinitrol. The later product came out top in a survey carried out by Practical Classics magazine and they also have the advantage that they produce an inexpensive application gun which does a proper job of atomising the fluid and putting a thorough misting inside each enclosed box section. If you don't own a compressor, you will have to hire one in order to power the Dinitrol applicator but the results will be better than can be obtained with any hand operated applicator.
(Courtesy Frost Auto Restoration Techniques)

2

AROUND THE CAR

Job 3. Chrome Trim

Some rustproofing fluids are available in aerosol form and since they generally contain thinner fluid, they are probably best for injecting behind chrome trim such as the rear side window surrounds on GT models, which are particularly prone to rust on the steel panel beneath. The clips behind the chrome trim along the sides and that on bonnet and boot lid are also know trouble spots.

Also remember to treat behind each of the bumpers and the insides of all of the over riders since all are particularly susceptible to corrosion.

3

Job 4. Inside Doors

To do this job properly, you will have to remove the door trim although some firms drill a hole in the end of the door and bung it later with a rubber grommet. By taking the door off, you can get at some of the worst areas, including that beneath the quarter light.

Job 5. Boot Lid and Tailgate

You'll be able to get behind the supporting ribs in the boot lid and tailgate although in the latter case, you will have to remove the trim panels. Ensure that fluid is injected in vaporised form all along the inside of the pressings on the tailgate, especially around the rear window. You may have to drill holes if the ribs are too close to allow you to inject fluid between rib and panel skin.

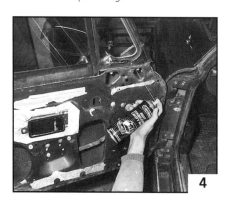

4

5

RUSTPROOFING

Job 6. Bonnet

You can get at most of the bonnet support panels through existing holes, depending on model, but if necessary, drill holes so that you can insert a lance along each of the supporting ribs.

Job 7. Sills

The MGB's sills are essential to the strength of the car so it's important that you understand where they go. The part of the sill that you see just beneath the door is less than half of the entire structure. The sills disappear behind front and rear wings and continue as far as the rear wheel arch and almost as far forward

as the front wheel arch. In addition, just beneath where the door seal clips on to the sill, there is a vertical panel inside the sill. (This is completely hidden from view, since it is right inside the sill structure.) This separates the outer section of the sill shown in the photograph for Job 7 and the inner section which is covered by rubber or carpet trim, depending on model. You must be prepared to drill holes both inside and outside this vertical strengthening panel and towards both the front and the back of each sill - four holes per sill - and to insert the injector nozzle as far as it will go in each direction, drawing it out slowly and injecting plenty of fluid.

Job 8. Door Hinge Posts

These are vertical box sections located behind the front wings and you can gain access with your injector above and below the hinges where they disappear into the hinge posts as the door is closed.

Job 9. Door Shut Pillars

These are not enclosed sections so you can gain access to the backs of them by taking off the trim behind each door.

Job 10. Front Bulkhead

This can be accessed through the air vent just in front of the windscreen and beneath the dash from inside the car.

Job 11. Toe Board Ends

It's easy to miss these box sections right at the front of the floor. After lifting the floor covering, you can drill holes to gain access into these box sections.

Job 12. Boot Floor

To avoid creating a sticky mess, it's best not to apply rustproofing materials over the whole of the boot floor, just over the edges at the back, and at the sides. Here you can see a hole that has been drilled in order to inject fluid into the rear "chassis" rail.

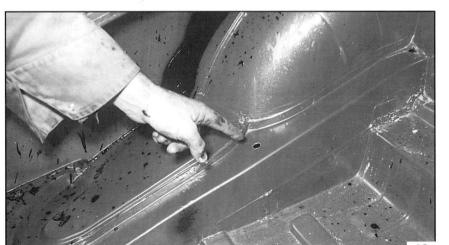

BENEATH THE CAR

Job 13. Inside Rear Wheel Arches

The insides of the rear wheel arches where they butt up against the rear wings and the tops of the rear wings are all susceptible to corrosion and should all be treated with fluid.

Job 14. Front Wheel Arches

Take a look at the illustration to Job 24C in *Chapter 3, Service Intervals Step-by-Step*, where you will see that there is a box section inside the top of each wheel arch and this is particularly susceptible to corrosion. You will be able to feel it if you run your hand inside each front wing so be sure to clean off any mud. You will also have to drill the splash panels, as shown here. The thinner type of fluid can be injected inside the splash panels while the heavier type of fluid can be sprayed over the whole underside of the front wing and wheel arch, paying special attention to the head light backs which are also rather good at corroding!

Job 15. Front Valance

Beneath the front of the car, behind the bumper and beneath the radiator are two panels that require a coating of fluid and injection of any box sections.

Job 16. Rear Wheel Arches

Give a coating of the heavier fluid inside the rear wheel arches, just as you did at the front.

Job 17. Rear Valance

This is a similar panel to that described in Job 15 and is equally prone to corrosion.

Job 18. Crossmembers

If you look beneath the car in line with the jacking points, you will see a box section that runs the width of the car and this must be thoroughly injected.

Job 19. Front Chassis Rails

Running from the crossmember right to the front of the car you will see more important box sections. In each case you may well have to drill holes so that the injector lance will reach every part of each rail.

13

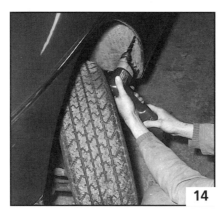

14

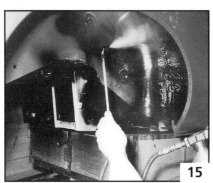

15

24

Job 20. Suspension Crossmember

This is such a heavily built component that it is not particularly susceptible to rusting but there are large holes in the bottom of it and applying rustproofing fluid is so easy that you really ought to do it.

Job 21. Castle Sections

These are relatively tiny box sections running the length of the sills and found just beneath them. They should have a series of holes already drilled in them through which you can easily inject the fluid.

Job 22. Rear Chassis Rails

These run back from the centre crossmember and sweep up and over the rear wheel arches so look hard to work out where they go. Once again you will probably have to drill some holes.

Job 23. Above Fuel Tank

The top of the fuel tank is particularly susceptible to rusting. Keep fluid away from the fuel pump and tank sender unit but inject fluid as well as you can between the top of the tank and the bodywork.

Job 24. Boot Floor

Once again, the underside of the boot floor should be treated in common with the whole of the rest of the flat areas of the car's floor panels, paying particular attention to all of the edges, joints and seams. The vehicle shown here is a stripped-out bodyshell: you'll need supports that are considerably more substantial in order to support a whole MGB - use axle stands!

INSIDE INFORMATION: i) Some car manufacturers coat the engine bay and the engine with protective clear (or yellow) wax when it is new. The wax is then washed off with a steam cleaner or with degreaser every two or three years and fresh wax applied. This makes the engine look dingy but protects metal surfaces against corrosion, screws against seizure and helps to keep rubber supple. Provided that you kept the wax off manifolds and any other very hot areas and away from any electrical or brake components and out of the brake master cylinder - covering each item individually with taped-on plastic bags should do it - you could preserve the components in your engine bay in the same way. Check that the makers of whichever rustproofing fluid you select don't recommend against using their product for this purpose.

ii) Always buy any blanking grommets you may want to use - a dozen or so are usually enough - before you drill any holes in the car's underbody. Grommets are often only available in a limited range of sizes and you will find it easier to match a drill to a given size of grommet than the other way around.

CHAPTER 6 - FAULT FINDING

This Chapter aims to help you to overcome the main faults that can affect the mobility or safety of your car. It also helps you to overcome the problem that has affected most mechanics – amateur and professional – at one time or another… Blind Spot Syndrome!

It goes like this: the car refuses to start one damp Sunday morning. You decide that there must be no fuel getting through. By the time you've stripped the fuel pump, carburetter, fuel lines and "unblocked" the fuel tank, it's time for bed. And the next day, the local garage finds that your main HT lead has dropped out of the coil! Something like that has happened to most of us!

Don't leap to assumptions: if your engine won't start or runs badly, if electrical components fail, follow the logical sequence of checks listed here and detailed overleaf, eliminating each "check" (by testing, not by "hunch") before moving on to the next. Remember that the great majority of failures are caused by electrical or ignition faults: only a minor proportion of engine failures come from the fuel system, follow the sequences shown here – and you'll have better success in finding that fault.

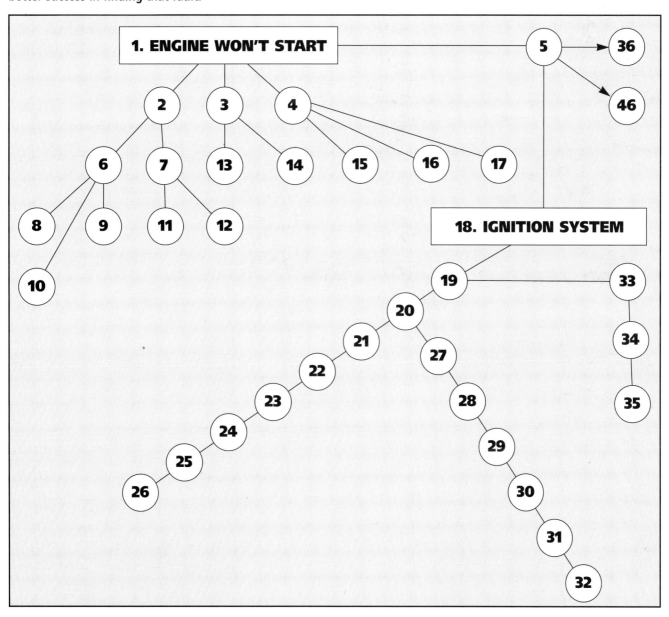

Before carrying out any of the work described in this Chapter please read carefully Chapter 1 Safety First!.

1. ENGINE WON'T START.

2. Starter motor doesn't turn.

3. Starter motor turns slowly.

4. Starter motor noisy or harsh.

5. Starter motor turns engine but car will not start.

6. Is battery okay?

7. Can engine be rotated by hand?

8. Check battery connections for cleanliness/tightness.

9. Test battery with voltmeter.

10. Have battery 'drop' test carried out by specialist.

11. If engine cannot be rotated by hand, check for mechanical seizure of power unit, or pinion gear jammed in mesh with flywheel - 'rock' car backwards and forwards until free, or apply spanner to square drive at front end of starter motor.

12. If engine can be rotated by hand, check for loose electrical connections at starter, faulty solenoid, or defective starter motor.

13. Battery low on charge or defective - recharge and have 'drop' test carried out by specialist.

14. Internal fault within starter motor - e.g. worn brushes.

15. Drive teeth on ring gear or starter pinion worn/broken.

16. Main drive spring broken.

17. Starter motor securing bolts loose.

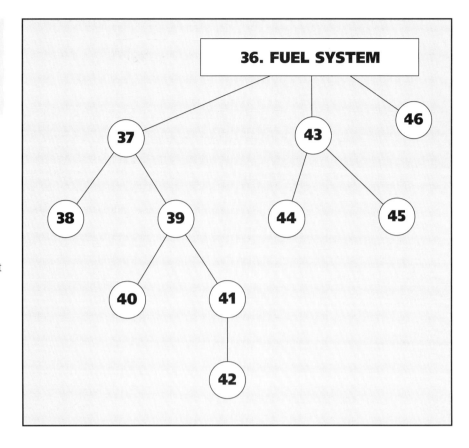

18. IGNITION SYSTEM.

19. Check for spark at plug (remove plug and prop it with threads resting on bare metal of cylinder block). Do not touch plug or lead while operating starter.

20. If no spark present at plug, check for spark at contact breaker points when 'flicked' open (ignition 'on'). Double-check to ensure that points are clean and correctly gapped, and try again.

21. If spark present at contact breaker points, check for spark at central high tension lead from coil.

22. If spark present at central high tension lead from coil, check distributor cap and rotor arm; replace if cracked or contacts badly worn.

23. If distributor cap and rotor arm are okay, check high tension leads and connections - replace leads if they are old, carbon core type suppressed variety.

24. If high tension leads are sound but dirty or damp, clean/dry them.

25. If high tension leads okay, check/clean/dry/re-gap sparking plugs.

26. Damp conditions? Apply water dispellant spray to ignition system.

27. If no spark present at contact breaker points, examine connections of low tension leads between ignition switch and coil, and from coil to contact breaker (including short low-tension lead within distributor).

28. If low tension circuit connections okay, examine wiring.

29. If low tension wiring is sound, is condenser okay? If in doubt, fit new condenser.

30. If condenser is okay, check for spark at central high tension lead from coil.

31. If no spark present at central high tension lead from coil, check for poor high tension lead connections.

32. If high tension lead connections okay, is coil okay? If in doubt, fit new coil.

33. If spark present at plug, is it powerful or weak? If weak, see '27'.

34. If spark is healthy, check ignition timing.

35. If ignition timing is okay, check fuel system (see 36).

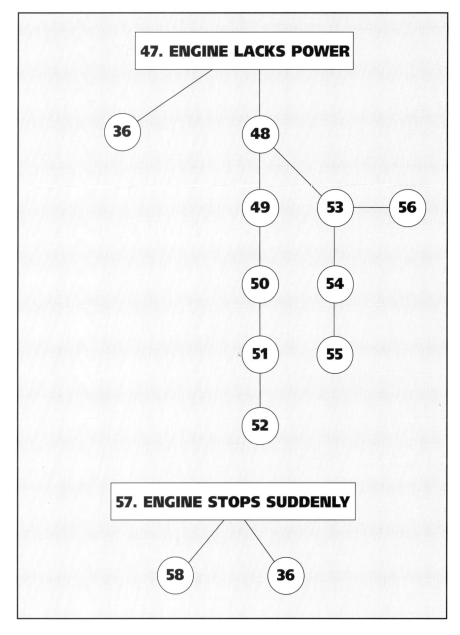

36. FUEL SYSTEM

Check fuel system for fuel at feel pipe to carbs. (Disconnect pipe and turn ignition 'on' very briefly, ensuring pipe is aimed away from hot engine and exhaust components).

37. If no fuel present at feed pipe, is petrol tank empty? (Rock car and listen for 'sloshing' in tank, as well as looking at gauge).

38. If tank is empty, replenish!

39. If there is petrol in the tank but none issues from the feed pipe, check for a defective fuel pump. (With outlet pipe disconnected AND AIMED AWAY FROM PUMP AND HOT EXHAUST COMPONENTS, ETC., turn ignition 'on' - pump should 'click' and fuel should issue from pump outlet).

40. If pump is okay, check for blocked filter or pipe, or major leak in pipe between tank and pump, or between pump and carbs.

41. If the filter is clean and the pump fails to operate, check for 12 volts at electrical supply to pump (with ignition 'on').

42. If 12 volts evident at pump supply, check for sticking and/or dirty pump contact points. Tapping pump with a spanner may re-start it to 'get you home'; cleaning or replacing points is long-term answer.

43. If fuel is present at carburettor feed pipe, remove spark plugs and check whether wet with unburnt fuel.

44. If the spark plugs are fuel-soaked, check that the choke linkage operates as it should and is not jammed 'shut'. Other possibilities include float needle valve(s) sticking 'open' or leaking, float(s) punctured, carburettors incorrectly adjusted or air filter totally blocked.

45. If the spark plugs are dry, check whether the float needle valve(s) are jammed 'shut'.

46. OTHER POSSIBILITIES. Severe air leak at inlet manifold gasket or carburettor gasket(s). Incorrectly set valve clearances. Leaking brake servo hose and/or connections.

47. ENGINE LACKS POWER.

48. OTHER POSSIBILITIES. Before following the rest of this sequence check that, if your car's carburation or fuel injection has an air inlet connected to a heater chamber on the exhaust manifold that: i) the pipe is in place and not split and, ii) any thermostatic valve or flap is operating correctly. If not the car can stop and restart intermittently because of inlet icing.

49. Engine overheating. Check temperature gauge for high reading.

50. Check for loss of coolant - WAIT UNTIL ENGINE HAS FULLY COOLED BEFORE ATTEMPTING TO REMOVE RADIATOR CAP. USE RAG TO PROTECT HANDS WHEN RELEASING CAP, AND KEEP FACE WELL CLEAR IN CASE COOLANT SPRAYS OUT. If low on coolant, check hoses and connections, water pump and cylinder block for leaks. Rectify and top up system.

51. If coolant level okay, check oil level. BEWARE - DIPSTICK AND OIL MAY BE VERY HOT.

52. If oil level okay, check for slipping fan belt, blocked radiator core/air grille, thermostat jammed 'shut', coolant hose obstructed, cylinder head gasket 'blown' (look for signs of mixing of oil and coolant), partial mechanical seizure of engine, blocked or damaged exhaust system.

53. If engine temperature is normal, check cylinder compressions.

54. If cylinder compression readings low, add a couple of teaspoons of engine oil to each cylinder in turn, and repeat test. If readings don't improve, suspect burnt valves/seats.

55. If compression readings improve after adding oil as described, suspect worn cylinder bores, pistons and rings.

56. If compression readings are normal, check for mechanical problems, for example, binding brakes, slipping clutch, partially seized transmission, etc.

57. ENGINE STOPS SUDDENLY

58. Check in particular for electrical disconnections, running out of fuel, blown fuse protecting petrol pump, and for sudden ingress of water/snow onto ignition components, in adverse weather conditions.

59. Go to 5 and follow subsequent checking sequence.

60. LIGHTS FAIL

61. Sudden failure. Check fuses.

62. If all lamps affected, check switch and main wiring feeds.

63. If not all lamps are affected, check bulbs on lamps concerned.

64. If bulbs appear to be okay, check bulb holder(s), local wiring and connections.

65. If bulb(s) blown, replace!

66. Intermittent operation, flickering or poor light output.

67. Check earth (ground) connections(s).

68. If earth(s) okay, check switch.

69. If switch okay, check wiring and connections.

70. HORN FAILURE

71. If horn does not operate, check fuse, all connections and cables. Remove horn cover and check/clean contact breaker points with fine file, wiping clean with petrol-dampened rag. Check current consumption - should be 3.5 amps if all is well.

72. If horn will not stop(!), check for earthing of horn button or cable between button and horn unit.

73. FUEL GAUGE

74. Gauge reads 'empty' - check for fuel in tank.

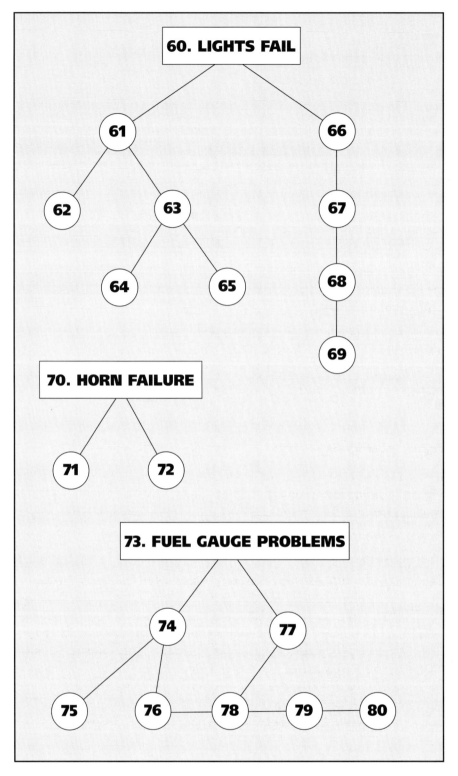

75. If not fuel present, replenish!

76. If fuel is present in tank, check for earthing of wiring from tank to gauge, and for wiring disconnections.

77. Gauge permanently reads 'full', regardless of tank contents. Check wiring and connections between tank sender unit and gauge.

78. If wiring and connections all okay, sender unit/fuel gauge defective.

79. With wiring disconnected, check for continuity between fuel gauge terminals. Do NOT test gauge by short-circuiting to earth. Replace unit if faulty.

80. If gauge is okay, disconnect wiring from tank sender unit and check for continuity between terminal and case. Replace sender unit if faulty.

CHAPTER 7
GETTING THROUGH THE MOT

Taking your beloved MGB for the annual MoT test can be rather like going to the dentist - you're not sure what to expect and the result could be painful - not only to your pocket! However, it needn't be like that...

This Chapter is for owners in Britain whose cars need to pass the 'MoT' test. The Test was first established in 1961 by the then-named Ministry of Transport: the name of the Test remains, even though the name of the government department does not!

The information in this Chapter could be very useful to non-UK owners in helping to carry out a detailed check of a car's condition - such as when checking over a car that you might be interested in buying, for instance. But it is MOST IMPORTANT that UK owners check for themselves that legislation has not changed since this book was written and that non-UK owners obtain information on the legal requirements in their own territory - and that they act upon them.

PASS THE MoT!

The aim of this chapter is to explain what is actually tested on an MGB, MGC, MGB V8 or MG RV8 and (if it is not obvious) how the test is done. This should enable you to identify and eliminate problems before they undermine the safety or diminish the performance of your car and long before they cause the expense and inconvenience of a test failure.

SAFETY FIRST!
The MoT tester will follow a set procedure and we will cover the ground in a similar way, starting inside the car, then continuing outside, under the bonnet, underneath the car etc. When preparing to go underneath the car, do ensure that it is jacked on firm level ground and then supported on axle stands or ramps which are adequate for the task. Wheels which remain on the ground should have chocks in front of and behind them, and while the rear wheels remain on the ground, the hand brake should be firmly ON. For most repair and replacement jobs under a car these normal precautions will suffice. However, the car needs to be even more stable than usual when carrying out these checks. There must be no risk of it toppling off its stands while suspension and steering components are being pushed and pulled in order to test them. Read carefully Chapter 1, Safety First! for further important information on raising and supporting the car above the ground.

The purpose of the MoT test is to try to ensure that vehicles using British roads reach minimum standards of safety. Accordingly, it is an offence to use a car without a current MoT certificate. Approximately 40 per cent of vehicles submitted for the test fail it, but many of these failures could be avoided by knowing what the car might 'fall down' on, and by taking appropriate remedial action before the test 'proper' is carried out. It is also worth noting that a car can be submitted for a test up to a month before the current certificate expires - if the vehicle passes, the new certificate will be valid until one year from the date of expiry of the old one, provided that the old certificate is produced at the time of the test.

It is true that the scope of the test has been considerably enlarged in the last few years, with the result that it is correspondingly more difficult to be sure that your MG will reach the required standards. In truth, however, a careful examination of the car in the relevant areas, perhaps a month or so before the current certificate expires, will highlight components which require attention, and enable any obvious faults to be rectified before you take the car for its test.

If the car is muddy or particularly dirty (especially underneath) it would be worth giving it a thorough clean a day or two before carrying out the inspection so that it has ample time to dry. Do the same before the real MoT test. A clean car makes a better impression on the examiner, who can refuse to test a car which is particularly dirty underneath.

GETTING THROUGH THE MOT

MoT testers do not dismantle assemblies during the test but you may wish to do so during your pre-test check-up for a better view of certain wearing parts, such as the rear brake shoes for example. See **Chapter 3, Service Intervals Step-by-Step** for information on how to check the brakes.

TOOL BOX

Dismantling apart, few tools are needed for testing. A light hammer is useful for tapping panels underneath the car when looking for rust. If this produces a bright metallic noise, then the area being tapped is sound. If the noise produced is dull, the area contains rust or filler. When tapping sills and box sections, listen also for the sound of debris (that is, rust flakes) on the inside of the panel. Use a screwdriver to prod weak parts of panels. This may produce holes of course, but if the panels have rusted to that extent, you really ought to know about it. A strong lever (such as a tyre lever) can be useful for applying the required force to suspension joints etc. when assessing whether there is any wear in the joints.

You will need an assistant to operate controls and perhaps to wobble the road wheels while you inspect components under the car.

Two more brief explanations are required before we start our informal test. Firstly, the age of the car determines exactly which lights, seat belts and other items it should have. Frequently in the next few pages you will come across the phrase "Cars first used ..." followed by a date. A car's "first used date" is either its date of first registration, or the date six months after it was manufactured, whichever was earlier. Or, if the car was originally used without being registered (such as a car which has been imported to the U.K. or an ex-H.M. Forces car etc.) the "first used date" is the date of manufacture.

Secondly, there must not be excessive rust, serious distortion or any fractures affecting certain prescribed areas of the bodywork. These prescribed areas are load-bearing parts of the bodywork within 30 cm (12 in.) of anchorages or mounting points associated with testable items such as seat belts, brake pedal assemblies, master cylinders, servos, suspension and steering components and also body mountings. Keep this rule in mind while inspecting the car, but remember also that even if such damage occurs outside a prescribed area, it can cause failure of the test. Failure will occur if the damage is judged to reduce the continuity or strength of a main load-bearing part of the bodywork sufficiently to have an adverse effect on the braking or steering.

The following notes are necessarily abbreviated, and are for assistance only. They are not a definitive guide to all the MoT regulations. It is also worth mentioning that the varying degrees of discretion of individual MoT testers can mean that there are variations between the standards as applied. However, the following points should help to make you aware of the aspects which will be examined. Now, if you have your clipboard, checklist and pencil handy, let's make a start...

THE 'EASY' BITS

Checking these items is straightforward and should not take more than a few minutes - it could avoid an embarrassingly simple failure...

LIGHTS

Within the scope of the test are headlamps, side and tail lights, brake lamps, direction indicators, and number plate lamps (plus rear fog lamps on all cars first used on or after 1 April, 1980, and any earlier cars subsequently so equipped, and also hazard warning lamps on any car so fitted). All must operate, must be clean and not significantly damaged; flickering is also not permitted. The switches should also all work properly. Pairs of lamps should give approximately the same intensity of light output, and operation of one set of lights should not affect the working of another - such trouble is usually due to bad earthing.

Indicators should flash at between 60 and 120 times per minute (rev the engine to encourage them, if a little slow, although the examiner might not let you get away with it!) Otherwise, renew the (inexpensive) flasher unit and check all wiring and earth connections.

Interior 'reminder' lamps, such as for indicators, rear fog lamps and hazard warning lamps should all operate in unison with their respective exterior lamps.

Head light aim must be correct - in particular, the lights should not dazzle other road users. An approximate guide can be obtained by shining the lights against a vertical wall, but final adjustment may be necessary by reference to the beam checking machine at the MoT station - if necessary, you may have to ask the examiner to adjust the lights so that they comply.

Reflectors must be unbroken, clean, and not obscured - for example, by stickers.

WHEELS AND TYRES

Check the wheels for loose nuts, cracks, and damaged rims. Missing wheel nuts or studs are also failure points, naturally enough!

There is no excuse for running on illegal tyres. The legal requirement is that there must be at least 1.6 mm of tread depth remaining, over the 'central' three-quarters of the width of the tyre all the way around. From this it can be deduced that there is no legal requirement to have

1.6 mm. (1/16 in.) of tread on the 'shoulders' of the tyre, but in practice, most MoT stations will be reluctant to pass a tyre in this condition. In any case, for optimum safety - especially 'wet grip' - you would be well advised to change tyres when they wear down to around 3 mm (1/8 in.) or so depth of remaining tread.

Visible 'tread wear indicator bars', found approximately every nine inches around the tread of the tyre, are highlighted when the tread reaches the critical 1.6 mm. point.

Tyres should not show signs of cuts or bulges, rubbing on the bodywork or running gear, and the valves should be in sound condition, and correctly aligned.

Cross-ply and radial tyre types must not be mixed on the same axle, and if pairs of cross-ply and radial tyres are fitted, the radials must be on the rear axle.

WINDSCREEN

The screen must not be damaged (by cracks, chips, etc.) or obscured so that the driver does not have a clear view of the road. Permissible size of damage points depends on where they occur. Within an area 290 mm. (nearly 12 in.) wide, ahead of the driver, and up to the top of the wiper arc, any damage must be confined within a circle less than 10 mm. (approx. 0.4 in.) in diameter. This is increased to 40 mm. (just over 1.5 in.) for damage within the rest of the screen area swept by the wipers.

WASHERS AND WIPERS

The wipers must clear an area big enough to give the driver a clear view forwards and to the side of the car. The wiper blades must be securely attached and sound, with no cracks or 'missing' sections. The wiper switch should also work properly. The screen washers must supply the screen with sufficient liquid to keep it clean, in conjunction with the use of the wipers.

MIRRORS

If your MG was first used before 1 August, 1978, it only needs to have one rear view mirror. Later cars must have at least two, one of which must be on the driver's side. The mirrors must be visible from the driver's seat, and not be damaged or obscured so that the view to the rear is affected. Therefore cracks, chips and discolouration can mean failure.

HORN

The horn must emit a uniform note which is loud enough to give adequate warning of approach, and the switch must operate correctly. Multi-tone horns playing 'in sequence' are not permitted, but two tones sounding together are fine.

SEAT SECURITY

The seats must be securely mounted, and the frames should be sound.

NUMBER (REGISTRATION) PLATES

Both front and rear number plates must be present, and in good condition, with no breaks or missing numbers or letters. The plates must not be obscured, and the digits must not be re-positioned to form names, for instance.

VEHICLE IDENTIFICATION NUMBERS (VIN)

MGBs first used on or after 1 August, 1980 are obliged to have a clearly displayed VIN - Vehicle Identification Number (or old-fashioned 'chassis number' for older cars), which is plainly legible. See *Chapter 8, Facts and Figures* for the correct location on your car.

EXHAUST SYSTEM

The entire system must be present, properly mounted, free of leaks and should not be noisy - which can happen when the internal baffles fail. 'Proper' repairs by welding, or exhaust cement, or bandage are acceptable, as long as no gas leaks are evident. Then again, although common sense, if not the MoT, dictates that exhaust bandage should only be a very short-term emergency measure. For safety's sake, fit a new exhaust if yours is reduced to this!

SEAT BELTS

Belts are not needed on 'Bs first used before 1 January, 1965. On cars after this date - and earlier examples, if subsequently fitted with seat belts - the belts must be in good condition (i.e. not frayed or otherwise damaged), and the buckles and catches should also operate correctly. Inertia reel types, where fitted, should retract properly.

Belt mountings must be secure, with no structural damage or corrosion within 30 cm. (12 in.) of them.

MORE DETAILS

You've checked the easy bits - now it's time for the detail! Some of the 'easy bits' referred to above are included here, but this is intended as a more complete check list to give your car the best possible chance of gaining a First Class Honours, MoT Pass!

INSIDE THE CAR

☐ 1. The steering wheel should be examined for cracks and for damage which might interfere with its use, or injure the driver's hands. It should also be pushed and pulled along the column axis, and also up and down, at 90 degrees to it. This will highlight any deficiencies in the wheel and upper column mounting/bearing, and also any excessive end float, and movement between the column shaft and the wheel. Rotate the steering wheel in both directions to test for free play at the wheel rim - this shouldn't exceed approximately 13 mm. (0.5 in.), assuming a 380 mm. (15 in.) diameter steering wheel. Look, too, for movement in the steering column couplings and fasteners (including the universal joint on the engine side of the bulkhead), and visually check their condition and security. They must be sound, and properly tightened.

☐ 2. Check that the switches for headlamps, sidelights, direction indicators, hazard warning lights, wipers, washers and horn, appear to be in good working order and check that the tell-tale lights or audible warnings are working where applicable.

☐ 3. Make sure that the windscreen wipers operate effectively with blades that are secure and in good condition. The windscreen washer should provide sufficient liquid to clear the screen in conjunction with the wipers.

☐ 4. Check for windscreen damage, especially in the area swept by the wipers. From the MoT tester's point of view, Zone A is part of this area, 290 mm (11.5 in.) wide and centred on the centre of the steering wheel. Damage to the screen within this area should be capable of fitting into a 10 mm (approx. 0.4 in.) diameter circle and the cumulative effect of more minor damage should not seriously restrict the driver's view. Windscreen stickers or other obstructions should not encroach more than 10 mm (approx 0.5 in.) into this area. In the remainder of the swept area the maximum diameter of damage or degree of encroachment by obstructions is 40 mm (approx. 1.6 in.) and there is no ruling regarding cumulative damage. Specialist windscreen companies can often repair a cracked screen for a lot less than the cost of replacement.

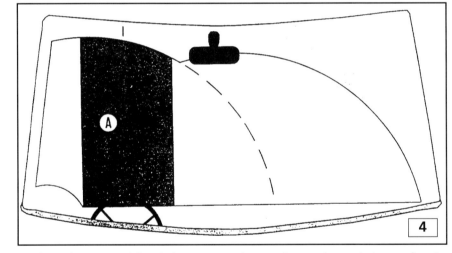

☐ 5. The horn control should be present, secure and readily accessible to the driver, and the horn(s) should be loud enough to be heard by other road users. Gongs, bells and sirens are not permitted (except as part of an anti-theft device) and two (or more) tone horns (which alternate between two or more notes) are not permitted at all. On cars first used after 1 August 1973, the horn should produce a constant, continuous or uniform note which is neither harsh nor grating.

☐ 6. There must be one exterior mirror on the driver's side of the vehicle and either an exterior mirror fitted to the passenger's side or an interior mirror. The required mirrors should be secure and in good condition.

☐ 7. Check that the hand brake operates effectively without coming to the end of its working travel. The lever and its mechanism must be complete, securely mounted, unobstructed in its travel and in a sufficiently good condition to remain firmly in the "On" position even when knocked from side to side. The 30 cm rule applies in the vicinity of the hand brake lever mounting.

☐ 8. The foot brake pedal assembly should be complete, unobstructed, and in a good working condition, including the pedal rubber (which should not have been worn smooth). There should be no excessive movement of the pedal at right angles to its normal direction (indicating a badly worn pedal bearing or pivot). When fully depressed, the pedal should not be at the end of its travel. The pedal should not feel spongy (indicating air in the hydraulic system), nor should it tend to creep downwards while held under pressure (which indicates a faulty master cylinder). However, if the pedal is depressed and held in this position while the engine is started, it should dip slightly as the engine starts. This indicates that the vacuum servo unit is working properly.

☐ 9. Seats must be secure on their mountings and seat backs must be capable of being locked in the upright position.

☐ 10. On MGBs first used on or after 1 January 1965, but before 1 April 1981, the driver's and front passenger's seats need belts, but these can be simple diagonal belts rather than the three-point belts (lap and diagonal belts for adults with at least three anchorage points) required by later cars. (For safety's sake, however, we do not recommend this type of belt.) Examine seat belt webbing and fittings to make sure that all are in good condition and that anchorages are firmly attached to the car's structure. Locking mechanisms should be capable of remaining locked, and of being released if required, when under load. Flexible buckle stalks (if fitted) should be free of corrosion, broken cable strands or other weaknesses.

☐ 11. Check that on retracting seat belts the webbing winds into the retracting unit automatically, albeit with some manual assistance to start with.

☐ 12. Note the point raised earlier regarding corrosion around seat belt anchorage points. The MoT tester will not carry out any dismantling here, but he will examine floor mounted anchorage points from underneath the car if that is possible.

☐ 13. Before getting out of the car, make sure that both doors can be opened from the inside.

OUTSIDE THE CAR

☐ 14. Before closing the driver's door check the condition of the inner sill. Usually the MoT tester will do this by applying finger or thumb pressure to various parts of the panel while the floor covering remains in place. For your own peace of mind, look beneath the sill covering, taking great care not to tear any rubber covers. Then close the driver's door and make sure that it latches securely and repeat these checks on the nearside inner sill and door.

Now check all of the lights, front and rear, (and the number plate lights) while your assistant operates the light switches.

☐ 15. As we said earlier, you can carry out a rough and ready check on head lamp alignment for yourself, although it will certainly not be as accurate as having it done for you at the MoT testing station. Drive your car near to a wall, as shown. Check that your tyres are correctly inflated and the car is on level ground.

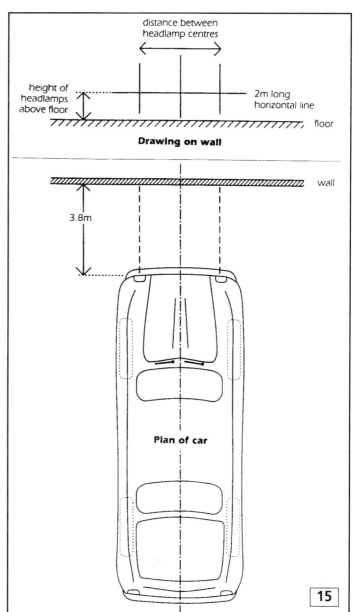

Draw on the wall, with chalk:

- a horizontal line about 2 metres long, and at same height as centre of head lamp lens.

- two vertical lines about 1 metre long, each forming a cross with the horizontal line and the same distance apart as the head lamp centres.

- another vertical line to form a cross on the horizontal line, midway between the others.

Now position your car so that:

- it faces the wall squarely, and its centre line is in line with centre line marked on the wall.

- the steering is straight.

- head light lenses are 3.8 metres (12.5 ft) from the wall.

Switch on the headlamps' 'main' and 'dipped' beams in turn, and measure their centre points. You will be able to judge any major discrepancies in intensity and aim prior to having the beams properly set by a garage with beam measuring equipment.

Headlamps should be complete, clean, securely mounted, in good working order and not adversely affected by the operation of another lamp, and these basic requirements affect all the lamps listed below. Headlamps must dip as a pair from a single switch. Their aim must be correctly adjusted and they should not be affected (even to the extent of flickering) when lightly tapped by hand. Each head lamp should match its partner in terms of size, colour and intensity of light, and can be white or yellow.

☐ 16. Side lights should show white light to the front and red light to the rear. Lenses should not be broken, cracked or incomplete.

☐ 17. Vehicles first used before 1 April 1986 do not have to have a hazard warning device, but if one is fitted, it must be tested, and it must operate with the ignition switch either on or off. The lights should flash 60-120 times per minute, and indicators must operate independently of any other lights.

☐ 18. Check your stop lights. Pre-1971 cars need only one, but when two are fitted, both are tested, so you will not get away with one that works and one that doesn't! Stop lamps should produce a steady red light when the foot brake is applied.

☐ 19. There must be two red rear reflectors - always fitted by the manufacturers, of course! - which are clean, and securely and symmetrically fitted to the car.

☐ 20. Cars first used on or after 1 April 1980 must have one rear fog lamp fitted to the centre or offside of the car and, so far as fog lamps are concerned, the MoT tester is interested in this lamp on these cars only. It must comply with the basic requirements (listed under headlamps) and emit a steady red light. Its tell-tale lamp, inside the car, must work to inform the driver that it is switched on.

☐ 21. There must be a registration number plate at the front and rear of the car and both must be clean, secure, complete and unobscured. Letters and figures must be correctly formed and correctly spaced and not likely to be misread due to an uncovered securing bolt or whatever. The year letter counts as a figure. The space between letters and figures must be at least twice that between adjacent letters or figures.

☐ 22. Number plate lamps must be present, working, and not flickering when tapped by hand, just as for other lamps. Where more than one lamp or bulb was fitted as original equipment, all must be working.

The MoT tester will examine tyres and wheels while walking around the car and again when he is under the car.

☐ 23. Front tyres should match each other and rear tyres should match each other, both sets matching in terms of size, aspect ratio and type of structure. For example, you must never fit tyres of different sizes or types, such as cross-ply or radial, on the same 'axle' - both front wheels counting as 'on the same axle' in this context. Cross-ply or bias belted tyres should not be fitted on the rear axle, with radials on the front, neither should cross-ply tyres be fitted to the rear, with bias belted tyres on the front.

☐ 24. Failure of the test can be caused by a cut, lump, tear or bulge in a tyre, exposed ply or cord, a badly seated tyre, a re-cut tyre, a tyre fouling part of the vehicle, or a seriously damaged or misaligned valve stem which could cause sudden deflation of the tyre. To pass the test, the grooves of the tread pattern must be at least 1.6 mm deep throughout a continuous band comprising the central three-quarters of the breadth of tread, and round the entire outer circumference of the tyre.

All of the following photographs and the information in this section have been supplied with grateful thanks to Dunlop/SP Tyres.

☐ 24A. Modern tyres have tread wear indicators built into the tread groves (usually about eight of them spread equidistantly around the circumference). These appear as continuous bars running across the tread when the original pattern depth has worn down to 1.6 mm. There will be a distinct reduction in wet grip well before the tread wear indicators start to show, and you should replace tyres before they get to this stage, even though this is the legal minimum in the UK.

☐ 24B. Lumps and bulges in the tyre wall usually arise from accidental damage or even

24A

TWI

NEW TYRE   **ILLEGAL TYRE**

because of faults in the tyre construction. You should run your hand all the way around the side wall of the tyre, with the car either jacked off the ground, or moving the car half a wheels revolution, so that you can check the part of the tyre that was previously resting on the ground. Since you can't easily check the insides of the tyres in day-to-day use, it is even more important that you spend time carefully checking the inside of each tyre - the MoT tester will certainly do so! Tyres with bulges in them must be scrapped and replaced with new, since they can fail suddenly, causing your car to lose control.

☐ 24C. Abrasion of the tyre side wall can take place either in conjunction with bulging, or by itself, and this invariably results from an impact, such as the tyre striking the edge of a kerb or a pothole in the road. Once again, the tyre may be at imminent risk or failure and you should take advice from a tyre specialist on whether the abrasion is just superficial, or whether the tyre will need replacement.

☐ 24D. All tyres will suffer progressively from cracking, albeit in most cases superficially, due to the effects of sunlight. If old age has caused

24B

the tyres on your car to degrade to this extent, replace them.

☐ 24E. If the outer edges of the tread are worn noticeably more than the centre, the tyres have been run under inflated which not only ruins tyres, but causes worse fuel consumption, dangerous handling and is, of course, illegal.

Over-inflation causes the centre part of the tyre to wear more quickly than the outer edges. This is also illegal but in addition, it causes the steering and grip to suffer and the tyre becomes more susceptible to concussion damage.

☐ 24F. Incorrect wheel alignment causes one side of the tyre to wear more severely than the other. If your car should ever hit a kerb or large pothole, it is worthwhile having the wheel alignment checked since this costs considerably less than new front tyres!

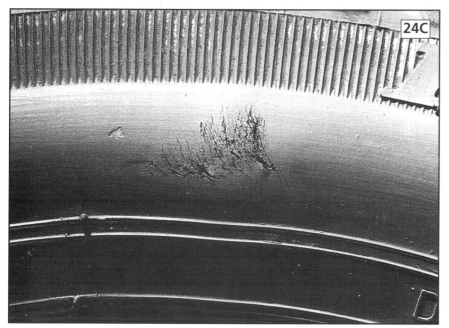

24C

24E

24D

24F

☐ 25. Road wheels must be secure and must not be badly damaged, distorted or cracked, or have badly distorted bead rims (perhaps due to "kerbing"), or loose or missing wheel nuts, studs or bolts.

☐ 26. Check the bodywork for any sharp edges or projections, caused by corrosion or damage, which could prove dangerous to other road users, including pedestrians.

GETTING THROUGH THE MOT

☐ 27. Check that the fuel cap fastens securely and that its sealing washer is neither torn nor deteriorated, or its mounting flange damaged sufficiently to allow fuel to escape (for example, while the car is cornering).

UNDER THE BONNET

☐ 28. The car should have a Chassis Number or Vehicle Identification Number fitted to the bodywork. The modern VIN plate is required on all vehicles first used on or after 1 August 1980. This can be on a plate secured to the vehicle or, etched or stamped on the bodywork. Others have a more traditional 'chassis number' which the tester will need to refer to. See **Chapter 8, Facts and Figures** for information on where they should be located on your car!

☐ 29. Check the steering column universal joint and clamp bolts for wear and looseness by asking your assistant to turn the steering wheel from side to side while you watch what happens under the bonnet. More than 13 mm (approx. 0.5 in.) of free play, on the MGB's rack and pinion systems, at the perimeter of the steering wheel, due to wear in the steering components, is sufficient grounds for a test failure. Note that the 13 mm criterion is based on a steering wheel of 380 mm (15 in.) diameter and will be less for smaller steering wheels. Also check for the presence and security of retaining and locking devices in the steering column assembly.

☐ 30. While peering under the bonnet check that hydraulic master cylinders and reservoirs are securely mounted and not severely corroded or otherwise damaged. Ensure that caps are present, that fluid levels are satisfactory and that there are no fluid leaks.

☐ 31. Also check that the servo is securely mounted and not damaged or corroded to an extent that would impair its operation. Vacuum pipes should be sound, that is, free from kinks, splits and excessive chafing and not collapsed internally.

☐ 32. Still under the bonnet, make a thorough search for evidence of excessive corrosion, severe distortion or fracture in any load bearing panelling within 30 cm (12 in.) of important mounting points such as the master cylinder/servo mounting, front suspension mountings etc.

UNDER THE CAR - FRONT END

☐ 33. Have an assistant turn the steering wheel from side to side while you watch for movement in the steering rack mountings (make sure too that they are secure), and within the ball joints. While in this vicinity, visually examine the rack gaiters - no leaks should be evident, and the rubbers must not be split. The ball joint dust covers should also be in sound condition. Ensure that all split pins, locking nuts and so on are in place and correctly fastened, throughout the steering and suspension systems.

> **SAFETY FIRST!**
> **On some occasions there is no alternative but for your assistant to sit in the car whilst you go beneath. Therefore:**
> **1) Place the car ramps as well as axle stands beneath the car's structure so that it cannot fall. 2) Don't allow your assistant to move vigorously or get in or out of the car while you are beneath it. If either of these are problematical, DON'T CARRY OUT THIS CHECK - leave it to your garage.**

☐ 34. Closely examine the wishbone support rubber bushes - they should not be severely squashed or breaking up. The rubber bushes supporting the anti-roll bar also require close scrutiny. Next, employ a suitable lever (such as a long screwdriver) to test for excessive movement in each rubber bush.

☐ 35. With the front of the car raised, and securely supported on axle stands (with the wheels clear of the ground), grasp each front wheel/tyre in turn at top and bottom, and attempt to 'rock' the wheel in and out. If more than just perceptible movement is evident at the rim, this could be due to wear in the king (swivel) pins and bushes, or in the front wheel bearings. Repeat the test while an assistant applies the foot brake. This will effectively lock the hub to the stub axle assembly, so any movement remaining will be in the king pins and bushes.

☐ 36. Spin each front wheel in turn, listening for roughness in the bearings. There must be none!

☐ 37. Visually inspect the shock absorbers and front coil springs. The lever arm type shock absorbers employed on the 'B can leak from the joints between the body of the unit and the twin operating arms - check each joint very carefully for wear, as well; leaks mean failure. Check also the small upper trunnion bushes (two on each side) where the shock absorber arm joins the top of the king pin. Where telescopic type shock absorbers are fitted, the same applies here; any signs of leaks mean failure. The coil springs must be sound and free from cracks or other visible damage.

☐ 38. With the wheels on the ground again, push down firmly a couple of times on each front wing of the car, then let go at the bottom of a stroke. The car should rise and then fall to approximately its original level. Continuing oscillations will earn your MG a 'failure' ticket for worn front 'shockers'!

UNDER THE CAR - REAR SUSPENSION

☐ 39. Check the condition and alignment of the spring leaves, and ensure that the central leaf retaining bolt is sound. Watch in particular for cracks in the main (upper) leaf. Look closely too at the condition of the spring eye bushes - these must be sound, as must the shackle assemblies. The lever arm rear shock absorbers can suffer from leaks around the operating arm - check carefully. Look too for deterioration in the bushes at each end of the link rod connecting the shock absorber with the spring, on each side of the car, also the bushes in the rear anti-roll bar and check that all mounting bolts and fixings are tight.

☐ 40. A 'bounce' test can be carried out as for the front shock absorbers as an approximate check on how efficient or otherwise the damping effect is!

☐ 41. With the back of the car raised on axle stands (both rear wheels off the ground), rotate the rear wheels and check, as well as you can, for roughness in the bearings, just as you did at the front.

BRAKES

☐ 42. The MoT brake test is carried out on a special 'rolling road' set-up, which measures the efficiency in terms of percentage. For the foot brake, the examiner is looking for 50 per cent; the hand brake must measure 25 per cent. Frankly, without a rolling road of your own, there is little that you can do to verify whether or not your car will come up to the required figures. What you can do, though, is carry out an entire check of the brake system, which will also cover all other aspects the examiner will be checking, and be as sure as you can that the system is working efficiently.

☐ 43. The MoT examiner will not dismantle any part of the system, but you can do so. So, take off each front wheel in turn, and examine the front brake discs (look for excessive grooving/crazing), the calliper pistons/dust seals (look for signs of fluid leakage and deterioration of the seals), and the brake pads - ideally, replace them if less than approximately 3 mm. (1/8th in.) friction material remains on each pad. At the rear, remove each brake drum and check the condition of the linings (renew if worn down to anywhere near the rivet heads), the brake drum (watch for cracking, ovality and serious scoring, etc.) and the wheel cylinders. Check the cylinder's dust covers to see if they contain brake fluid. If so, or if it is obvious that the cylinder(s) have been leaking, replace them or - ONLY if the cylinder bore is in perfect condition - fit a new seal kit.

IMPORTANT!
See **Chapter 3, Service Intervals, Step-by-Step** for important information, including **SAFETY FIRST!** information before working on your car's brakes.

☐ 44. Ensure that the rear brake adjusters (where fitted) are free to rotate (i.e. not seized!). If they are stuck fast, apply a little penetrating oil to the backs of the adjusters (but only from behind the backplate, not inside the brake drum where there would be some risk of getting oil onto the brake shoes), and gently 'work' the adjuster backwards and forwards with a brake adjuster spanner. Eventually the adjusters should free, and a little brake grease can be applied to the threads to keep them in this condition. With the rear brakes correctly adjusted, check hand brake action. The lever should rise three or four 'clicks' before the brake operates fully - if it goes further, the cable requires adjustment. Ensure too that the hand brake lever remains locked in the 'on' position when fully applied, even if the lever is knocked sideways.

☐ 45. As a very approximate check on brake operation, with the car securely supported with either both front or both rear wheels clear of the ground, get an assistant to apply the foot brake, then attempt to rotate each wheel in turn - they should not, of course, move! Repeat the test with the hand brake applied, but on the rear wheels only this time...

☐ 46. Closely check the state of ALL visible hydraulic and fuel-line pipework. If any section of the steel tubing shows signs of corrosion, replace it, for safety as well as to gain an MoT pass. Look too for leakage of fluid around pipe joints, and from the master cylinder. The fluid level in the master cylinder reservoir must also be at its correct level - if not, find out why and rectify the problem! At the front of the car, bend the flexible hydraulic pipes through 180 degrees (by hand) near each end of each pipe, checking for signs of cracking. If any is evident, or if the pipes have been chafing on the tyres, wheels, steering or suspension components, replace them with new items, re-routing them to avoid future problems. Also, where fuel line retaining clips were fitted by the manufacturer, they must be present and effective.

☐ 47. Have an assistant press down hard on the brake pedal while you check all flexible pipes for bulges. As an additional check, firmly apply the foot brake and hold the pedal down for a few minutes. It should not slowly sink to the floor (if it does, you have a hydraulic system problem). Press and release the pedal a few times - it should not feel 'spongy' (due to the presence of air in the system). Now start the engine while the pedal is being held down. If all is well, as the vacuum servo starts to operate, the pedal should move a short distance towards the floor. Check the condition of the servo unit and its hoses - all MUST be sound. If there is the risk of any problems with the braking system's hydraulics, have a qualified mechanic check it over before using the car.

☐ 48. A test drive should reveal obvious faults (such as pulling to one side, due to a seized calliper piston, for example), but otherwise all will be revealed on the rollers at the MoT station...

BODYWORK STRUCTURE

A structurally deficient car is a dangerous vehicle, and rust can affect many important areas, including the inner and outer sills (which literally hold the car together, especially on MGB roadsters), floor pans and the quarter panels, and in front of the rear wheels. Examine these areas, also the inner wings and 'turret' reinforcing sections at the upper, and the rear corners underneath the front wings (these can be 'felt' by hand), since weakness here will bring MoT disappointment. See **Chapter 3, Service Intervals Step-by-Step** for illustrations.

49. Essentially, fractures, cracks or serious corrosion in any load bearing panel or member (to the extent that the affected sections are weakened) need to be dealt with. In addition, failure will result from any deficiencies in the structural metalwork within 30 cm. (12 in.) of the seat belt mountings, and also the steering and suspension component attachment points. Repairs made to any structural areas must be carried out by 'continuous' seam welding, and the repair should restore the affected section to at least its original strength.

50. The MoT examiner will be looking for metal which gives way under squeezing pressure between finger and thumb, and will use his wicked little 'Corrosion Assessment Tool' (i.e. a plastic-headed hammer!), which in theory at least should be used for detecting rust by lightly tapping the surface. If scraping the surface of the metal shows weakness beneath, the car will fail.

51. Note that the security of doors and other openings must also be assessed, including the hinges, locks and catches. Corrosion damage or other weakness in the vicinity of these items can mean failure. It must be possible to open both doors from inside and outside the car.

EXTERIOR BODYWORK

52. Check for another area which can cause problems. Look out for surface rust, or accident damage, on the exterior bodywork, which leaves sharp/jagged edges and which may be liable to cause injury. Ideally, repairs should be carried out by welding in new metal, but for non-structural areas, riveting a plate over a hole, bridging the gap with glass fibre/body filler or even taping over the gap can be legally acceptable, at least as far as the MoT test is concerned.

FUEL SYSTEM

53. Another recent extension of the regulations brings the whole of the fuel system under scrutiny, from the tank to the engine. The system should be examined with and without the engine running, and there must be no leaks from any of the components. The tank must be securely mounted, and the filler cap must fit properly - 'temporary' caps are not permitted.

EMISSIONS

Oh dear - even the thought of this aspect can cause headaches. In almost every case, a proper 'engine tune' will help to ensure that your car is running at optimum efficiency, and there should be no difficulty in passing the test, unless your engine, the distributor or the carburettors really are well worn. However, MGBs can be more difficult than most in this regard – see below.

54. For cars first used before 1 August, 1975, the only test carried out is for 'visual smoke emission'. The engine must be fully warmed up, allowed to idle, then revved slightly. If smoke emitted is regarded by the examiner as being 'excessive', the car will fail. Often smoke emitted during this test is as a result of worn valve stem seals, allowing oil into the combustion chambers during tickover, to be blown out of the exhaust as 'blue smoke' when the engine is revved. In practice, attitudes vary widely between MoT stations on this aspect of the test.

55. For cars first used between 1 August, 1975 and 31 July, 1983, a 'smoke' test also applies. Again, the engine must be fully warmed up, and allowed to idle, before being revved to around 2,500 rpm for 20 seconds (to 'purge' the system). If dense blue or black smoke is emitted for more than five seconds, the car will fail. In addition, the exhaust gas is analysed. A maximum of 6 per cent carbon monoxide (CO), and 1,200 parts per million (ppm) hydrocarbons is allowable. The percentage of these gases are established using an exhaust gas analyser - home user versions are available for testing CO readings.

56. Normally, if the CO reading is within limits, the hydrocarbon emissions will be acceptable, but unfortunately, some cars fitted with twin S.U. carburettors (MGBs included) give excessive hydrocarbon percentage readings when checked with the engine idling - EVEN WITH NEW CARBURETTORS! Therefore, many cars were 'failing' the test and in some cases their owners were persuaded to spend vast sums of money on replacement carburettors they didn't need, and which in any case had a marginal effect on the hydrocarbon levels in the exhaust gas.

Therefore, a little-known, but vitally important, exemption was introduced by the Vehicle Inspectorate Executive Agency, in the form of Special Notice SN 18/19, Section 2. Copies should have been circulated to all MoT Testing Stations, but an unofficial survey by members of the MG Owners' Club revealed that many examiners were apparently unaware of the exemption. Under this, it is acknowledged that some vehicles were unable to meet the specified hydrocarbon limit, even when new. These vehicles include twin-carburettor MGBs, all MGCs and V8s, but not the fuel-injected MG RV8 of course! If such vehicles meet the CO requirements at normal idling speed, but fail the hydrocarbon test at the same speed, the hydrocarbon test should be repeated at an engine speed of 2,000 rpm, using the throttle, NOT cold start/cold running mechanisms to increase the engine speed. If the hydrocarbon reading is then 1,200 ppm or less, the car will pass. So, if you should have difficulties in this respect, politely show the examiner this book, and quote SN 18/19, Section 2!

INSIDE INFORMATION: Bromsgrove MG Centre claim that they have a higher success rate if the vacuum advance pipe to the distributor is temporarily disconnected and the end of the pipe leading to the inlet manifold blocked off - temporarily again. Worth a try!

CHAPTER 8 - FACTS AND FIGURES

This Chapter serves two main purposes. First, we aim to show you how to find the identification numbers on your car and then we show you which settings you will need to use in order to carry out servicing.

The "Data" sections of this chapter will also make essential reading when you come to carrying out the servicing on your car since you will then need to know things like tappet settings, spark plug gap, torque settings and a whole host of other adjustments and measurements that you will need to carry out in the course of maintaining your car.

SECTION 1 - IDENTIFICATION NUMBERS

For location of the numbers and plates mentioned in this section please refer to the line drawings in *Chapter 2, Buying Spares*.

MGB - ALL MODELS

BMC and British Leyland used to recommend that when parts were being purchased, the correct part numbers were referred to and as we've said earlier, with the passage of time and the possibility of parts being interchanged, this becomes even more important.

The most important number of all is the car's chassis or car number. On some models of MGB, this number can be found in alternative positions: stamped onto a plate fixed to the right hand inner wing panel, near to, and in front of, the radiator. On later cars (from August, 1976 on), the plate is located on the right hand side of the bonnet 'shut' panel.

The engine number is stamped on a plate secured to the right-hand of the cylinder block or is stamped directly onto the cylinder block, depending on the age of the vehicle.

The gearbox number is stamped on the right-hand side of the gearbox casing while the overdrive number is stamped on a plate secured to the underside of the overdrive.

The rear axle number is stamped on the left-hand side of the rear axle tube (later, tube-axle type models) and on the casting of the axle casing (earlier, banjo-type axle casing models) and on earlier models the number is to be found near the spring seating.

MGC - ALL MODELS

The chassis/VIN number is stamped onto a plate fixed to the left-hand inner wing panel, near to and behind, the radiator 'diaphragm' panel, adjacent to the coolant expansion tank.

The engine number is stamped on a plate attached to the right-hand side of the cylinder block.

The gearbox number is stamped directly into the top of the gearbox casing.

MGB GT V8

There are two main car identification numbers on these models. There is the car number stamped on a plate fixed to the right-hand valance and partly concealed by the oil cooler hose and the commission number, something that we have previously referred to as a chassis number, stamped on a plate secured to the bonnet "shut" panel.

The engine number is stamped on the left-hand side of the cylinder block located directly behind the left-hand cylinder head.

The gearbox number, overdrive unit number and rear axle number are all in the same location as for the standard MGB models.

MG RV8

The Vehicle Identification Number (VIN) is stamped on a plate secured to the bonnet "shut" panel. The VIN number is also chemically etched on the windscreen so it is important to remember when having a new windscreen fitted to have the number etched onto the new screen. Please also note that the body colour and trim codes are also stamped on the VIN plate.

The engine number is stamped on the cylinder block behind the dipstick tube.

The gearbox number is stamped on the bottom right-hand side of the gearbox.

SECTION 2 - WHAT THE NUMBERS MEAN

CHASSIS NUMBERS:

Translation of the BMC/BL codings is as follows:

1st digit denotes make, i.e. G = MG.

2nd digit denotes type of power unit, e.g. H = BMC 'B' Series engine, C = 'C' Series engine.

3rd digit denotes type of bodywork, i.e. either N = tourer, or D = fixed head GT.

4th digit denotes Series, e.g. in the case of the MGB: 3 = First Series, 4 = Second Series MGB, 5 = Third Series (with no changes to Series made after October, 1979). (Note, numbers 1 and 2 referred to the earlier MGA).

5th digit denotes differences from standard right hand drive model, e.g L = L.H.D; U = U.S.A.

6th digit denotes model year, 1970 on, e.g. A = 1970, B = 1971, C = 1972, D = 1973, etc, etc.

ENGINE NUMBER:

Translation of BMC/BL codings is as follows:

First (prefix) group of digits:
1st two digits denote engine capacity - e.g. 18 = 1800cc.
3rd digit denotes make - i.e. G = MG.

Second group of digits:
U = centrally positioned floor gearchange.
R = overdrive.
RC = automatic.

Third group of digits (in each case followed by the engine's individual serial number):
H = High compression.
L = Low compression.

MGC: Prefix 29 denotes engine capacity, 2912cc, 'G' = MG, etc. '29A' indicates the presence of an Austin 3 Litre engine...

1st and 2nd Prefix letters (marque and model) GV-MGB

3rd Prefix letter (class): A = Base Line; G = GT; J = Japanese; L = Canadian; V = North America; Z = California

4th Prefix Letter (body): D = 2 Door Sports Open; E = 2 Door Sports Closed

5th Prefix Letter (engine): J = 1800cc

6th Prefix Letter (transmission and steering): 1 = Manual 4 speed R.H.D.; 2 = Manual 4 speed L.H.D.

7th Prefix Letter (model change): A = 1980 Model Year

8th Prefix Letter (assembly plant): G = Abingdon

Later engines, with an 18V prefix (V for Vertical, not V8!) have a string of numbers and letters in the second group whose meaning is rather complex and obscure. If three numbers are followed by the letter 'F', this means that twin-carburettors were originally fitted.

SECTION 3 – MAINTENANCE INFORMATION AND SETTINGS

The following information will be required when carrying out certain service jobs. The model headings used are:

MGB = all models
MGC = all models
MGB GT V8
MG RV8

ENGINE

Compression pressure at cranking speed:

These are the manufacturer's "when new" figures. Expect yours to be different especially if the engine is worn (lower) or if the cylinder head has been skimmed (higher) but these figures are a good guide.

MGB

8.0:1 compression ratio	130 p.s.i. (9.15 kg/cm².)
8.8:1 compression ratio	160 p.s.i. (11.25 kg/cm².)
9.0:1 compression ratio	170 p.s.i. (11.95 kg/cm².)

MGC

9.0:1 compression ratio	175 p.s.i. (12.3 kg/cm².)

MGB GT V8

8.26:1 compression ratio	155 p.s.i. (10.9 kg/cm²) @ 200 rpm

MG RV8

9.35:1 compression ratio	160 to 180 p.s.i. (11.2 to 12.6 kg/cm²)

Firing Order

MGB	1,3,4,2 (No. 1 cylinder next to radiator)
MGC	1,5,3,6,2,4 (No. 1 cylinder next to radiator)
MGB GT V8	1,8,4,3,6,5,7,2 (No. 1 cylinder next to radiator on left bank)
MG RV8	1,8,4,3,6,5,7,2 (No. 1 cylinder next to radiator on left bank)

Valve clearance (exhaust and inlet)

MGB	0.015 in. (0.38 mm) cold
MGC	0.015 in. (0.38 mm) cold
MGB GT V8	Not adjustable
MG RV8	Not adjustable

IGNITION SYSTEM

Distributor

MGB	Lucas 25D4 (early models), Lucas 45D4 (later models), or Lucas 45DE4 electronic (later US models)
MGC	Lucas 25D6
MGB GT V8	Lucas 35D8
MG RV8	Lucas 35DLM8 electronic

Contact breaker gap

MGB	0.014 to 0.016 in. (0.35 to 0.40 mm)
MGC	0.014 to 0.016 in. (0.35 to 0.40 mm)
MGB GT V8	0.014 to 0.016 in. (0.35 to 0.40 mm)
MG RV8	Not applicable, electronic ignition

Dwell angle

MGB	Lucas 25D4 Distributor: 60° ± 3° Lucas 45D4 Distributor: 51° ± 5°
MGC	Lucas 25D6 Distributor: 35° ± 2°
MGB GT V8	Lucas 35D8 Distributor: 26° to 28°
MG RV8	Not applicable

Coil

MGB	Lucas HA12 (oil filled)
MGC	Lucas HA12
MGB GT V8	Lucas 16C6 with ballast resistor
MG RV8	Bosch 0-221-122-392

Spark plugs

We have quoted the recommended NGK spark plugs but other manufacturers equivalents can be used.

MGB	NGK-BP6ES gap setting 0.024 in. (0.6 mm)
MGC	NGK-BP6ES gap setting 0.024 in. (0.6 mm)
MGB GT V8	NGK-BP5HS gap setting 0.028 in. (0.7 mm)
MG RV8	NGK-BPR6ES gap setting 0.035 in. (0.9 mm)

Ignition timing (static)

MGB   18G series engines:
      High compression: 10° B.T.D.C.
      Low compression: 8° B.T.D.C.

      18v series engines (non-emission control type):
      581F/582F/583F/581Y/582Y/583Y:
        High compression: 10° B.T.D.C.
        Low compression: 10° B.T.D.C.

      18v series engines (to emission control requirements ECE15):
        18V: 5° B.T.D.C.
        779F/780F: 6° B.T.D.C.
        846F/847F: 7° B.T.D.C.
        847 (1976 on): Stroboscopic timing only (see below)

MGC   8° B.T.D.C.

Ignition timing (stroboscopic)

MGB   18G series engines:
      High compression: 14° B.T.D.C. @ 600 r.p.m.
      Low compression: 12° B.T.D.C. @ 600 r.p.m.

      18V series engines (non emission control type) - 581F/582F/583F/581Y/582Y/583Y:
        High compression: 13° B.T.D.C. @ 600 r.p.m.
        Low compression: 13° B.T.D.C. @ 600 r.p.m.

      18V series engines (to emission control requirements ECE15)
        18V: 15° B.T.D.C. @ 1000 r.p.m.
        779F/780F: 11° B.T.D.C. @ 1000 r.p.m.
        846F/847F: 10° B.T.D.C. @ 1000 r.p.m.
        847F (1976 on): 10° B.T.D.C. @ 1000 r.p.m.

MGC	20° B.T.D.C. @ 1,000 r.p.m.
MGB GT V8	8° B.T.D.C. @ 1,000 r.p.m.
MG RV8	5° ± 1° B.T.D.C. @ 800 r.p.m.

ELECTRICAL EQUIPMENT

Batteries

MGB	Two 6 volt Lucas SG9E, STG29E, BT9E, BTZ9E, CA9E, Exide 3XCK9L (later cars). 1975 models on: Lucas P250 single 12 volt Positive earth on car prior to chassis prefix numbers GHN4 or GHD4. Negative earth on cars with chassis prefix number GHN4 or GHD4 on.
MGC	Two 6 volt, Lucas FG11E
MGB GT V8	Two 6 volt
MG RV8	12 volt sealed for life

Battery capacity

MGB	51 amp hour at 10 hr rate (early cars) 58 amp hour at 20 hr rate (early cars) 53 amp hour at 10 hr rate (CA9E batteries) 60 amp hour at 20 hr rate (CA9E batteries) 66 amp hour at 20 hr rate (single 12 volt)

MGC   64 amp hour at 10 hr rate
72 amp hour at 20 hr rate

MGB GT V8   67 amp hour at 20 hr rate

MG RV8   Cold crank capacity 405 amps, reserve capacity 70 mins.

Dynamo
MGB   Lucas C40/1

Regulator
MGB   Lucas RB34

NB MGBs fitted with alternators did not have regulators.

Alternator
MGB   Lucas 16AC or 16ACR (replaces dynamo)
MGC   Lucas 16AC
MGB GT V8   A.C. Delco 7982707
MG RV8   Magneti Marelli A127-65

Control box
MGB   Lucas 4TR
MGC   Lucas 4TR
MGB GT V8   Not applicable
MG RV8   Not applicable

Windscreen wiper motor
MGB   Lucas DR3A, single speed
Lucas 14W, two-speed (later models)
MGC   Lucas 14W, two speed
MGB GT V8   Lucas 54071811
MG RV8   Lucas 14W, two speed

Horns
MGB   Lucas 9H
MGC   Lucas 9H Windtone
MGB GT V8   Lucas 9H
MG RV8   Claxon   (Part Nos. GGE151: low note)
(Part Nos. GGE152: high note)

Starter motor
MGB   Lucas M418G inertia type, Lucas M418G pre-engaged type or Lucas 2M100, pre-engaged type.
MGC   Lucas M418G pre-engaged
MGB GT V8   Lucas 3M100
MG RV8   Bosch AMR 2165 pre-engaged

Fuses
MGB Early models:

A1-A2 (35 amp) - All items not controlled through ignition switch eg. horns, lights etc.

A3-A4 (35 amp) - Ignition switch and items controlled by ignition switch - stop lights, fuel gauge, traffic indicators, windscreen wiper motor, etc.

Separate line-fuse, GT model only (35 amp) - Heated rear screen.

Later models with Lucas 7FJ fusebox (GHN5/GHD5 cars) - fuses listed from top to bottom:

No 1 and No 2 (17 amp current rating, 35 amp blow rating) - side and tail lights.

No 3 (17 amp current rating, 35 amp blow rating) - Items controlled by ignition switch eg. stop lights, reverse lights, etc.

No 4 (17 amp current rating, 35 amp blow rating) - Items not controlled by ignition switch eg. horns, interior light, cigarette lighter.

Separate line-fuse below fusebox (35 amp) - Windscreen wipers/washers, heater blower, radio, heated rear screen (GT model only).

Separate line-fuse behind hazard warning light switch - Hazard warning lights.

Latest models (all fuses 17 amp current rated, 35 amp blow rated)

Fuse No 2 - One parking light, one tail light and one number plate light.

Fuse No 3 - As above for lights not covered.

Fuse No 4 - Circuits controlled by ignition switch eg. direction indicators, stop lights, reverse lights, seat belt warning, temperature and fuel gauges, heated rear window (where applicable).

Fuse No 5 - Circuits not covered by ignition switch eg. horns, interior lights, head light flasher, and radio (if fitted).

Separate line-fuses:

Fuse No 7 - Hazard warning lights.

Fuse No 8 - Fan thermostat circuit.

MGC

A1-A2 (35 amp) - All items not controlled through ignition switch e.g. horns, lights etc.

A3-A4 (35 amp) - Ignition switch and items controlled by ignition switch - stop lights, fuel gauge, traffic indicators, windscreen wiper motor, etc.

Separate line-fuse (25 amp) - protects electrically heated back-light (GT).

MGB GT V8

1-2 - protects one parking light, one tail light and one number-plate light.

3-4 - protects one parking light, one tail light and one number-plate light.

5-6 - Ignition switch and items controlled by ignition switch - cooling fans, traffic indicators, brake stop lights reverse lights, temperature and fuel gauges, heated rear window.

7-8 - All items not controlled through ignition switch - horns, interior and luggage compartment lights, head light flasher, cigarette lighter.

MG RV8

Nos 4, 13, 16, 20 and 23 are all spare fuses.

1 (10 amp) - Fuel, ignition coil, anti-theft alarm.

2 (10 amp) - Right hand side tail and number plate lights, interior light, fascia illumination.

3 (10 amp) - Temperature gauge, fuel gauge and tachometer.

5 (15 amp) - Right hand head light - main beam.

6 (10 amp) - Brake lights, warning lights and voltmeter.

7 (10 amp) - Front fog lights.

8 (15 amp) - Cigarette lighter.

9 (10 amp) - Warning lights, indicators and reverse lights.

10 (10 amp) - Rear fog lights.

11 (20 amp) - Cooling fan.

12 (15 amp) - Radio cassette memory, electric boot switch warning light, clock, interior light, horn, engine management and anti-theft indicator.

14 (15 amp) - Heater blower motor.

15 (15 amp) - Windscreen wiper/washer.

17 (10 amp) - Fuel pump.

18 (15 amp) - Left hand head light - main beam.

19 (20 amp) - Headlights, sidelights, anti-theft alarm and boot release.

21 (15 amp) - Hazards.

22 (15 amp) - Radio cassette and rear amplifier.

24 (10 amp) - Right hand head light - dip beam.

25 (10 amp) - Left hand head light - dip beam.

26 (10 amp) - Left hand side, tail and number plate lights, radio cassette illumination, fascia illumination.

FUEL SYSTEM

Carburettor

MGB	18G series engines and earlier - Twin SU HS4 semi-downdraught
	18V - 581F/582F/583F/ engines - Twin SU HS4 semi-downdraught
	All other 18V series engines - Twin SU HIF4 or single Zenith/Stromberg 175 CD semi-downdraught
MGC	Twin SU HS6
MGB GT V8	Twin SU type HIF 6
MG RV8	Not applicable, fuel injection system fitted

Idle speed

MGB	500 r.p.m. (18G series engines) 750 to 850 r.p.m. (18V series engines) 1300 r.p.m. (fast idle speed)
MGC	700 r.p.m. (manual gearbox) 800 r.p.m. (automatic gearbox) 1000 r.p.m. (fast idle speed)
MGB GT V8	800 to 850 r.p.m 1400 to 1500 r.p.m. (fast idle speed)
MG RV8	700 r.p.m. ± 25 r.p.m. Fast idle speed not applicable

Fuel pump

MGB	SU type HP or AUF 300 or AUF 305 electric
MGC	SU type AUF 301 electric
MGB GT V8	SU type AUF 305 electric
MG RV8	Lucas 14 CUX

COOLING SYSTEM

Pressure cap setting

MGB	7 p.s.i. (early models), 15 p.s.i. (later models)
MGC	10 p.s.i.
MGB GT V8	15 p.s.i.
MG RV8	15 p.s.i.

CLUTCH

Fluid type

MGB	As for braking system specifications.
MGC	As for braking system specifications.
MGB GT V8	As for braking system specifications.
MG RV8	As for braking system specifications.

BRAKING SYSTEM

Brake disc thickness

MGB	Disc thickness when new: 0.35 in. (8.89 mm.) Minimum disc thickness: 0.31 in. (7.87 mm.)* * This reflects the maximum amount recommended by Rover to be ground off. If removal of this much material does not remove all scoring, the discs should be scrapped and replaced.
MGC	Disc thickness when new: 0.5 in. (12.7 mm.) Minimum disc thickness: 0.45 in. (11.4 mm.)
MGB GT V8	Disc thickness when new: 0.5 in. (12.7 mm.) Minimum disc thickness: 0.45 in. (11.4 mm.)
MG RV8	Disc thickness when new: information not supplied by manufacturer Minimum disc thickness: 0.955 in. (24.25 mm.)

Fluid type

MGB	All models, Castrol Universal Brake & Clutch fluid or equivalent.
MGC	Castrol Universal Brake & Clutch fluid or equivalent.
MGB GT V8	Castrol Universal Brake & Clutch fluid or equivalent.
MG RV8	Castrol Universal DOT 4 brake fluid

LUBRICATION SYSTEM

Oil pressure (when hot)

MGB	Idling: 10 to 15 p.s.i. (0.7 to 1.7 kg/cm².) Normal motoring: 50 to 80 p.s.i. (3.5 to 5.6 kg/cm².)
MGC	Idling: 10 to 20 p.s.i. (0.7 to 1.4 kg/cm².) Normal motoring: 55 p.s.i. (3.87 kg/cm².)
MGB GT V8	Normal motoring: 30 to 40 p.s.i. (2 to 2.8 kg/cm².)
MG RV8	30 to 40 p.s.i. (2 to 2.8 kg/cm².) above 82°C, @ 2,400 r.p.m.

CAPACITIES

Coolant capacity (inc. heater)

MGB	Up to car number 410002 - 10 pints (5.6 litres) Car number 410002 on - 12 pints (6.8 litres)
MGC	18.5 pints (10.5 litres)
MGB GT V8	16 pints (9.08 litres)
MG RV8	8.8 pints (5.0 litres)

Manual gearbox oil capacity

MGB	4.5 pints (2.56 litres) early cars * 5.25 pints (3 litres) later cars * * Add 0.75 pint (0.426 litre) where overdrive is fitted
MGC	5.25 pints (3 litres) * * Add 0.75 pint (0.426 litre) where overdrive is fitted
MGB GT V8	6 pints (3.4. litres) inc. overdrive
MG RV8	4.8 pints (2.7 litres)

Automatic transmission fluid capacity

MGB	10.5 pints (6 litres)
MGC	14.5 pints (7.3 litres)
MGB GT V8	Not applicable
MG RV8	Not applicable

Rear axle oil capacity

MGB	2.25 pints (1.28 litres) early cars with "banjo" axle 1.5 pints (0.84 litre) later cars with "tubed" axle
MGC	1.75 pints (1.14 litres)
MGB GT V8	1.5 pints (0.84 litre)

Sump capacity (with oil cooler)

MGB	7.5 pints (4.26 litres)
MGC	12 pints (6.8 litres)
MGB GT V8	8 pints (4.54 litres)
MG RV8	9.7 pints (5.5 litres)

Oil cooler capacity

MGB	0.75 pint (0.42 litre)
MGC	2.5 pints (1.42 litres)

Steering rack capacity

MGB	1/3 pint (0.19 litre)
MGC	1/3 pint (0.19 litre)
MGB GT V8	1/3 pint (0.19 litre)

GENERAL DATA

Tyre pressures (normal)

(For sustained high speeds, the tyre pressures for all models except MG RV8 should be increased by 6 p.s.i. (0.4 kg/cm².).)

MGB	Cross-ply 5.60 - 14S
	Front: 19 p.s.i. (1.34 kg/cm².)
	Rear: 22 p.s.i. (1.55 kg/cm².)
	Radial-ply 155SR-14 and 165SR-14
	Front: 21 p.s.i. (1.48 kg/cm².
	Rear: 24 p.s.i. (1.69 kg/cm².)
MGC Tourer	Front: 26 p.s.i. (1.8 kg/cm².)
	Rear: 22 p.s.i. (1.5 kg/cm².)
GT	Front: 26 p.s.i. (1.8 kg/cm².)
	Rear: 26 p.s.i. (1.8 kg/cm².)
MGB GT V8	Front: 21 p.s.i. (1.5 kg/cm².)
	Rear: 25 p.s.i. (1.8 kg/cm².)
MG RV8	Front: 22 p.s.i. (1.5 kg/cm².)
	Rear: 24 p.s.i. (1.7 kg/cm².)

Steering gear - toe-in

(otherwise known as wheel alignment or tracking)

MGB	1/16 to 3/32 in. (1.5 to 2.3 mm.)
MGC	1/16 to 3/32 in. (1.5 to 2.3 mm.)
MGB GT V8	1/16 to 3/32 in. (1.5 to 2.3 mm.)
MG RV8	0° 5' to 0° 10'.

TORQUE WRENCH SETTINGS

Only those settings relating to this book are shown here. If you wish to carry out further work, refer to torque wrench settings shown in the appropriate workshop manual.

MGB (With 18G/18GA series engines)

Engine
> Cylinder head nuts: 45 to 50 lb. ft. (6.2 to 6.9 kg. m.)
> Rocker bracket nuts: 25 lb. ft. (3.4 kg. m.)
> Sump to crankcase: 6 lb. ft. (0.8 kg. m.)
> Cylinder side cover screws: 2 lb. ft. (0.28 kg. m.)
> Second type: deep pressed cover - 5 lb. ft. (0.7 kg. m.)
> Rocker cover nuts: 4 lb. ft. (0.56 kg. m.)
> Manifold nuts: 15 lb. ft. (2.1 kg. m.)
> Oil filter centre bolt: 15 lb. ft. (2.1 kg. m.)
> Carburettor stud nuts: 2 lb. ft. (0.28 kg. m.)
> Spark plugs: 18 lb. ft. (2.5 kg. m.)

Rear Axle
> Rear brake adjuster securing nuts: 5 to 7 lb ft (0.69 to 0.97 kg m)

Rear Suspension
> Rear shock absorber bolts: 55 to 60 lb. ft. (7.6 to 8.3 kg. m.)

Front Suspension
> Front shock absorber bolts: 43 to 45 lb. ft. (5.9 to 6.2 kg. m.)
> Cross-member to body: 54 to 56 lb. ft. (7.5 to 7.7 kg. m.)

Steering
> Steering arm bolts: 60 to 65 lb. ft. (8.3 to 8.9 kg. m.)
> Steering track-rod lock nut: 33.3 to 37.5 lb. ft. (4.6 to 5.2 kg. m.)
> Steering track-rod end balljoint nut: 34 to 35 lb. ft. (4.7 to 4.8 kg. m.)
> Steering universal joint bolt: 20 to 22 lb. ft. (2.8 to 3.0 kg. m.)

Road Wheels
> Road wheel nuts: 60 to 65 lb. ft. (8.3 to 9 kg. m)

MGB (With 18GD/18GG/18GF/18GH series engines)

Automatic gearbox
> Oil pan to gearbox bolts: 8 to 13 lb. ft. (1.1 to 1.8 kg. m.)
> Drain plug: 8 to 10 lb. ft. (1.1. to 1.38 kg. m.)

General
> Stiffnut to cross-member mounting bolt: 44 to 46 lb. ft. (6.08 to 6.36 kg. m.)

MGB (With 18V series engines)

Engine
> Camshaft nut: 65 lb. ft. (8.9 kg. m.)
> Carburettor - stud nuts: 15 lb. ft. (2.1 kg. m.)
> Spark plugs: 18 lb. ft. (2.5 kg. m.)

MGB (all models)

> Interior mirror special screw: 5 lb. in. (5.7 kg. cm.)
> Steering-column universal joint bolts: 20 to 22 lb. ft. (2.8 to 3.04 kg. m.)

MGC

Engine
> Cylinder head nuts: 75 lb. ft. (10.4 kg. m.)
> Rocker bracket bolts: 25 to 27 lb. ft. (3.4 to 3.7 kg. m.)
> Sump to crankcase: 6 lb. ft. (0.8 kg. m.)
> Cylinder side covers:
>> Front: 15 lb. ft. (2.1 kg. m.)
>> Centre and Rear: 4 lb. ft. (0.5 kg. m.)
> Manifold nuts: 42 lb. ft. (5.8 kg. m.)
> Oil filter centre-bolt: 15 lb. ft. (2.1 kg. m.)
> Carburettor stud nuts: 15 lb. ft. (2.1 kg. m.)
> Float chamber bolt: 7.5 lb. ft. (1 kg. m.)
> Distributor clamp nut: 2.5 lb. ft. (0.35 kg. m.)
> Sparking plugs: 30 lb. ft. (4.1 kg. m.)

Automatic gearbox
> Oil pan to gearbox bolt: 8 to 13 lb. ft. (1.1 to 1.8 kg. m.)
> Drain plug: 9 to 12 lb. ft. (1.24 to 1.66 kg. m.)

Steering
> Top arm studs: 60 to 70 lb. in. (0.691 to 0.807 kg. m.)
> Top arm bolt nut: 18 to 20 lb. ft. (2.49 to 2.77 kg. m.)
> Steering-arm bolt: 60 to 65 lb. ft. (8.3 to 8.9 kg. m.)
> Steering track-rod locknut: 33 to 37 lb. ft. (4.62 to 5.18 kg. m.)
> Steering track-rod end ball joint nut: 35 lb. ft. (4.8 kg. m.)
> Steering universal joint bolt: 20 lb. ft. (2.8 kg. m.)

Rear Suspension
> Rear damper bolts: 55 to 60 lb. ft. (7.6 to 8.3 kg. m.)

Road Wheels
> Road wheel nuts: 60 to 65 lb. ft. (8.3 to 9 kg. m.)

Alternator
> Through-bolts: 45 to 60 lb. in. (0.52 to 6.58 kg. m.)

MGB GT V8

Engine
> Cylinder head bolts: 68 lb. ft. (9.40 kg. m.)
> Rocker shaft bolts: 28 lb. ft. (3.87 kg. m.)
> Exhaust manifold bolts: 13 lb. ft. (1.80 kg. m.)
> Induction manifold bolts: 28 lb. ft. (3.87 kg. m.)
> Induction manifold gasket clamp bolt: 13 lb. ft. (1.80 kg. m.)
> Carburettor adaptor nuts: 18 lb. ft. (2.49 kg. m.)

Rear Suspension
> Shock absorber to side-member nut: 58 lb. ft. (8.01 kg. m.)

Front Suspension
> Bottom wishbone pivot to cross-member nut: 45 lb. ft. (6.22 kg. m.)
> Front shock absorber to cross-member bolt: 44 lb. ft. (6.08 kg. m.)
> Cross-member to side member nut:
>> Top: 55 lb. ft. (7.60 kg. m.)
>> Bottom: 45 lb. ft. (6.22 kg. m.)

Steering
> Rack to tie-rod ball joint nut: 35 lb. ft. (4.84 kg. m.)

Road Wheels
> Stud nut: 60 lb. ft. (8.30 kg. m.)

MG RV8

General
> For unspecified nuts and bolts:
>> M5: 4 Nm
>> M6: 6 Nm
>> M8: 18 Nm
>> M10: 35 Nm

M12: 65 Nm
M14: 80 Nm
M16: 130 Nm
1/4 UNC/UNF: 8 Nm/10 Nm
5/16 UNC and UNF: 25 Nm
3/8 UNC and UNF: 40 Nm
7/16 UNC and UNF: 75 Nm
1/2 UNC and UNF: 90 Nm
5/8 UNC and UNF: 135 Nm

Engine
Rocker cover bolts: 7 Nm
Rocker shaft to cylinder head bolts: 38 Nm
Spark plug: 15 Nm
Cylinder head bolts: *
    Outer row: 60 Nm
    Centre row: 90 Nm
    Inner row: 90 Nm
Oil sump drain plug: 45 Nm
* Coat first three threads with thread locking compound

Manifold and Exhausts
Exhaust manifold to cylinder head bolts: 40 Nm
Exhaust front pipe to manifold bolts: 45 Nm
Exhaust pipe nuts: 35 Nm
Inlet manifolds gasket clamp bolt: 15 Nm
Inlet manifolds to cylinder head bolts: 35 Nm
Ram housing to inlet manifold bolts: 20 Nm

Manual Gearbox
Gearbox drain plug: 40 Nm
Gearbox filler level plug: 45 Nm
Gearbox crossmember to body bolts: 40 Nm

Rear Axle
Filler/level plug: 15 Nm
Drain plug: 30 Nm
Differential cover bolts: 28 Nm
Cross-member to body nuts: 75 Nm

Steering
Track rod end ball joint to steering arm nut: 35 Nm
Track rod end ball joint to track rod locknut: 55 Nm
Steering rack to crossmember bolts: 25 Nm

Front Suspension
Spring pan to wishbone bolts: 30 Nm
Lower arm pivot shaft nut: 65 Nm
Pivot shaft to crossmember: 45 Nm
Road wheel nuts: 70 Nm
Damper to top fixing assembly locknut: 40 Nm (Locknut should be flush with top of piston rod thread.)
Crossmember to body nuts: 75 Nm

Rear Suspension
Anti-roll bar clamp bolts: 45 Nm
Anti-roll bar link to axle bracket bolts:
    3/8 UNF: 40 Nm
    M10: 45 Nm
Anti-roll bar line to bar: 45 Nm
Damper mounting bracket to body bolts: 75 Nm
Damper to upper and lower mounting brackets: 75 Nm
Spring to hanger bracket bolt: 75 Nm
Spring to hanger body bolt: 75 Nm
Spring shackle to body bolt: 40 Nm
Spring shackle to spring bolt: 40 Nm
Torque control arm to spring hanger bolt: 75 Nm
Torque control arm to axle bracket nut: 75 Nm
Road wheel nuts: 70 Nm
Spring to axle 'U' bolt nuts: 40 Nm

Brakes
Rear wheel cylinder bleed nipple - 6 Nm
Brake drum retaining screw - 4 Nm

Electrical
Alternator pivot, link bolts: 25 Nm
Drive belt tensioner bolt: 45 Nm

REPLACEMENT BULBS

Early MGBs
50/40 watts: Head light, L.H.D. (except North America & Europe)
45/45 watts: Head lights (Europe except France)
45/40 watts: Head light (France only)
6 watts: Side light
21 watts: Direction indicator, front
21 watts: Direction indicator, rear
21/6 watts: Stop and tail lights
6 watts: Number plate illumination light
2.2 watts: Panel and warning lights
21 watts: Reverse light

Late Chrome Bumper MGBs
5 watts: Pilot lights (capless-type bulbs)
5/21 watts: Tail and stop lights
18 watts: Reverse lights
21 watts: Direction indicators
2 watts: Warning lights - fascia
2.2 watts: Warning light - heated rear window
2.2 watts: Instrument illumination
2.2 watts: Cigarette lighter illumination
6 watts: Courtesy light
6 watts: Interior light
6 watts: Number-plate lights

MGC
45/40 watts: Head lights (L.H.D. Europe - except France - dip vertical
45/40 watts: Head lights (L.H.D. France - dip vertical - yellow)
50/40 watts: Head lights (L.H.D. - except Europe - dip vertical)
6 watts: Side lights
6/21 watts: Stop and tail lights
21 watts - Direction indicator lights
21 watts: Reverse light
6 watts: Number-plate illumination light
2.2 watts: Map light
6 watts: Selector lever illumination light
2.2 watts: Panel and warning lights
6 watts: Interior light

MGB GT V8
5 watts: Side lights
5/21 watts: Tail and stop lights
18 watts: Reverse lights
21 watts: Direction indicators
2 watts: Warning lights - fascia
2.2 watts: Warning light - heated rear window
2.2 watts: Instrument illumination
2.2 watts: Cigarette lighter illumination
6 watts: Courtesy light
6 watts: Interior light
5 watts: Number-plate lights: early cars
4 watts: Number-plate lights: later cars
75/50 watts: Head lights (sealed beam unit)

MG RV8
60/55 watts: Head light - dip/main
5 watts: Side light
21 watts: Direction indicators
5 watts: Side repeater lights
55 watts: Front fog light
21/5 watts: Brake - tail light
21 watts: Reversing light
21 watts: Fog guard light
5 watts: Number-plate light
5 watts: Glovebox light
5 watts: Interior light
10 watts: Luggage compartment light

CHAPTER 9 - TOOLS AND EQUIPMENT

Basic maintenance on any MGB can be carried out using a fairly simple, relatively inexpensive tool kit. There is no need to spend a fortune all at once - most owners who do their own servicing acquire their implements over a long period of time. However, there are some items you simply cannot do without in order properly to carry out the work necessary to keep your MG on the road. Therefore, in the following lists, we have concentrated on those items which are likely to be valuable aids to maintaining your car in a good state of tune, and to keep it running sweetly and safely and in addition we have featured some of the tools that are 'nice-to-have' rather than 'must have' because as your tool chest grows, there are some tools that help to make servicing just that bit easier and more thorough to carry out.

One vital point - always buy the best quality tools you can afford. 'Cheap and cheerful' items may look similar to more expensive implements, but experience shows that they often fail when the going gets tough, and some can even be dangerous. With proper care, good quality tools will last a lifetime, and can be regarded as an investment. The extra outlay is well worth it, in the long run.

The following lists are shown under headings indicating the type of use applicable to each group of tools and equipment.

LIFTING:

It is inevitable that you will need to raise the car from the ground in order to gain access to the underside of it.

SAFETY FIRST! There are, of course, important safety implications when working underneath any vehicle. Sadly, many d-i-y enthusiasts have been killed or seriously injured when maintaining their automotive pride and joy, usually for the want of a few moments' thought. So - THINK SAFETY! In particular, NEVER venture beneath any vehicle supported only by a jack - of ANY type. A jack is ONLY intended to be a means of lifting a vehicle, NOT for holding it 'airborne' while being worked on.

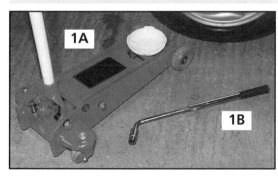

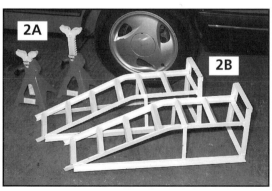

We strongly recommend that you invest in a good quality trolley jack, such as the Kamasa 2¼ ton unit shown here (1A) while alongside is an excellent 'nice-to-have' extendable wheel nut spanner from the same company (1B). This is also ideal for carrying in the car in case of punctures. If you've ever tried removing a wheel nut tightened by a garage gorilla, you know why this tool is so good!

Having raised the vehicle from the floor, always support it under a sound section of the 'chassis', or, if working at the rear of the car, beneath the rear axle. Use only proper axle stands (2A), intended for the purpose, with solid wooden blocks on top, if necessary, to spread the load. These Kamasa stands are exceptionally strong and are very rapidly adjusted, using the built-in ratchet stops. Screw-type stands have an infinite amount of adjustments but are fiddly and time-consuming to use. *NEVER, NEVER* use bricks to support a car - they can crumble without warning, with horrifying results. Always chock all wheels not in the air, to prevent the car from rolling.

Frankly, if you don't need to remove the road wheels for a particular job, the use of car ramps (2B), which are generally more stable than axle stands - is preferable, in order to gain the necessary working height. However, even then there are dangers. Ensure that the car is 'square' to the ramps before attempting to drive up onto them, and preferably place the ramps on two long lengths of old carpet, extending towards the vehicle. The carpet should help prevent the ramps from sliding as the wheels mount them. If you have an assistant guiding you onto the ramps, be absolutely sure that he/she is well out of the way as you

---

**Thanks are due to Kamasa Tools for their kind assistance with this chapter.
Almost all of the tools shown here and in Chapter 3 were kindly supplied by them.**

drive forwards. **NEVER** allow anyone to stand in front of the car, or immediately beside it - the ramps could tip. Be very careful, too, not to 'overshoot' the ramps. When the car is safely positioned on the ramps, fully apply the handbrake, and firmly chock the pair of wheels still on the ground. See Introduction to Chapter 3.

In conclusion, here's a few more words on using and choosing jacks and supports.

JACKS: Manufacturer's jack - for emergency wheel changing ONLY - NOT to be used when working on the vehicle.

'Bottle' jack - screw or hydraulic types - can be used as a means of lifting the car, in conjunction with axle stands to hold it clear of the ground. Ensure that the jack you buy is low enough to pass beneath the 'chassis' of your MG.

Trolley jack - extremely useful as it is so easily manoeuvrable. Again, use only for lifting the vehicle, in conjunction with axle stands to support it clear of the ground. Ensure that the lifting head of the jack will pass beneath the lowest points on the 'chassis' of your MG. Aim for the highest quality jack you can afford. Cheap types seldom last long, and can be **VERY** dangerous (suddenly allowing a car to drop to ground level, without warning, for example).

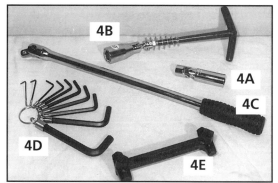

AXLE STANDS: Available in a range of sizes. Ensure that those you buy are sturdy, with a good wide base, and with a useful range of height adjustment.

CAR RAMPS: Available in several heights - high ones are easier for working beneath the car, but too steep a ramp angle can cause problems with the low build of the MGB (the front/rear valances can catch on the ramps as you drive on/off) - bear this in mind when buying.

The ultimate ramps are the 'wind-up' variety - easy to drive onto at their lowest height setting, then raised by means of screw threads to a convenient working height.

SPANNERS:

Inside Information: Most fasteners on the MGB have UNF (Unified National Fine) threads, compatible with AF (American Fine) or SAE threads. Some have UNC (Unified National Coarse) threads, and a very few use the BSF or BSW (British Standard Fine, and British Standard Whitworth - coarse, respectively. BA (British Association) screws are also employed, as are BSP (British Standard Pipe) threads, in the fuel, lubrication and cooling systems. Metric threads were used on Lucas electrical components from 1969, and on many of the fasteners used on the MG RV8. Therefore, for most jobs, spanners in 'AF' sizes, measured across the flats of the spanner in fractions of an inch, will be required, with some items requiring the use of implements designed for the other systems mentioned above.

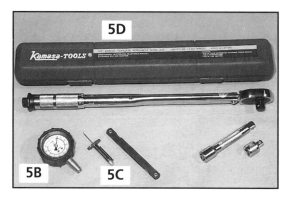

This Kamasa spanner set (3A) is very unusual in that it includes the more unusual types of spanner size in the same set. There are also 'stubby' ratchet handles available (3B) for that cramped engine bay!

Note - in every case, ring spanners provide a more positive grip on a nut/bolt head than open-ended types, which can spread and/or slip when used on tight fasteners. Similarly, 'impact' type socket spanners with hexagonal apertures give better grip on a tight fastener than the normal 12 point 'bi-hex' variety.

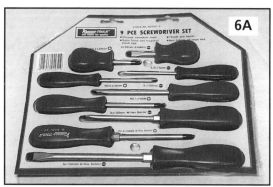

Open-ended spanners - set(s) covering the range ⅜ to 15⁄16in AF.

Ring spanners - set(s) covering the range ⅜ to 15⁄16in AF (alternatively, combination spanner set(s) (with one ring end, and one 'open' end of the same AF size, for each spanner) covering the same range.

Socket spanners - ⅜in and ½in square drive, covering the same range.

A long extension bar is a typical 'nice-to-have' tool. (4C)

Adjustable spanner - nine inch, to start off with. (8F)

Allen key set. (4D)

Spark plug spanner, with rubber 'plug grip' insert either for use with the ratchet set (3A) or the harder to use T-bar type. (4B)

Rear axle drain plug spanner. 4E)

Brake adjuster spanner.

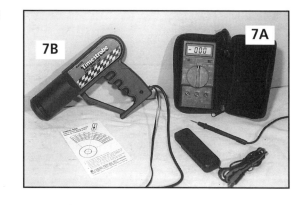

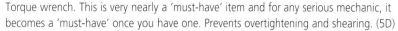

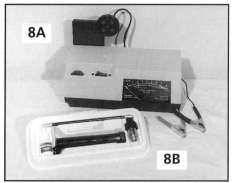

Torque wrench. This is very nearly a 'must-have' item and for any serious mechanic, it becomes a 'must-have' once you have one. Prevents overtightening and shearing. (5D)

SCREWDRIVERS:

General-purpose set of cross-head variety and flat-bladed variety. (All available in various-sized sets.) (6A)

Impact driver (useful for releasing seized screws in brake drums, etc.). (12A)

'TUNING' AIDS:

Depending on how much of the servicing you want to carry out yourself, you'll need all of these - see **Chapter 3, Service Intervals Step-by-Step** for information on how to use them. The more expensive can be purchased gradually, as you save more money by doing your own servicing!

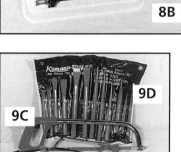

Compression gauge, preferably screw-in, rather than 'push-in' variety.

Set of feeler gauges.

'Automatic' valve clearance adjuster (can help to correctly set valve clearances when rockers have worn pads).

Spark plug adjuster tool. (Although many people lever the spark-plug electrode with a screwdriver, it's best gripped and bent with pliers if you don't have an adjuster.)

Dwell meter/multi-meter (preferably with built-in tachometer). (7A)

Xenon stroboscopic timing light (neon types can be used, but the orange light produced is less bright than the white light produced by the xenon lamps, so that the timing marks are correspondingly less easy to see). This is one of several from the highly regarded Gunson range. 7B)

Carburettor balancing/adjusting tool.

Simple CO meter. Gunson have now introduced an accurate exhaust gas analyser that is expensive but affordable. (8A)

Colortune. This enables you to see the spark - which changes colour as you adjust the carburettor and to set the carburation accordingly. (8B)

SUNDRY ITEMS:

Tool box - steel types are sturdiest..

Extension lead.

Small/medium ball pein hammer. This one is part of the huge Kamasa range. (9A).

Soft-faced hammer (available here, from Kamasa Tools, as a set). (9B)

Special, brass bristle wire brush for cleaning spark plugs. (10A)

12 volt test lamp (can be made using 12 volt bulb, bulb holder, two short lengths of cable and two small crocodile clips).

Copper-based anti-seize compound - useful during assembly of threaded components, including spark plugs, to make future dismantling easier!

Grease gun.

Oil can (with 15W/50 multigrade oil, for general purpose lubrication).

Water dispellant 'electrical' aerosol spray.

Pair of pliers ('standard' jaw). (11A)

Pair of 'long-nosed' pliers. (11B)

Pair of 'side cutters'. (11C)

Kamasa also sell pliers in sets, as this shoal indicates. (11D)

Self-grip wrench or -preferably - set of three. (11E)

Junior hacksaw. (9C)

Oil filter removal tool.

Stud removing tools. A 'nice-to-have' when studs shear and all else fails. (12B)

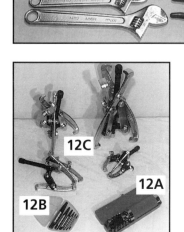

Tyre pump.

Tyre tread depth gauge. (5B)

Tyre pressure gauge. (5C)

Drifts - a set is an extremely useful 'nice-to-have'. (9D)

Hub pullers, useful when you go beyond the straightforward servicing stage. (12C)

Electric drill. Not a servicing tool as such but a 'must-have' nevertheless. The Kamasa rechargeable drill (13A) is superb, enabling you to reach tight spots without trailing leads - and much safer out of doors. Recommended!

APPENDIX 1 – RECOMMENDED CASTROL LUBRICANTS
for MGB, MGC and MGB GT V8

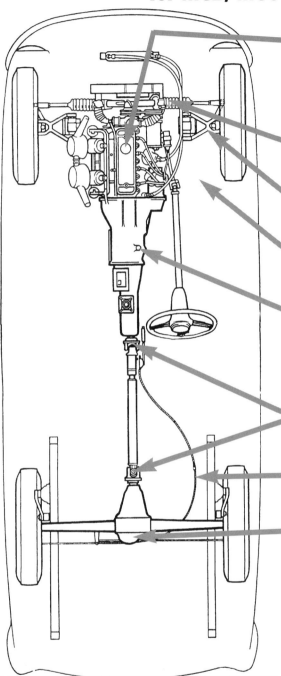

1 Engine
See Jobs 36 to 39
Castrol GTX

Overseas For territories with regular air temperatures below 5°C, there are various grades of Castrol lubricants available. Consult your local supplier.

2 Steering Rack
See Jobs 34, 131 and 168
Castrol EPX 80W/90

3 Front Suspension
See Job 44
Castrol LM Grease (High Melting Point)

4 Brake and Clutch Fluid
See Jobs 2, 3 and 158
Castrol Universal Brake & Clutch Fluid

5 Gearbox and overdrive
See Jobs 72 and 153
Castrol GTX, or for auto transmission, TQF

Overseas For territories with regular air temperatures below 5°C, there are various grades of Castrol lubricants available. Consult your local supplier.

6 Universal Joints *(where applicable)*
See Job 91
Castrol LM Grease (High Melting Point)

7 Handbrake cable
See Job 90
Castrol LM Grease (High Melting Point)

8 Rear Axle
See Jobs 92 and 159
Castrol EPX 80W/90
Overseas For territories with regular air temperatures below 5°C, there are various grades of Castrol lubricants available. Consult your local supplier.

9 Brake Mechanism - areas of metal-to-metal contact
See Jobs 43 and 136
Proprietary brand of high melting point brake grease such as Castrol PH Grease – not conventional high point melting grease

10 General
Castrol Flick Easing Oil (aerosol)
Castrol Everyman Oil (in a can)

Issued by:
Castrol (UK) Limited,
Burmah Castrol House,
Pipers Way, Swindon SN3 1RE

CASTROL GRADES recommended for MGB RV8

Engine	**Castrol Formula RS or Castrol GTX3 Lightec**
Power Steering	**Castrol TQ Dexron RIIE**
Gearbox	**Castrol TQ Dexron RIIE**
Rear Axle	**Castrol EPX 80W/90**
Brake Fluid	**Castrol Universal Brake & Clutch Fluid**
Wheel Bearings	**Castrol LM Grease**

APPENDIX 2
AMERICAN AND BRITISH TERMS

It was Mark Twain who described the British and the Americans as, "two nations divided by a common language". such cynicism has no place here but we do acknowledge that our common language evolves in different directions. We hope that this glossary of terms, commonly encountered when servicing your car, will be of assistance to American owners and, in some cases, English speaking owners in other parts of the world, too.

American	British
Antenna	Antenna
Axleshaft	Halfshaft
Back-up	Reverse
Carburetor	Carburettor
Cotter pin	Split pin
Damper	Shock absorber
DC Generator	Dynamo
Defog	Demist
Drive line	Transmission
Driveshaft	Propeller shaft
Fender	Wing or mudguard
Firewall	Bulkhead
First gear	Bottom gear
Float bowl	Float chamber
Freeway, turnpike	Motorway
Frozen	Seized
Gas tank	Petrol tank
Gas pedal	Accelerator or throttle pedal
Gasoline, Gas or Fuel	Petrol or fuel
Ground (electricity)	Earth
Hard top	Fast back
Header	Exhaust manifold
Headlight dimmer	Headlamp dipswitch
High gear	Top gear
Hood	Bonnet
Industrial Alcohol or Denatured Alcohol	Methylated spirit
Kerosene	Paraffin
Lash	Free-play
License plate	Number plate
Lug nut	Wheel nut
Mineral spirit	White spirit
Muffler	Silencer
Oil pan	Sump
Panel wagon/van	Van
Parking light	Side light
Parking brake	Hand brake
'Pinging'	'Pinking'
Quarter window	Quarterlight
Recap (tire)	Remould or retread
Rocker panel	Sill panel

American	British
Rotor or disk (brake)	Disc
Sedan	Saloon
Sheet metal	Bodywork
Shift lever	Gear lever
Side marker lights, side turn signal or position indicator	Side indicator lights
Soft-top	Hood
Spindle arm	Steering arm
Stabiliser or sway bar	Anti-roll bar
Throw-out bearing	Release or thrust bearing
Tie-rod (or connecting rod)	Track rod (or steering)
Tire	Tyre
Transmission	Drive line
Trouble shooting	Fault finding/diagnosis
Trunk	Boot
Turn signal	Indicator
Valve lifter	Tappet
Valve cover	Rocker cover
Valve lifter or tappet	Cam follower or tappet
Vise	Vice
Windshield	Windscreen
Wrench	Spanner

Useful conversions:

	Multiply by
US gallons to Litres	3.785
Litres to US gallons	0.2642
UK gallons to US gallons	1.20095
US gallons to UK gallons	0.832674

Fahrenheit to Celsius (Centigrade) -
Subtract 32, multiply by 0.5555

Celsius to Fahrenheit -
Multiply by 1.8, add 32

APPENDIX 3
SPECIALISTS AND SUPPLIERS

All of the products and specialists listed below have contributed in various ways to this book. All of the consumer products used are available through regular high street outlets.

Autoline (Dinitrol)
Eagle House, Redstone Industrial Estate, Boston, Lincs, PE21 8EA.
Tel: 0205 354500
Rust prevention treatment of various grades.

Automotive Chemicals Ltd,
Bevis Green Works, Wallmersley, Bury, Lancs, BL9 8RE.
Tel: 061 797 5899
Aerosol spray paint.

Automotive Products,
Tachbrook Road, Leamington Spa, Warwicks, CV31 3ER.
Tel: 0926 472251
Manufacturers of AP Lockheed 'original equipment' brakes.

Bromsgrove MG Centre
Unit 10, Sugarbrook Road, Aston Fields Industrial Estate, Bromsgrove, B61 3DW.
Tel: 0529 879909
MGB, C and V8 servicing, spares and repair for callers and mail order.

Castrol (UK) Ltd
Burmah House, Pipers Way, Swindon, Wiltshire, SN3 1RE
Tel: 0793 452222
Contact Castrol's Consumer Technical Department Help Line on the above number for assistance with lubrication recommendations.

Gunson Ltd
Pudding Mill Lane, Stratford, London, E15 2PJ
Tel: 081 555 7421
Electrical and electronic engine tuning equipment.

Kamasa Tools
Saxon Industries, Lower Everland Road, Hungerford, Berkshire, RG17 0DX
Wide range of hand and power tools, used throughout this book.

MG Car Club
Kimber House, PO Box 251, Abingdon, Oxon, OX14 1FF.
Tel: 0235 555552
The oldest MG car club and excellent for motor sport.

MG Owners Club
Octagon House, 2-4 Station Road, Swavesey, Cambridge, CB4 5QZ.
Tel: 0954 231125
The largest car club in the world. Monthly magazine. Excellent for MGB owners.

NGK Spark Plugs (UK) Ltd
7-8-9 Garrick Industrial Centre, Hendon, London, NW9 6AQ
Tel: 081 202 2151
Top quality spark plugs.

Partco
See *Yellow Pages* for your local Partco centre (look under Motor Factors).
Suppliers of most types of consumable and regular service items used in automotive repair.

SP Tyres UK Ltd
Fort Dunlop, Birmingham, B24 9QT.
Tel: 021 384 4444
Manufacturers of Dunlop tyres in both modern and 'period' patterns.

W David & Sons Ltd (Isopon)
Ridgemount House, 1 Totteridge Lane, Whetstone, London, N20 0EY.
Tel: 081 445 0372
Manufacturers of Isopon filler and ancillaries - top quality products.

APPENDIX 4
SERVICE HISTORY

This Chapter helps you keep track of all the servicing carried out on your car and can even save you money! A car with a 'service history' is always worth more than one without. Although this book's main purpose is to give invaluable advice to anyone carrying out his or her own servicing, you could make full use of this section, even if you have a garage or mechanic carry out the work for you. It enables you to specify the jobs you want to have carried out to your car and, once again, it enables you to keep that all-important service history. And even if your car doesn't have a 'history' going back to when it was new, keeping this Chapter complete will add to your car's value when you come to sell it. Mind you, it obviously won't be enough to just to tick the boxes: keep all your receipts when you buy oil, filters and other consumables or parts. That way, you'll also be able to return any faulty parts if needs be.

IMPORTANT NOTE! The Service Jobs listed here are intended as a check list and a means of keeping a record of your car's service history. It is most important that you refer to *Chapter 3, Service Intervals, Step-by-Step* for full details of how to carry out each Job listed here and for essential SAFETY information, all of which will be essential when you come to carry out the work.

Before carrying out a service on your car, you will need to purchase the right parts. Please refer to *Chapter 2, Buying Spares* for information on how to buy the right parts at the right prices and for information on how to find your car's model type, 'identity numbers', and so on: information that you will need in order to buy the right parts, first time!

Wherever possible, the Jobs listed in this section have been placed in a logical order or placed into groups that will help you make progress on the car. We have tried to save you too much in the way of unnecessary movement by grouping Jobs around areas of the car and also - most important, this! - into groups of jobs that apply when the car is on the ground, when the front or rear of the car is off the ground, and so on. Therefore, at each Service Interval, you will see the work grouped into Jobs that need carrying out in the engine bay, around the car or under the car and another division into Bodywork and Interior Jobs, and Mechanical and Electrical Jobs.

You'll also see space at each Service Interval for you to write down the date, price and seller's name every time you buy consumables or accessories. And once again, do remember to keep your receipts! There's also space for you to date and sign the Service Record or for a garage's stamp to be applied.

As you move through the Service Intervals, you will notice that the work carried out at, say, 1,500 Miles or Every Month, whichever comes first, is repeated at each one of the following Service Intervals. The same applies to the 6,000 Miles or Every Six Months interval: much of it is repeated at 12,000 Miles or Every Twelve Months. Every time a Job or set of Jobs is 'repeated' from an earlier Interval, we show it in a tinted area on the page. You can then see more clearly which Jobs are unique to the level of Service Interval that you are on. And you may be surprised to find that all the major Service Intervals, right up to 36,000 Miles or Every Thirty Six Months contain Jobs that are unique to that Service Interval. That's why we have continued this Service History right up to the Thirty Six Month Interval. There are sufficient Service History sheets for you to keep a record of your car's servicing for three years, and when that is full, you can purchase a set of continuation sheets from Porter Publishing at the address and telephone number shown at the end of this Chapter. If you keep your car and wish to continue your service record, you will be able to start the three year sequence all over again, in the knowledge that your car has been serviced as well as anyone could wish for!

SERVICE HISTORY

500 MILES, WEEKLY OR BEFORE A LONG JOURNEY

This list is shown, complete, only once. It would have been a bit much to have provided the list 52 times over for use once a week throughout the year! They are, however, included with every longer Service list from 3,000 miles/Three Months-on so that each of the 'weekly' Jobs is carried out as part of every Service.

500 miles Mechanical and Electrical - The Engine Bay

- [ ] Job 1. Engine oil level
- [ ] Job 2. Clutch fluid level
- [ ] Job 3. Brake fluid level
- [ ] Job 4. Battery electrolyte
- [ ] Job 5. Washer reservoir
- [ ] Job 6. Coolant system

500 miles Mechanical and Electrical - Around the Car

- [ ] Job 7. Check horns
- [ ] Job 8. Windscreen washers
- [ ] Job 9. Windscreen wipers
- [ ] Job 10. Tyre pressures
- [ ] Job 11. Check headlamps
- [ ] Job 12. Check front sidelamps
- [ ] Job 13. Check rear sidelamps
- [ ] Job 14. Number plate lamps
- [ ] Job 15. Reversing lamps
- [ ] Job 16. Check wheel spinners

500 miles Bodywork and Interior - Around the Car

- [ ] Job 17. Valet bodywork

1,500 MILES - OR EVERY MONTH, whichever comes first

These jobs are similar to the 500 Mile jobs but don't need carrying out quite so regularly. Once again, these Jobs are not shown with a separate listing for each 1,500 miles/1 Month interval but they are included as part of every 3,000 miles/Three Month Service list and for every longer Service interval.

1,500 miles Mechanical and Electrical - Around the Car

- [ ] Job 18. Check tyres
- [ ] Job 19. Check spare tyre

1,500 miles Bodywork and Interior - Around the Car

- [ ] Job 20. Touch-up paintwork
- [ ] Job 21. Aerial/antenna
- [ ] Job 22. Valet interior
- [ ] Job 23. Improve visibility!

1,500 miles Bodywork - Under the Car

- [ ] Job 24. Clean mud traps

Date serviced: ....

Carried out by: ....

Garage stamp or signature:

Parts/Accessories Purchased (Date, Parts, Source)..
....
....
....
....
....
....
....

3,000 MILES - OR EVERY THREE MONTHS, whichever comes first

All the Service Jobs in the tinted area have been carried forward from earlier service intervals and are to be repeated at this Service.

3,000 miles Mechanical and Electrical - The Engine Bay

First carry out all Jobs listed under earlier Service Intervals.

- [ ] Job 2. Clutch fluid level
- [ ] Job 3. Brake fluid level
- [ ] Job 4. Battery electrolyte
- [ ] Job 5. Washer reservoir
- [ ] Job 6. Coolant system

- [ ] Job 25. Adjust spark plugs
- [ ] Job 26. Check HT circuit
- [ ] Job 27. Distributor
- [ ] Job 28. Generator belt
- [ ] Job 29. **OPTIONAL** SU carburettors
- [ ] Job 30. Check air filters
- [ ] Job 31. **MG RV8, US AND EXPORT CARS ONLY** Check drive belts
- [ ] Job 32. Pipes and hoses

3,000 miles Mechanical and Electrical - Around the Car

First, carry out all Jobs listed under earlier Service Intervals

- [ ] Job 7. Check horns
- [ ] Job 8. Windscreen washers
- [ ] Job 9. Windscreen wipers
- [ ] Job 10. Tyre pressures
- [ ] Job 11. Check headlamps
- [ ] Job 12. Check front sidelamps
- [ ] Job 13. Check rear sidelamps
- [ ] Job 14. Number plate lamps
- [ ] Job 15. Reversing lamps

Job 16. Check wheel spinners

Job 18. Check tyres

Job 19. Check spare tyre

Job 33. Hand brake travel

3,000 miles Mechanical and Electrical - Under the Car

Job 34. Steering rack

Job 35. Track rod ends

Optional - Carry out Job 1

Job 1. Engine oil level

or

Job 36. Drain engine oil

Job 37. Remove oil filter

Job 38. New oil filter

Job 39. Pour fresh oil

Job 40. **AUTOMATICS ONLY**
Auto-box park lock

Job 41. Check oil level

Job 42. Check for oil leaks

Job 43. Check brake pads

Job 44. **MGB AND MGC ONLY**
Lube front suspension

Job 45. **MGB ONLY**
Adjust rear brakes

3,000 miles Mechanical and Electrical - Road Test

Job 46. Clean controls

Job 47. Check instruments

Job 48. Throttle pedal

Job 49. Hand brake function

Job 50. Brakes and steering

3,000 miles Bodywork and Interior - Around the Car

First carry out all Jobs listed under earlier Service Intervals.

Job 17. Valet bodywork

Job 20. Touch-up paintwork

Job 21. Aerial/antenna

Job 22. Valet interior

Job 23. Improve visibility!

Job 51. Wiper blades and arms

Job 52. Check windscreen

Job 53. Rear view mirrors

Job 54. Check floors

Job 55. Chrome trim and badges

3,000 miles Bodywork - Under The Car

First carry out all Jobs listed under earlier Service Intervals.

Job 24. Clean mud traps.

Job 56. Inspect underside

Date serviced: ....

Carried out by: ....

Garage stamp or signature:

Parts/Accessories Purchased (Date, Parts, Source) ....

....

....

....

....

....

....

....

....

....

....

....

....

6,000 MILES - OR EVERY SIX MONTHS, whichever comes first

All the Service Jobs in the tinted area have been carried forward from earlier service intervals and are to be repeated at this Service.

6,000 miles Mechanical and Electrical - The Engine Bay

First carry out all Jobs listed under earlier Service Intervals.

Job 2. Clutch fluid level

Job 3. Brake fluid level

Job 4. Battery electrolyte

Job 5. Washer reservoir

Job 6. Coolant system

Job 26. Check HT circuit

Job 28. Generator belt

Job 30. Check air filters

Job 31. **MG RV8, US AND EXPORT CARS ONLY**
Check drive belts

Job 32. Pipes and hoses

Job 57. Cooling system

Job 58. Coolant check

Job 59. Heater valve

Job 60. Check water pump

Job 61. Battery terminals

Job 62. Accelerator controls

Job 63. Dynamo bearings

Job 64. Fit new spark plugs

Job 65. Renew cb points

Job 66. Ignition timing

Job 67. Fit fuel filter

Job 68. Fuel connections

Job 69. Top-up dashpots

Job 70. Set carburettors

Job 71. **SPECIALIST SERVICE**
Exhaust emissions

6,000 miles Mechanical and Electrical - Around the Car

First, carry out all Jobs listed under earlier Service Intervals.

- Job 7. Check horns
- Job 8. Windscreen washers
- Job 9. Windscreen wipers
- Job 10. Tyre pressures
- Job 11. Check headlamps
- Job 12. Check front sidelamps
- Job 13. Check rear sidelamps
- Job 14. Number plate lamps
- Job 15. Reversing lamps
- Job 16. Check wheel spinners
- Job 18. Check tyres
- Job 19. Check spare tyre
- Job 33. Handbrake travel

- Job 72. Top-up gearbox oil
- Job 73. **SPECIALIST SERVICE** Adjust headlamps
- Job 74. Fuel filler pipe
- Job 75. **SPECIALIST SERVICE** Front wheel alignment
- Job 76. Rear ride height
- Job 77. Front ride height
- Job 78. Check tyre clearance
- Job 79. Check wheel nuts

6,000 miles Mechanical and Electrical - Under the Car

First carry out all Jobs listed under earlier Service Intervals.

- Job 34. Steering rack
- Job 35. Track rod ends
- Job 36. Drain engine oil
- Job 37. Remove oil filter
- Job 38. New oil filter
- Job 39. Pour fresh oil
- Job 40. **AUTOMATICS ONLY** Auto.-box park lock
- Job 41. Check oil level
- Job 42. Check for oil leaks

- Job 43. Check brake pads
- Job 44. **MGB AND MGC ONLY** Lube Front suspension
- Job 45. **MGB ONLY** Adjust rear brakes

- Job 80. Front fuel lines
- Job 81. Front brake lines
- Job 82. Brake pedal adjust
- Job 83. Exhaust manifold
- Job 84. Front dampers
- Job 85. Clutch hydraulics
- Job 86. Rear brake lines
- Job 87. Rear fuel lines
- Job 88. Exhaust system
- Job 89. Rear dampers
- Job 90. Hand brake mechanism
- Job 91. Universal joints
- Job 92. Rear axle oil
- Job 93. Rear springs

6,000 miles Mechanical and Electrical - Road Test

- Job 46. Clean controls
- Job 47. Check instruments
- Job 48. Throttle pedal
- Job 49. Hand brake function
- Job 50. Brakes and steering

6,000 miles Bodywork and Interior - Around the Car

First carry out all Jobs listed under earlier Service Intervals.

- Job 17. Valet bodywork
- Job 20. Touch-up paintwork
- Job 21. Aerial/antenna
- Job 22. Valet interior
- Job 23. Improve visibility!
- Job 51. Wiper blades and arms
- Job 52. Check windscreen
- Job 53. Rear view mirrors
- Job 54. Check floors
- Job 55. Chrome trim and badges

- Job 94. Bonnet release
- Job 95. Door locks
- Job 96. Boot lock
- Job 97. Seats and seat belts

6,000 miles Bodywork - Under the Car

First carry out all Jobs listed under earlier Service Intervals.

- Job 24. Clean mud traps

- Job 56. Inspect underside
- Job 98. Rustproof underbody

Be sure to carry out Job 99 after Job 98.

- Job 99. Clear drain holes

Date serviced: ....

Carried out by: ....

Garage stamp or signature:

Parts/Accessories Purchased (Date, Parts, Source) ....

....
....
....
....
....
....
....
....
....
....
....
....
....
....

9,000 MILES - OR EVERY NINE MONTHS, whichever comes first

All the Service Jobs at this Service Interval have been carried forward from earlier service intervals and are to be repeated at this Service.

9,000 miles Mechanical and Electrical - The Engine Bay

- [ ] Job 2. Clutch fluid level
- [ ] Job 3. Brake fluid level
- [ ] Job 4. Battery electrolyte
- [ ] Job 5. Washer reservoir
- [ ] Job 6. Coolant system
- [ ] Job 25. Adjust spark plugs
- [ ] Job 26. Check HT circuit
- [ ] Job 27. Distributor
- [ ] Job 28. Generator belt
- [ ] Job 29. SU carburettors
- [ ] Job 30. Check air filters
- [ ] Job 31. **MG RV8, US AND EXPORT CARS ONLY** Check drive belts
- [ ] Job 32. Pipes and hoses

9,000 miles Mechanical and Electrical - Around the Car

- [ ] Job 7. Check horns
- [ ] Job 8. Windscreen washers
- [ ] Job 9. Windscreen wipers
- [ ] Job 10. Tyre pressures
- [ ] Job 11. Check headlamps
- [ ] Job 12. Check front sidelamps
- [ ] Job 13. Check rear sidelamps
- [ ] Job 14. Number plate lamps
- [ ] Job 15. Reversing lamps
- [ ] Job 16. Check wheel spinners
- [ ] Job 18. Check tyres
- [ ] Job 19. Check spare tyre
- [ ] Job 33. Hand brake travel

9,000 miles Mechanical and Electrical - Under the Car

- [ ] Job 34. Steering rack
- [ ] Job 35. Track rod ends

Optional - Carry out Job 1

- [ ] Job 1. Engine oil level

or

- [ ] Job 36. Drain engine oil
- [ ] Job 37. Remove oil filter
- [ ] Job 38. New oil filter
- [ ] Job 39. Pour fresh oil
- [ ] Job 40. **AUTOMATICS ONLY** Auto.-box park lock
- [ ] Job 41. Check oil level
- [ ] Job 42. Check for oil leaks
- [ ] Job 43. Check brake pads
- [ ] Job 44. **MGB AND MGC ONLY** Lube front suspension
- [ ] Job 45. **MGB ONLY** Adjust rear brakes

9,000 miles Mechanical and Electrical - Road Test

- [ ] Job 46. Clean controls
- [ ] Job 47. Check instruments
- [ ] Job 48. Throttle pedal
- [ ] Job 49. Hand brake function
- [ ] Job 50. Brakes and steering

9,000 miles Bodywork and Interior - Around the Car

- [ ] Job 17. Valet bodywork
- [ ] Job 20. Touch-up paintwork
- [ ] Job 21. Aerial/antenna
- [ ] Job 22. Valet interior
- [ ] Job 23. Improve visibility!
- [ ] Job 51. Wiper blades and arms
- [ ] Job 52. Check windscreen
- [ ] Job 53. Rear view mirrors
- [ ] Job 54. Check floors
- [ ] Job 55. Chrome trim and badges

9,000 miles Bodywork and Interior - Under the Car

- [ ] Job 24. Clean mud traps
- [ ] Job 56. Inspect underside

Date serviced: ....

Carried out by: ....

Garage stamp or signature:

Parts/Accessories Purchased (Date, Parts, Source) ....
....
....
....
....
....
....
....
....
....
....
....
....
....
....

12,000 MILES - OR EVERY TWELVE MONTHS, whichever comes first

All the Service Jobs in the tinted area have been carried forward from earlier service intervals and are to be repeated at this Service.

12,000 miles Mechanical and Electrical - Emission Control Equipment

- [ ] Job 100. **EARLIER CARS**
  Crankcase breather
- [ ] Job 101. Hoses and connectors
- [ ] Job 102. Oil filler cap
- [ ] Job 103. Air valve filter
- [ ] Job 104. **US CARS ONLY**
  Adsorption canister
- [ ] Job 105. **US CARS ONLY**
  Second fuel filter
- [ ] Job 106. **US CARS ONLY**
  Air pump belt
- [ ] Job 107. **US CARS ONLY**
  Air pump filter
- [ ] Job 108. **US CARS ONLY**
  Test check valve
- [ ] Job 109. **US CARS ONLY**
  Fuel filler cap
- [ ] Job 110. **SPECIALIST SERVICE**
  Emission system

12,000 miles Mechanical and Electrical - The Engine Bay

First carry out all jobs listed under earlier Service Intervals.

- [ ] Job 2. Clutch fluid level
- [ ] Job 3. Brake fluid level
- [ ] Job 4. Battery electrolyte
- [ ] Job 5. Washer reservoir
- [ ] Job 6. Coolant system
- [ ] Job 26. Check HT circuit
- [ ] Job 28. Generator belt
- [ ] Job 30. Check air filters
- [ ] Job 32. Pipes and hoses

- [ ] Job 57. Cooling system
- [ ] Job 58. Coolant check
- [ ] Job 59. Heater valve
- [ ] Job 60. Check water pump
- [ ] Job 61. Battery terminals
- [ ] Job 62. Accelerator controls
- [ ] Job 63. Dynamo bearings
- [ ] Job 64. Fit new spark plugs
- [ ] Job 65. Renew cb points
- [ ] Job 66. Ignition timing
- [ ] Job 67. Fit fuel filter
- [ ] Job 68. Fuel connections
- [ ] Job 69. Top-up dashpots
- [ ] Job 70. Set carburettors
- [ ] Job 71. **SPECIALIST SERVICE**
  Exhaust emissions

- [ ] Job 111. **US CARS ONLY**
  Zenith/Stromberg carbs
- [ ] Job 112. **MGB ONLY**
  Check heat shields
- [ ] Job 113. **LATER MODELS ONLY**
  Carb. poppet valves
- [ ] Job 114. **V8 ENGINES ONLY**
  V8 flame traps
- [ ] Job 115. Oil leaks
- [ ] Job 116. Clean radiators
- [ ] Job 117. **EARLY MODELS ONLY**
  Grease water pump
- [ ] Job 118. **MGB ONLY**
  Remote brake servo filter
- [ ] Job 119. **MGB ONLY**
  In-line brake servo filter
- [ ] Job 120. **NOT MGB GT V8 OR MG RV8**
  Valve clearances
- [ ] Job 121. Rocker cover gasket
- [ ] Job 122. Check cylinder compressions
- [ ] Job 123. Exhaust manifold bolts

12,000 miles Mechanical and Electrical - Around the Car

First, carry out all Jobs listed under earlier Service Intervals.

- [ ] Job 7. Check horns

- [ ] Job 8. Windscreen washers
- [ ] Job 9. Windscreen wipers
- [ ] Job 10. Tyre pressures
- [ ] Job 11. Check headlamps
- [ ] Job 12. Check front sidelamps
- [ ] Job 13. Check rear sidelamps
- [ ] Job 14. Number plate lamps
- [ ] Job 15. Reversing lamps
- [ ] Job 16. Check wheel spinners
- [ ] Job 18. Check tyres
- [ ] Job 19. Check spare tyre
- [ ] Job 33. Hand brake travel
- [ ] Job 72. Top-up gearbox oil
- [ ] Job 73. **SPECIALIST SERVICE**
  Adjust headlamps
- [ ] Job 74. Fuel filler pipe
- [ ] Job 75. Front wheel alignment
- [ ] Job 76. Rear ride height
- [ ] Job 77. Front ride height
- [ ] Job 78. Check tyre clearance
- [ ] Job 79. Check wheel nuts

- [ ] Job 124. Test dampers
- [ ] Job 125. Alarm remote units

12,000 miles Mechanical and Electrical - Under the Car

Of all the Service intervals, this is the one that involves most working under the car. For that reason, we have grouped areas of work together so that the work is in logical groups rather than strict numerical order.

FRONT OF CAR

First carry out all Jobs listed under earlier Service Intervals.

- [ ] Job 34. Steering rack
- [ ] Job 35. Track rod ends
- [ ] Job 36. Drain engine oil
- [ ] Job 37. Remove oil filter
- [ ] Job 38. New oil filter
- [ ] Job 39. Pour fresh oil
- [ ] Job 40. **AUTOMATICS ONLY**
  Auto.-box park lock

☐ Job 41. Check oil level

☐ Job 42. Check for oil leaks

☐ Job 43. Check brake pads

☐ Job 44. **MGB AND MGC ONLY**
Lube front suspension

☐ Job 80. Front fuel lines

☐ Job 81. Front brake lines

☐ Job 82. Brake pedal adjust

☐ Job 83. Exhaust manifold

☐ Job 84. Front dampers

☐ Job 85. Clutch hydraulics

☐ Job 126. Wishbone bushes

☐ Job 127. Damper pivots

☐ Job 128. Kingpins

☐ Job 129. Check front hubs

☐ Job 130. Front brake callipers

☐ Job 131. **EARLY CARS ONLY**
Lubricate steering

☐ Job 132. Steering mountings

☐ Job 133. Check free play

☐ Job 134. Check ball joints

☐ Job 135. **MG RV8 ONLY**
Adjust dampers

REAR OF CAR

☐ Job 86. Rear brake lines

☐ Job 87. Rear fuel lines

☐ Job 88. Exhaust system

☐ Job 89. Rear dampers

☐ Job 90. Hand brake mechanism

☐ Job 91. Universal joints

☐ Job 92. Rear axle oil

☐ Job 93. Rear springs

☐ Job 136. Rear brake inspection

☐ Job 137. Rear wheel cylinders

☐ Job 138. 'U'-bolt tightness

☐ Job 139. Top-up dampers

☐ Job 140. Universal joint flanges

12,000 miles Mechanical and Electrical - Road Test

☐ Job 46. Clean controls

☐ Job 47. Check instruments

☐ Job 48. Throttle pedal

☐ Job 49. Hand brake function

☐ Job 50. Brakes and steering

12,000 miles Bodywork and Interior - Around the Car

First carry out all jobs listed under earlier Service Intervals.

☐ Job 17. Valet bodywork

☐ Job 20. Touch-up paintwork

☐ Job 21. Aerial/antenna

☐ Job 22. Valet interior

☐ Job 23. Improve visibility!

☐ Job 51. Wiper blades and arms

☐ Job 52. Check windscreen

☐ Job 53. Rear view mirrors

☐ Job 54. Check floors

☐ Job 55. Chrome trim and badges

☐ Job 94. Bonnet release

☐ Job 95. Door locks

☐ Job 96. Boot lock

☐ Job 97. Seats and seat belts

☐ Job 141. Seat runners

☐ Job 142. Toolkit and jack

☐ Job 143. **WIRE WHEELED CARS ONLY**
Wire wheel splines

☐ Job 144. Wire wheel spokes

12,000 miles Bodywork - Under the Car

First carry out all Jobs listed under earlier Service Intervals.

☐ Job 24. Clean mud traps

☐ Job 56. Inspect underside

☐ Job 145. Top-up rustproofing

Be sure to carry out Job 99 after Job 145.

☐ Job 99. Clear drain holes

Date serviced: ....

Carried out by: ....

Garage stamp or signature:

Parts/Accessories Purchased (Date, Parts, Source) ....

....

....

....

....

....

....

....

....

....

....

....

....

....

15,000 MILES - OR EVERY FIFTEEN MONTHS, whichever comes first

All the Service Jobs at this Service Interval have been carried forward from earlier service intervals and are to be repeated at this Service.

15,000 miles Mechanical and Electrical - The Engine Bay

- [ ] Job 2. Clutch fluid level
- [ ] Job 3. Brake fluid level
- [ ] Job 4. Battery electrolyte
- [ ] Job 5. Washer reservoir
- [ ] Job 6. Coolant system
- [ ] Job 25. Adjust spark plugs
- [ ] Job 26. Check HT circuit
- [ ] Job 27. Distributor
- [ ] Job 28. Generator belt
- [ ] Job 29. SU carburettors
- [ ] Job 30. Check air filters
- [ ] Job 31. **MG RV8, US AND EXPORT CARS ONLY** Check drive belts
- [ ] Job 32. Pipes and hoses

15,000 miles Mechanical and Electrical - Around the Car

- [ ] Job 7. Check horns
- [ ] Job 8. Windscreen washers
- [ ] Job 9. Windscreen wipers
- [ ] Job 10. Tyre pressures
- [ ] Job 11. Check headlamps
- [ ] Job 12. Check front sidelamps
- [ ] Job 13. Check rear sidelamps
- [ ] Job 14. Number plate lamps
- [ ] Job 15. Reversing lamps
- [ ] Job 16. Check wheel spinners
- [ ] Job 18. Check tyres
- [ ] Job 19. Check spare tyre
- [ ] Job 33. Hand brake travel

15,000 miles Mechanical and Electrical - Under the Car

- [ ] Job 34. Steering rack
- [ ] Job 35. Track rod ends

Optional - Carry out Job 1

- [ ] Job 1. Engine oil level

or

- [ ] Job 36. Drain engine oil
- [ ] Job 37. Remove oil filter
- [ ] Job 38. New oil filter
- [ ] Job 39. Pour fresh oil
- [ ] Job 40. **AUTOMATICS ONLY** Auto.-box park lock
- [ ] Job 41. Check oil level
- [ ] Job 42. Check for oil leaks
- [ ] Job 43. Check brake pads
- [ ] Job 44. **MGB AND MGC ONLY** Lube front suspension
- [ ] Job 45. **MGB ONLY** Adjust rear brakes

15,000 miles Mechanical and Electrical - Road Test

- [ ] Job 46. Clean controls
- [ ] Job 47. Check instruments
- [ ] Job 48. Throttle pedal
- [ ] Job 49. Hand brake function
- [ ] Job 50. Brakes and steering

15,000 miles Bodywork and Interior - Around the Car

- [ ] Job 17. Valet bodywork
- [ ] Job 20. Touch-up paintwork
- [ ] Job 21. Aerial/antenna
- [ ] Job 22. Valet interior
- [ ] Job 23. Improve visibility!
- [ ] Job 51. Wiper blades and arms
- [ ] Job 52. Check windscreen
- [ ] Job 53. Rear view mirrors
- [ ] Job 54. Check floors
- [ ] Job 55. Chrome trim and badges

15,000 miles Bodywork and Interior - Under the Car

- [ ] Job 24. Clean mud traps
- [ ] Job 56. Inspect underside

Date serviced: ....

Carried out by: ....

Garage stamp or signature:

Parts/Accessories Purchased (Date, Parts, Source) ....

....
....
....
....
....
....
....
....
....
....
....
....
....
....
....

18,000 MILES - OR EVERY EIGHTEEN MONTHS, whichever comes first

All the Service jobs at this Service Interval have been carried forward from earlier service intervals and are to be repeated at this Service.

18,000 miles Mechanical and Electrical - The Engine Bay

- [ ] Job 2. Clutch fluid level
- [ ] Job 3. Brake fluid level
- [ ] Job 4. Battery electrolyte
- [ ] Job 5. Washer reservoir
- [ ] Job 6. Coolant system
- [ ] Job 26. Check HT circuit
- [ ] Job 28. Generator belt
- [ ] Job 30. Check air filters
- [ ] Job 31. **MG RV8, US & EXPORT CARS ONLY**
      Check drive belts
- [ ] Job 32. Pipes and hoses
- [ ] Job 57. Cooling system
- [ ] Job 58. Coolant check
- [ ] Job 59. Heater valve
- [ ] Job 60. Check water pump
- [ ] Job 61. Battery terminals
- [ ] Job 62. Accelerator controls
- [ ] Job 63. Dynamo bearings
- [ ] Job 64. Fit new spark plugs
- [ ] Job 65. Renew cb points
- [ ] Job 66. Ignition timing
- [ ] Job 67. Fit fuel filter
- [ ] Job 68. Fuel connections
- [ ] Job 69. Top-up dashpots
- [ ] Job 70. Set carburettors
- [ ] Job 71. **SPECIALIST SERVICE**
      Exhaust emissions

18,000 miles Mechanical and Electrical - Around the Car

- [ ] Job 7. Check horns
- [ ] Job 8. Windscreen washers
- [ ] Job 9. Windscreen wipers
- [ ] Job 10. Tyre pressures
- [ ] Job 11. Check headlamps
- [ ] Job 12. Check front sidelamps
- [ ] Job 13. Check rear sidelamps
- [ ] Job 14. Number plate lamps
- [ ] Job 15. Reversing lamps
- [ ] Job 16. Check wheel spinners
- [ ] Job 18. Check tyres
- [ ] Job 19. Check spare tyre
- [ ] Job 33. Handbrake travel
- [ ] Job 72. Top-up gearbox oil
- [ ] Job 73. **SPECIALIST SERVICE**
      Adjust headlamps
- [ ] Job 74. Fuel filler pipe
- [ ] Job 75. **SPECIALIST SERVICE**
      Front wheel alignment
- [ ] Job 76. Rear ride height
- [ ] Job 77. Front ride height
- [ ] Job 78. Check tyre clearance
- [ ] Job 79. Check wheel nuts

18,000 miles Mechanical and Electrical - Under the Car

- [ ] Job 34. Steering rack
- [ ] Job 35. Track rod ends
- [ ] Job 36. Drain engine oil
- [ ] Job 37. Remove oil filter
- [ ] Job 38. New oil filter
- [ ] Job 39. Pour fresh oil
- [ ] Job 40. **AUTOMATICS ONLY**
      Auto.-box park lock
- [ ] Job 41. Check oil level
- [ ] Job 42. Check for oil leaks
- [ ] Job 43. Check brake pads
- [ ] Job 44. **MGB AND MGC ONLY**
      Lube Front suspension

- [ ] Job 45. **MGB ONLY**
      Adjust rear brakes
- [ ] Job 80. Front fuel lines
- [ ] Job 81. Front brake lines
- [ ] Job 82. Brake pedal adjust
- [ ] Job 83. Exhaust manifold
- [ ] Job 84. Front dampers
- [ ] Job 85. Clutch hydraulics
- [ ] Job 86. Rear brake lines
- [ ] Job 87. Rear fuel lines
- [ ] Job 88. Exhaust system
- [ ] Job 89. Rear dampers
- [ ] Job 90. Hand brake mechanism
- [ ] Job 91. Universal joints
- [ ] Job 92. Rear axle oil
- [ ] Job 93. Rear springs

18,000 miles Mechanical and Electrical - Road Test

- [ ] Job 46. Clean controls
- [ ] Job 47. Check instruments
- [ ] Job 48. Throttle pedal
- [ ] Job 49. Hand brake function
- [ ] Job 50. Brakes and steering

18,000 miles Bodywork and Interior - Around the Car

- [ ] Job 17. Valet bodywork
- [ ] Job 20. Touch-up paintwork
- [ ] Job 21. Aerial/antenna
- [ ] Job 22. Valet interior
- [ ] Job 23. Improve visibility!
- [ ] Job 51. Wiper blades and arms
- [ ] Job 52. Check windscreen
- [ ] Job 53. Rear view mirrors
- [ ] Job 54. Check floors
- [ ] Job 55. Chrome trim and badges
- [ ] Job 94. Bonnet release
- [ ] Job 95. Door locks
- [ ] Job 96. Boot lock
- [ ] Job 97. Seats and seat belts

18,000 miles Bodywork - Under the Car

- [ ] Job 24. Clean mud traps
- [ ] Job 56. Inspect underside
- [ ] Job 98. Rustproof underbody

Be sure to carry out Job 99 after Job 98.

- [ ] Job 99. Clear drain holes

Date serviced: ....

Carried out by: ....

Garage stamp or signature:

Parts/Accessories Purchased (Date, Parts, Source) ....

....
....
....
....
....
....
....
....
....
....
....
....
....

21,000 MILES - OR EVERY TWENTY-ONE MONTHS, whichever comes first

All the Service jobs at this Service Interval have been carried forward from earlier service intervals and are to be repeated at this Service.

21,000 miles Mechanical and Electrical - The Engine Bay

- [ ] Job 2. Clutch fluid level
- [ ] Job 3. Brake fluid level
- [ ] Job 4. Battery electrolyte
- [ ] Job 5. Washer reservoir
- [ ] Job 6. Coolant system
- [ ] Job 25. Adjust spark plugs
- [ ] Job 26. Check HT circuit
- [ ] Job 27. Distributor
- [ ] Job 28. Generator belt
- [ ] Job 29. SU carburettors
- [ ] Job 30. Check air filters
- [ ] Job 31. **MG RV8, US AND EXPORT CARS ONLY**
  Check drive belts
- [ ] Job 32. Pipes and hoses

21,000 miles Mechanical and Electrical - Around the Car

- [ ] Job 7. Check horns
- [ ] Job 8. Windscreen washers
- [ ] Job 9. Windscreen wipers
- [ ] Job 10. Tyre pressures
- [ ] Job 11. Check headlamps
- [ ] Job 12. Check front sidelamps
- [ ] Job 13. Check rear sidelamps
- [ ] Job 14. Number plate lamps
- [ ] Job 15. Reversing lamps
- [ ] Job 16. Check wheel spinners
- [ ] Job 18. Check tyres
- [ ] Job 19. Check spare tyre
- [ ] Job 33. Hand brake travel

21,000 miles Mechanical and Electrical - Under the Car

- [ ] Job 34. Steering rack
- [ ] Job 35. Track rod ends

Optional - Carry out Job 1

- [ ] Job 1. Engine oil level

or

- [ ] Job 36. Drain engine oil
- [ ] Job 37. Remove oil filter
- [ ] Job 38. New oil filter
- [ ] Job 39. Pour fresh oil
- [ ] Job 40. **AUTOMATICS ONLY**
  Auto.-box park lock
- [ ] Job 41. Check oil level
- [ ] Job 42. Check for oil leaks
- [ ] Job 43. Check brake pads
- [ ] Job 44. **MGB AND MGC ONLY**
  Lube front suspension
- [ ] Job 45. **MGB ONLY**
  Adjust rear brakes

21,000 miles Mechanical and Electrical - Road Test

- [ ] Job 46. Clean controls
- [ ] Job 47. Check instruments
- [ ] Job 48. Throttle pedal
- [ ] Job 49. Hand brake function
- [ ] Job 50. Brakes and steering

21,000 miles Bodywork and Interior - Around the Car

- [ ] Job 17. Valet bodywork
- [ ] Job 20. Touch-up paintwork
- [ ] Job 21. Aerial/antenna
- [ ] Job 22. Valet interior
- [ ] Job 23. Improve visibility!
- [ ] Job 51. Wiper blades and arms
- [ ] Job 52. Check windscreen
- [ ] Job 53. Rear view mirrors
- [ ] Job 54. Check floors
- [ ] Job 55. Chrome trim and badges

21,000 miles
Bodywork - Under the Car

☐ Job 24. Clean mud traps.

☐ Job 56. Inspect underside

Date serviced: ....

Carried out by: ....

Garage stamp or signature:

Parts/Accessories Purchased (Date, Parts, Source) ....

....
....
....
....
....
....
....
....
....
....
....
....
....
....

24,000 MILES - OR EVERY TWENTY FOUR MONTHS, whichever comes first

All the Service jobs in the tinted area have been carried forward from earlier service intervals and are to be repeated at this Service.

24,000 miles Mechanical and Electrical - Emission Control Equipment

☐ Job 100. **EARLIER CARS**
Crankcase breather

☐ Job 101. Hoses and connectors

☐ Job 102. Oil filler cap

☐ Job 103. Air valve filter

☐ Job 104. **US CARS ONLY**
Adsorption canister

☐ Job 105. **US CARS ONLY**
Second fuel filter

☐ Job 106. **US CARS ONLY**
Air pump belt

☐ Job 107. **US CARS ONLY**
Air pump filter

☐ Job 108. **US CARS ONLY**
Test check valve

☐ Job 109. **US CARS ONLY**
Fuel filler cap

☐ Job 110. **SPECIALIST SERVICE**
Emission system

24,000 miles Mechanical and Electrical - The Engine Bay

First carry out all jobs listed under earlier Service Intervals.

☐ Job 2. Clutch fluid level

☐ Job 3. Brake fluid level

☐ Job 4. Battery electrolyte

☐ Job 5. Washer reservoir

☐ Job 6. Coolant system

☐ Job 26. Check HT circuit

☐ Job 28. Generator belt

☐ Job 30. Check air filters

☐ Job 32. Pipes and hoses

☐ Job 57. Cooling system

☐ Job 58. Coolant check

☐ Job 59. Heater valve

☐ Job 60. Check water pump

☐ Job 61. Battery terminals

☐ Job 62. Accelerator controls

☐ Job 63. Dynamo bearings

☐ Job 64. Fit new spark plugs

☐ Job 65. Renew cb points

☐ Job 66. Ignition timing

☐ Job 67. Fit fuel filter

☐ Job 68. Fuel connections

☐ Job 69. Top-up dashpots

☐ Job 70. Set carburettors

☐ Job 71. **SPECIALIST SERVICE**
Exhaust emissions

☐ Job 111. **US CARS ONLY**
Zenith/Stromberg carbs

☐ Job 112. **MGB ONLY**
Check heat shields

☐ Job 113. **LATER MODELS ONLY**
Carb. poppet valves

☐ Job 114. **V8 ENGINES ONLY**
V8 flame traps

☐ Job 115. Oil leaks

☐ Job 116. Clean radiators

☐ Job 117. **EARLY MODELS ONLY**
Grease water pump

☐ Job 118. **MGB ONLY**
Remote brake servo filter

☐ Job 119. **MGB ONLY**
In-line brake servo filter

☐ Job 120. **NOT MGB GT V8 OR MG RV8**
Valve clearances

☐ Job 121. Rocker cover gasket

☐ Job 122. Check cylinder compressions

☐ Job 123. Exhaust manifold bolts

☐ Job 146. Engine mountings

☐ Job 147. Refill cooling system

☐ Job 148. Radiator pressure cap

☐ Job 149. Drive belts

☐ Job 150. **V8 ENGINES ONLY**
V8 engine breather

☐ Job 151. **US CARS ONLY**
Renew adsorption canister

24,000 miles Mechanical and Electrical - Around the Car

First, carry out all jobs listed under earlier Service Intervals.

- [ ] Job 7. Check horns
- [ ] Job 8. Windscreen washers
- [ ] Job 9. Windscreen wipers
- [ ] Job 10. Tyre pressures
- [ ] Job 11. Check headlamps
- [ ] Job 12. Check front sidelamps
- [ ] Job 13. Check rear sidelamps
- [ ] Job 14. Number plate lamps
- [ ] Job 15. Reversing lamps
- [ ] Job 16. Check wheel spinners
- [ ] Job 18. Check tyres
- [ ] Job 19. Check spare tyre
- [ ] Job 33. Hand brake travel
- [ ] Job 72. Top-up gearbox oil
- [ ] Job 73. **SPECIALIST SERVICE** Adjust headlamps
- [ ] Job 74. Fuel filler pipe
- [ ] Job 75. Front wheel alignment
- [ ] Job 76. Rear ride height
- [ ] Job 77. Front ride height
- [ ] Job 78. Check tyre clearance
- [ ] Job 79. Check wheel nuts
- [ ] Job 124. Test dampers
- [ ] Job 125. Alarm remote units

24,000 miles Mechanical and Electrical - Under the Car

Of all the Service intervals, this is the one that involves most working under the car. For that reason, we have grouped areas of work together so that the work is in logical groups rather than strict numerical order.

FRONT OF CAR

First carry out all jobs listed under earlier Service Intervals.

- [ ] Job 34. Steering rack
- [ ] Job 35. Track rod ends
- [ ] Job 36. Drain engine oil
- [ ] Job 37. Remove oil filter

- [ ] Job 38. New oil filter
- [ ] Job 39. Pour fresh oil
- [ ] Job 40. **AUTOMATICS ONLY** Auto.-box park lock
- [ ] Job 41. Check oil level
- [ ] Job 42. Check for oil leaks
- [ ] Job 43. Check brake pads
- [ ] Job 44. **MGB AND MGC ONLY** Lube front suspension
- [ ] Job 80. Front fuel lines
- [ ] Job 81. Front brake lines
- [ ] Job 82. Brake pedal adjust
- [ ] Job 83. Exhaust manifold
- [ ] Job 84. Front dampers
- [ ] Job 85. Clutch hydraulics
- [ ] Job 126. Wishbone bushes
- [ ] Job 127. Damper pivots
- [ ] Job 128. Kingpins
- [ ] Job 129. Check front hubs
- [ ] Job 130. Front brake callipers
- [ ] Job 131. **EARLY CARS ONLY** Lubricate steering
- [ ] Job 132. Steering mountings
- [ ] Job 133. Check free play
- [ ] Job 134. Check ball joints
- [ ] Job 135. **MG RV8 ONLY** Adjust dampers

- [ ] Job 152. Engine flushing oil
- [ ] Job 153. Gearbox oil
- [ ] Job 154. **OVERDRIVE GEARBOXES ONLY** Service overdrive
- [ ] Job 155. Suspension mountings
- [ ] Job 156. Check brake discs
- [ ] Job 157. Brake callipers
- [ ] Job 158. Renew brake fluid

REAR OF CAR

- [ ] Job 86. Rear brake lines
- [ ] Job 87. Rear fuel lines
- [ ] Job 88. Exhaust system
- [ ] Job 89. Rear dampers

- [ ] Job 90. Hand brake mechanism
- [ ] Job 91. Universal joints
- [ ] Job 92. Rear axle oil
- [ ] Job 93. Rear springs
- [ ] Job 136. Rear brake inspection
- [ ] Job 137. Rear wheel cylinders
- [ ] Job 138. 'U'-bolt tightness
- [ ] Job 139. Top-up dampers
- [ ] Job 140. Universal joint flanges

- [ ] Job 159. Rear axle oil.
- [ ] Job 160. Check brake drums
- [ ] Job 161. Brake back plates

24,000 miles Mechanical and Electrical - Road Test

- [ ] Job 46. Clean controls
- [ ] Job 47. Check instruments
- [ ] Job 48. Throttle pedal
- [ ] Job 49. Hand brake function
- [ ] Job 50. Brakes and steering

24,000 miles Bodywork and Interior - Around the Car

First carry out all jobs listed under earlier Service Intervals.

- [ ] Job 17. Valet bodywork
- [ ] Job 20. Touch-up paintwork
- [ ] Job 21. Aerial antenna
- [ ] Job 22. Valet interior
- [ ] Job 23. Improve visibility!
- [ ] Job 51. Wiper blades and arms
- [ ] Job 52. Check windscreen
- [ ] Job 53. Rear view mirrors
- [ ] Job 54. Check floors
- [ ] Job 55. Chrome trim and badges
- [ ] Job 94. Bonnet release
- [ ] Job 95. Door locks
- [ ] Job 96. Boot lock
- [ ] Job 97. Seats and seat belts
- [ ] Job 141. Seat runners
- [ ] Job 142. Toolkit and jack

☐ Job 143. **WIRE WHEELED CARS ONLY**
Wire wheel splines

☐ Job 144. Wire wheel spokes

☐ Job 162. Maintain window mechanism

☐ Job 163. Maintain door gear

☐ Job 164. Lamp seals

24,000 miles Bodywork - Under the Car

First carry out all jobs listed under earlier Service Intervals.

☐ Job 24. Clean mud traps

☐ Job 56. Inspect underside

☐ Job 145. Top-up rustproofing
Be sure to carry out Job 99 after Job 145.

☐ Job 99. Clear drain holes.

Date serviced: ....

Carried out by: ....

Garage stamp or signature:

Parts/Accessories Purchased (Date, Parts, Source) ....
....
....
....
....
....
....
....
....
....
....
....
....
....

27,000 MILES - OR EVERY TWENTY SEVEN MONTHS, whichever comes first

All the Service jobs at this Service Interval have been carried forward from earlier service intervals and are to be repeated at this Service.

27,000 miles Mechanical and Electrical - The Engine Bay

☐ Job 2. Clutch fluid level

☐ Job 3. Brake fluid level

☐ Job 4. Battery electrolyte

☐ Job 5. Washer reservoir

☐ Job 6. Coolant system

☐ Job 25. Adjust spark plugs

☐ Job 26. Check HT circuit

☐ Job 27. Distributor

☐ Job 28. Generator belt

☐ Job 29. **OPTIONAL**
SU carburettors

☐ Job 30. Check air filters

☐ Job 31. **MG RV8, US AND EXPORT CARS ONLY**
Check drive belts

☐ Job 32. Pipes and hoses

27,000 miles Mechanical and Electrical - Around the Car

☐ Job 7. Check horns

☐ Job 8. Windscreen washers

☐ Job 9. Windscreen wipers

☐ Job 10. Tyre pressures

☐ Job 11. Check headlamps

☐ Job 12. Check front sidelamps

☐ Job 13. Check rear sidelamps

☐ Job 14. Number plate lamps

☐ Job 15. Reversing lamps

☐ Job 16. Check wheel spinners

☐ Job 18. Check tyres

☐ Job 19. Check spare tyre

☐ Job 33. Hand brake travel

27,000 miles Mechanical and Electrical - Under the Car

☐ Job 34. Steering rack

☐ Job 35. Track rod ends

Optional - Carry out Job 1

☐ Job 1. Engine oil level
or

☐ Job 36. Drain engine oil

☐ Job 37. Remove oil filter

☐ Job 38. New oil filter

☐ Job 39. Pour fresh oil

☐ Job 40. **AUTOMATICS ONLY**
Auto.-box park lock

☐ Job 41. Check oil level

☐ Job 42. Check for oil leaks

☐ Job 43. Check brake pads

☐ Job 44. **MGB AND MGC ONLY**
Lube front suspension

☐ Job 45. **MGB ONLY**
Adjust rear brakes

27,000 miles Mechanical and Electrical - Road Test

☐ Job 46. Clean controls

☐ Job 47. Check instruments

☐ Job 48. Throttle pedal

☐ Job 49. Hand brake function

☐ Job 50. Brakes and steering

27,000 miles Bodywork and Interior - Around the Car

☐ Job 17. Valet bodywork

☐ Job 20. Touch-up paintwork

☐ Job 21. Aerial/antenna

☐ Job 22. Valet interior

☐ Job 23. Improve visibility!

☐ Job 51. Wiper blades and arms

☐ Job 52. Check windscreen

☐ Job 53. Rear view mirrors

☐ Job 54. Check floors

☐ Job 55. Chrome trim and badges

27,000 miles
Bodywork - Under the Car

- [ ] Job 24. Clean mud traps.
- [ ] Job 56. Inspect underside

Date serviced: ....

Carried out by: ....

Garage stamp or signature:

Parts/Accessories Purchased (Date, Parts, Source) ....

....
....
....
....
....
....
....
....
....
....
....
....
....
....

30,000 MILES - OR EVERY THIRTY MONTHS, whichever comes first

All the Service jobs at this Service Interval have been carried forward from earlier service intervals and are to be repeated at this Service.

30,000 miles Mechanical and Electrical - The Engine Bay

- [ ] Job 2. Clutch fluid level
- [ ] Job 3. Brake fluid level
- [ ] Job 4. Battery electrolyte
- [ ] Job 5. Washer reservoir
- [ ] Job 6. Coolant system
- [ ] Job 26. Check HT circuit
- [ ] Job 28. Generator belt
- [ ] Job 30. Check air filters
- [ ] Job 31. **MG RV8, US AND EXPORT CARS ONLY**
  Check drive belts
- [ ] Job 32. Pipes and hoses
- [ ] Job 57. Cooling system
- [ ] Job 58. Coolant check
- [ ] Job 59. Heater valve
- [ ] Job 60. Check water pump
- [ ] Job 61. Battery terminals
- [ ] Job 62. Accelerator controls
- [ ] Job 63. Dynamo bearings
- [ ] Job 64. Fit new spark plugs
- [ ] Job 65. Renew cb points
- [ ] Job 66. Ignition timing
- [ ] Job 67. Fit fuel filter
- [ ] Job 68. Fuel connections
- [ ] Job 69. Top-up dashpots
- [ ] Job 70. Set carburettors
- [ ] Job 71. **SPECIALIST SERVICE**
  Exhaust emissions

30,000 miles Mechanical and Electrical - Around the Car

- [ ] Job 7. Check horns
- [ ] Job 8. Windscreen washers
- [ ] Job 9. Windscreen wipers

- [ ] Job 10. Tyre pressures
- [ ] Job 11. Check headlamps
- [ ] Job 12. Check front sidelamps
- [ ] Job 13. Check rear sidelamps
- [ ] Job 14. Number plate lamps
- [ ] Job 15. Reversing lamps
- [ ] Job 16. Check wheel spinners
- [ ] Job 18. Check tyres
- [ ] Job 19. Check spare tyre
- [ ] Job 33. Handbrake travel
- [ ] Job 72. Top-up gearbox oil
- [ ] Job 73. **SPECIALIST SERVICE**
  Adjust headlamps
- [ ] Job 74. Fuel filler pipe
- [ ] Job 75. **SPECIALIST SERVICE**
  Front wheel alignment
- [ ] Job 76. Rear ride height
- [ ] Job 77. Front ride height
- [ ] Job 78. Check tyre clearance
- [ ] Job 79. Check wheel nuts

30,000 miles Mechanical and Electrical - Under the Car

- [ ] Job 34. Steering rack
- [ ] Job 35. Track rod ends
- [ ] Job 36. Drain engine oil
- [ ] Job 37. Remove oil filter
- [ ] Job 38. New oil filter
- [ ] Job 39. Pour fresh oil
- [ ] Job 40. **AUTOMATICS ONLY**
  Auto.-box park lock
- [ ] Job 41. Check oil level
- [ ] Job 42. Check for oil leaks
- [ ] Job 43. Check brake pads
- [ ] Job 44. **MGB AND MGC ONLY**
  Lube Front suspension
- [ ] Job 45. **MGB ONLY**
  Adjust rear brakes
- [ ] Job 80. Front fuel lines
- [ ] Job 81. Front brake lines
- [ ] Job 82. Brake pedal adjust
- [ ] Job 83. Exhaust manifold

☐ Job 84. Front dampers

☐ Job 85. Clutch hydraulics

☐ Job 86. Rear brake lines

☐ Job 87. Rear fuel lines

☐ Job 88. Exhaust system

☐ Job 89. Rear dampers

☐ Job 90. Hand brake mechanism

☐ Job 91. Universal joints

☐ Job 92. Rear axle oil

☐ Job 93. Rear springs

30,000 miles Mechanical and Electrical - Road Test

☐ Job 46. Clean controls

☐ Job 47. Check instruments

☐ Job 48. Throttle pedal

☐ Job 49. Hand brake function

☐ Job 50. Brakes and steering

30,000 miles Bodywork and Interior - Around the Car

☐ Job 17. Valet bodywork

☐ Job 20. Touch-up paintwork

☐ Job 21. Aerial/antenna

☐ Job 22. Valet interior

☐ Job 23. Improve visibility!

☐ Job 51. Wiper blades and arms

☐ Job 52. Check windscreen

☐ Job 53. Rear view mirrors

☐ Job 54. Check floors

☐ Job 55. Chrome trim and badges

☐ Job 94. Bonnet release

☐ Job 95. Door locks

☐ Job 96. Boot lock

☐ Job 97. Seats and seat belts

30,000 miles Bodywork - Under the Car

☐ Job 24. Clean mud traps

☐ Job 56. Inspect underside

☐ Job 98. Rustproof underbody

Be sure to carry out Job 99 after Job 98.

☐ Job 99. Clear drain holes

Date serviced: ....

Carried out by: ....

Garage stamp or signature:

Parts/Accessories Purchased (Date, Parts, Source) ....
....
....
....
....
....
....
....
....
....
....
....
....
....
....

33,000 MILES - OR EVERY THIRTY THREE MONTHS, whichever comes first

All the Service jobs at this Service Interval have been carried forward from earlier service intervals and are to be repeated at this Service.

33,000 miles Mechanical and Electrical - The Engine Bay

☐ Job 2. Clutch fluid level

☐ Job 3. Brake fluid level

☐ Job 4. Battery electrolyte

☐ Job 5. Washer reservoir

☐ Job 6. Coolant system

☐ Job 25. Adjust spark plugs

☐ Job 26. Check HT circuit

☐ Job 27. Distributor

☐ Job 28. Generator belt

☐ Job 29. **OPTIONAL**
SU carburettors

☐ Job 30. Check air filters

☐ Job 31. **MG RV8, US AND EXPORT CARS ONLY**
Check drive belts

☐ Job 32. Pipes and hoses

33,000 miles Mechanical and Electrical - Around the Car

☐ Job 7. Check horns

☐ Job 8. Windscreen washers

☐ Job 9. Windscreen wipers

☐ Job 10. Tyre pressures

☐ Job 11. Check headlamps

☐ Job 12. Check front sidelamps

☐ Job 13. Check rear sidelamps

☐ Job 14. Number plate lamps

☐ Job 15. Reversing lamps

☐ Job 16. Check wheel spinners

☐ Job 18. Check tyres

☐ Job 19. Check spare tyre

☐ Job 33. Hand brake travel

33,000 miles Mechanical and Electrical - Under the Car

- [ ] Job 34. Steering rack
- [ ] Job 35. Track rod ends

Optional - Carry out Job 1

- [ ] Job 1. Engine oil level

or

- [ ] Job 36. Drain engine oil
- [ ] Job 37. Remove oil filter
- [ ] Job 38. New oil filter
- [ ] Job 39. Pour fresh oil
- [ ] Job 40. **AUTOMATICS ONLY** Auto.-box park lock
- [ ] Job 41. Check oil level
- [ ] Job 42. Check for oil leaks
- [ ] Job 43. Check brake pads
- [ ] Job 44. **MGB AND MGC ONLY** Lube front suspension
- [ ] Job 45. **MGB ONLY** Adjust rear brakes

33,000 miles Mechanical and Electrical - Road Test

- [ ] Job 46. Clean controls
- [ ] Job 47. Check instruments
- [ ] Job 48. Throttle pedal
- [ ] Job 49. Hand brake function
- [ ] Job 50. Brakes and steering

33,000 miles Bodywork and Interior - Around the Car

- [ ] Job 17. Valet bodywork
- [ ] Job 20. Touch-up paintwork
- [ ] Job 21. Aerial/antenna
- [ ] Job 22. Valet interior
- [ ] Job 23. Improve visibility!
- [ ] Job 51. Wiper blades and arms
- [ ] Job 52. Check windscreen
- [ ] Job 53. Rear view mirrors
- [ ] Job 54. Check floors
- [ ] Job 55. Chrome trim and badges

33,000 miles Bodywork - Under the Car

- [ ] Job 24. Clean mud traps.
- [ ] Job 56. Inspect underside

Date serviced: ....

Carried out by: ....

Garage stamp or signature:

Parts/Accessories Purchased (Date, Parts, Source) ....
....
....
....
....
....
....
....
....
....
....
....
....
....

36,000 MILES - OR EVERY THIRTY SIX MONTHS, whichever comes first

All the Service jobs in the tinted area have been carried forward from earlier service intervals and are to be repeated at this Service.

36,000 miles Mechanical and Electrical - Emission Control Equipment

- [ ] Job 100. **EARLIER CARS** Crankcase breather
- [ ] Job 101. Hoses and connectors
- [ ] Job 102. Oil filler cap
- [ ] Job 103. Air valve filter
- [ ] Job 104. **US CARS ONLY** Adsorption canister
- [ ] Job 105. **US CARS ONLY** Second fuel filter
- [ ] Job 106. **US CARS ONLY** Air pump belt
- [ ] Job 107. **US CARS ONLY** Air pump filter
- [ ] Job 108. **US CARS ONLY** Test check valve
- [ ] Job 109. **US CARS ONLY** Fuel filler cap
- [ ] Job 110. **SPECIALIST SERVICE** Emission system

36,000 miles Mechanical and Electrical - The Engine Bay

First carry out all jobs listed under earlier Service Intervals.

- [ ] Job 2. Clutch fluid level
- [ ] Job 3. Brake fluid level
- [ ] Job 4. Battery electrolyte
- [ ] Job 5. Washer reservoir
- [ ] Job 6. Coolant system
- [ ] Job 26. Check HT circuit
- [ ] Job 28. Generator belt
- [ ] Job 30. Check air filters
- [ ] Job 32. Pipes and hoses

- [ ] Job 57. Cooling system
- [ ] Job 58. Coolant check
- [ ] Job 59. Heater valve
- [ ] Job 60. Check water pump
- [ ] Job 61. Battery terminals
- [ ] Job 62. Accelerator controls
- [ ] Job 63. Dynamo bearings
- [ ] Job 64. Fit new spark plugs
- [ ] Job 65. Renew cb points
- [ ] Job 66. Ignition timing
- [ ] Job 67. Fit fuel filter
- [ ] Job 68. Fuel connections
- [ ] Job 69. Top-up dashpots
- [ ] Job 70. Set carburettors
- [ ] Job 71. **SPECIALIST SERVICE** Exhaust emissions
- [ ] Job 111. **US CARS ONLY** Zenith/Stromberg carbs
- [ ] Job 112. **MGB ONLY** Check heat shields
- [ ] Job 113. **LATER MODELS ONLY** Carb. poppet valves
- [ ] Job 114. **V8 ENGINES ONLY** V8 flame traps
- [ ] Job 115. Oil leaks
- [ ] Job 116. Clean radiators
- [ ] Job 117. **EARLY MODELS ONLY** Grease water pump
- [ ] Job 118. **MGB ONLY** Remote brake servo filter
- [ ] Job 119. **MGB ONLY** In-line brake servo filter
- [ ] Job 120. **NOT MGB GT V8 OR MG RV8** Valve clearances
- [ ] Job 121. Rocker cover gasket
- [ ] Job 122. Check cylinder compressions
- [ ] Job 123. Exhaust manifold bolts

- [ ] Job 165. **MGC ONLY** MGC brake servo
- [ ] Job 166. Overhaul ignition
- [ ] Job 167. Clean float bowls

36,000 miles Mechanical and Electrical - Around the Car

First, carry out all jobs listed under earlier Service Intervals.

- [ ] Job 7. Check horns
- [ ] Job 8. Windscreen washers
- [ ] Job 9. Windscreen wipers
- [ ] Job 10. Tyre pressures
- [ ] Job 11. Check headlamps
- [ ] Job 12. Check front sidelamps
- [ ] Job 13. Check rear sidelamps
- [ ] Job 14. Number plate lamps
- [ ] Job 15. Reversing lamps
- [ ] Job 16. Check wheel spinners
- [ ] Job 18. Check tyres
- [ ] Job 19. Check spare tyre
- [ ] Job 33. Hand brake travel
- [ ] Job 72. Top-up gearbox oil
- [ ] Job 73. **SPECIALIST SERVICE** Adjust headlamps
- [ ] Job 74. Fuel filler pipe
- [ ] Job 75. Front wheel alignment
- [ ] Job 76. Rear ride height
- [ ] Job 77. Front ride height
- [ ] Job 78. Check tyre clearance
- [ ] Job 79. Check wheel nuts
- [ ] Job 124. Test dampers
- [ ] Job 125. Alarm remote units

36,000 miles MECHANICAL and ELECTRICAL - Under The Car

Of all the Service intervals, this is the one that involves most working under the car. For that reason, we have grouped areas of work together so that the work is in logical groups rather than strict numerical order.

FRONT OF CAR

First carry out all jobs listed under earlier Service Intervals.

- [ ] Job 34. Steering rack
- [ ] Job 35. Track rod ends
- [ ] Job 36. Drain engine oil
- [ ] Job 37. Remove oil filter

- [ ] Job 38. New oil filter
- [ ] Job 39. Pour fresh oil
- [ ] Job 40. **AUTOMATICS ONLY** Auto.-box park lock
- [ ] Job 41. Check oil level
- [ ] Job 42. Check for oil leaks
- [ ] Job 43. Check brake pads
- [ ] Job 44. **MGB AND MGC ONLY** Lube front suspension
- [ ] Job 80. Front fuel lines
- [ ] Job 81. Front brake lines
- [ ] Job 82. Brake pedal adjust
- [ ] Job 83. Exhaust manifold
- [ ] Job 84. Front dampers
- [ ] Job 85. Clutch hydraulics
- [ ] Job 126. Wishbone bushes
- [ ] Job 127. Damper pivots
- [ ] Job 128. Kingpins
- [ ] Job 129. Check front hubs
- [ ] Job 130. Front brake callipers
- [ ] Job 131. **EARLY CARS ONLY** Lubricate steering
- [ ] Job 132. Steering mountings
- [ ] Job 133. Check free play
- [ ] Job 134. Check ball joints
- [ ] Job 135. **MG RV8 ONLY** Adjust dampers

- [ ] Job 168. Steering rack oil
- [ ] Job 169. Hub lubrication

REAR OF CAR

- [ ] Job 86. Rear brake lines
- [ ] Job 87. Rear fuel lines
- [ ] Job 88. Exhaust system
- [ ] Job 89. Rear dampers
- [ ] Job 90. Hand brake mechanism
- [ ] Job 91. Universal joints
- [ ] Job 92. Rear axle oil
- [ ] Job 93. Rear springs
- [ ] Job 136. Rear brake inspection
- [ ] Job 137. Rear wheel cylinders

SERVICE HISTORY

Job 138. 'U'-bolt tightness

Job 139. Top-up dampers

Job 140. Universal joint flanges

36,000 miles Mechanical and Electrical - Road Test

Job 46. Clean controls

Job 47. Check instruments

Job 48. Throttle pedal

Job 49. Hand brake function

Job 50. Brakes and steering

36,000 miles Bodywork and Interior - Around the Car

First carry out all jobs listed under earlier Service Intervals.

Job 17. Valet bodywork

Job 20. Touch-up paintwork

Job 21. Aerial/antenna

Job 22. Valet interior

Job 23. Improve visibility!

Job 51. Wiper blades and arms

Job 52. Check windscreen

Job 53. Rear view mirrors

Job 54. Check floors

Job 55. Chrome trim and badges

Job 94. Bonnet release

Job 95. Door locks

Job 96. Boot lock

Job 97. Seats and seat belts

Job 141. Seat runners

Job 142. Toolkit and jack

Job 143. **WIRE WHEELED CARS ONLY** Wire wheel splines

Job 144. Wire wheel spokes

36,000 miles Bodywork - Under the Car

First carry out all jobs listed under earlier Service Intervals.

Job 24. Clean mud traps

Job 56. Inspect underside

Job 145. Top-up rustproofing

Be sure to carry out Job 99 after Job 145.

Job 99. Clear drain holes

Date serviced: ....

Carried out by: ....

Garage stamp or signature:

Parts/Accessories Purchased (Date, Parts, Source) ....

....

....

....

....

....

....

....

....

....

....

....

....

....

....

....

....

LONGER TERM SERVICING

48,000 miles

Job 170. **MG RV8 ONLY** Fit new filters

60,000 miles

Job 171. Auxiliary drive belts

YOU HAVE NOW COMPLETED ALL OF THE SERVICE JOBS LISTED IN THIS SERVICE GUIDE, THE 'LONGEST' INTERVAL BETWEEN ANY JOBS BEING 3 YEARS OR 36,000 MILES. WHEN YOU HAVE FILLED IN EACH OF THE SERVICE INTERVALS SHOWN HERE, YOU MAY PURCHASE CONTINUATION SHEETS TO ENABLE YOU TO CONTINUE AND COMPLETE YOUR SERVICE HISTORY FOR AS LONG AS YOU OWN THE CAR.
PLEASE CONTACT
PORTER PUBLISHING
at
**The Storehouse,
Little Hereford Street,
Bromyard,
Hereford, HR7 4DE,
England.
Tel: 0885 488800.**